D0900188

Law School Publications

of

WEST PUBLISHING COMPANY

St. Paul 2, Minnesota

ACCOUNTING

Shannon's Accounting and the Law, 604 pages, 1957.

Shannon's Legal Accounting, 366 pages, 1951.

ADMINISTRATIVE LAW

Davis' Cases, 592 pages, 1959.

Davis Text, 617 pages, 1959.

Davis' Cases, Text and Problems, 609 pages, 1960.

Merrill's Cases, 720 pages, 1954.

ADMIRALTY

Robinson's Text, 1025 pages, 1939.

Sprague and Healy's Cases, 859 pages, 1950.

AGENCY

Seavey and Hall's Cases, 431 pages 1956.

Seavey's Studies, 451 pages, 1949.

Steffen's Cases, 2nd Ed., 902 pages, 1952.

Tiffany's Text, 2nd Ed., 485 pages, 1924.

AGENCY AND PARTNERSHIP

Seavey, Reuschlein & Hall's Cases, 599 pages, 1962.

BANKRUPTCY

MacLachlan's Text, 500 pages, 1956.

Nadler's Cases on Creditor-Debtor Relations, 698 pages, 1956.

Nadler's Supp., 233 pages, 1959.

Sturges' Cases on Debtors' Estates, 4th Ed., 1291 pages, 1949.

See Creditors' Rights.

BILLS AND NOTES

Aigler and Steinheimer's Cases, 670 pages, 1962.

Britton's Text, 2nd Ed., 783 pages, 1961.

Smith & Moore's Cases, 4th Ed. 1070 pages, 1941.

CODE PLEADING

Clark's Cases on Modern Pleading, 1042 pages, 1952.

Clark's Text, 2nd Ed., 874 pages, 1947.

Cleary's Cases on Pleading, 2d Ed., 434 pages, 1958.

Elliott & Karlen's Cases, 438 pages, 1961.

Stayton's Cases, Texas Pleading, 851 pages, 1953.

COMMON LAW PLEADING

McBaine's Cases, Introduction to Civil Procedure. 399 pages, 1950.

Shipman's Text, 3rd Ed., 644 pages, 1923.

Stayton's Cases (Texas), 1952.

I

LAW SCHOOL PUBLICATIONS — Continued

COMMUNITY PROPERTY

Burby's Cases, 4th Ed., 342 pages, 1955.

Huie's Texas Cases on Marital Rights, 781 pages, 1955.

Verrall's Cases, California Community Property, 320 pages, 1960.

CONFLICT OF LAWS

Ehrenzweig's Text, 824 pages, 1962.

Goodrich's Text, 3rd Ed., 662 pages, 1949.

Lorenzen's Cases, 6th Ed., 918 pages, 1951.

Selected Readings, 1151 pages, 1956.

Stumberg's Cases, 497 pages, 1956.

CONSTITUTIONAL LAW

Dodd's Cases, 5th Ed., 1438 pages, 1954.

Dodd's Cases, 5th Ed., Shorter Ed., 969 pages, 1954.

Dodd's Supplement.

Forrester's Cases, 879 pages, 1959.

Forrester's Supplement.

Rottschaefer's Text, 982 pages, 1939.

CONTRACTS

Corbin's Cases, 3rd Ed., 1381 pages, 1947. 1953 Supplement, 36 pages.

Corbin's Text, Student Edition, 1224 pages, 1952.

Fuller's Cases, 994 pages, 1947.

Simpson's Cases, 592 pages, 1956.

Simpson's Text, 692 pages, 1954.

ΓORPORATIONS

Henn's Text, 665 pages, 1961.

Richard's Cases, Rev. 3rd Ed., 1067 pages, 1940.

Stevens & Larson's Cases, 2nd Ed., 741 pages, 1955.

Stevens' Text, 2nd Ed., 1125 pages, 1949.

CREDIT TRANSACTIONS

Maxwell & Riesenfeld's California Cases on Security Transactions, 371 pages, 1957.

Sturges' Cases, 4th Ed., 599 pages, 1955.

CREDITORS' RIGHTS

Nadler's Cases on Creditor and Debtor Relations, 698 pages, 1956.

Nadler's Supp., 233 pages, 1959.

Sturges' Cases Debtors' Estates, 4th Ed., 1291 pages, 1949.

CRIMINAL LAW

Hall & Glueck's Cases, 2d Ed., 699 pages, 1958.

Miller's Text, 649 pages, 1934.

Stumberg's Texas Cases, 505 pages, 1954.

DAMAGES

Crane's Cases, 3rd Ed., 337 pages, 1955.

McCormick's Text, 811 pages, 1935.

DICTIONARIES

Black's, one volume.

Bouvier's, two volumes.

DOMESTIC RELATIONS

Compton's Cases, 638 pages, 1951.

Huie's Texas Cases, 781 pages, 1955.

Madden's Text, 748 pp., 1931.

DRUGS AND DRUGGISTS

Arthur's Text, 4th Ed., 399 pp., 1955.

ENGINEERING LAW

Simpson & Dillavou's Text, 4th Ed., 506 pages, 1958.

EQUITY

Cook's Cases, 4th Ed., 1192 pp., 1948.

McClintock's Text, 2nd Ed., 643 pages, 1948.

Van Hecke's Cases on Equitable Remedies, 651 pages, 1959.

II

LAW SCHOOL PUBLICATIONS — Continued

EVIDENCE

McCormick's Cases, 3rd Ed., 663 pages, 1956.

McCormick's Text, 774 pages, 1954.

Selected Writings, 1232 pages, 1957.

FEDERAL ANTI-TRUST LAWS

Oppenheim's Cases, 1188 pages, 1959.

FEDERAL JURISDICTION AND PROCE-DURE

Bunn's U. S. Courts, Text, 5th Ed., 408 pages, 1949.

Forrester's Dobie & Ladd Cases, 968 pages, 1950.

FRAUD AND MISTAKE

Keeton's Cases, 514 pages, 1954.

FUTURE INTERESTS

Gulliver's Cases, 624 pages, 1959.

Powell's Cases, 3rd Ed., 1961.

Simes Text, 495 pages, 1951.

INSURANCE

Keeton's Basic Insurance Law, 655 pages, 1960.

Vance's Text, 3rd Ed., 1290 pages, 1951.

Vance's Cases, 4th Ed., 994 pages, 1952.

INTERNATIONAL LAW

Hudson's Cases, 3rd Ed., 770 pages, 1951.

Wilson's Text, 3rd Ed., 623 pages, 1939.

INTRODUCTION TO LAW

Bowman's Text, 307 pages, 1929.

Smith's Text, 2nd Ed., 468 pages, 1939.

See Legal Method

JUDICIAL REMEDIES

Cribbet's Cases, 762 pages, 1954.

JURISPRUDENCE

Simpson and Stone's Cases Law and Society, Book I, Law and Society in Evolution, 692 pages, 1948. Book II, Law in Modern Democratic Society, 902 pages, 1949. Book III, Law, Totalitarianism and Democracy, 796 pages, 1949.

Wu's Cases, 719 pages, 1958.

LABOR LAW

Handler & Hays' Cases, 3rd Ed., 824 pages, 1959.

Handler & Hays' Supp., 58 pages, 1930.

LANDLORD AND TENANT

Jacobs' Cases, 2nd Ed., 815 pages, 1941.

LEGAL ACCOUNTING

See Accounting.

LEGAL BIBLIOGRAPHY

How to Find the Law, 5th Ed., 207 pages, 1957.

LEGAL ETHICS

Pirsig's Cases on the Legal Profession, 211 pages, 1957.

Selected Readings Legal Profession, 556 pages, 1962.

LEGAL HISTORY

Radin's Text, 612 pages, 1936.

LEGAL METHOD

Fryer and Benson's Legal Method and Legal System, 1 volume Ed., 843 pages, 1950.

LEGAL WRITING STYLE

Weihofen's Text, 302 pages, 1961.

LEGISLATION

Nutting and Elliott's Cases, 2nd Ed., 402 pages, 1955.

MILITARY LAW
Schiller's Cases, 590 pages, 1952.

MORTGAGES
Osborne's Cases Property Security, 2nd Ed., 725 pages, 1954.
Osborne's Text, 1117 pages, 1951.
Sturges' Cases Credit Transactions, 4th Ed., 599 pages, 1955.

MUNICIPAL CORPORATIONS
Stason and Kauper's Cases, 3rd Ed., 692 pages, 1959.

NATURAL RESOURCES
Martz's Cases, 1124 pages, 1951.

OIL AND GAS
Huie, Walker and Woodward's Cases, 848 pages, 1960.
Kulp's Cases, 3rd Ed., 910 pages, 1947. Supplement, 1953.
Summer's Cases, 781 pages, 1952.

PARTNERSHIP
Crane's Text, 2d Ed., 655 pages, 1952.
Gilmore's Cases, 3rd Ed., 501 pages, 1949.
Reuschlein's Cases on Partnership & Unincorporated Business, 660 pages, 1952.
Seavey, Reuschlein & Hall, Cases on Agency and Partnership, 599 pages, 1962.

PERSONAL PROPERTY
Aigler, Smith and Tefft's Cases on Property, 2 Vols., 1339 pages, 1960.
Bigelow's Cases, 3rd Ed., 500 pages, 1942.
Fryer's Readings, 3rd Ed., 1184 pages, 1938.

PLEADING
See Code Pleading.
See Common Law Pleading.

PRESS, LAW OF
Hale's Text, 3rd Ed., 691 pages, 1948.

PROPERTY SECURITY
Osborne's Cases, 2nd Ed., 725 pages, 1954.
See also Mortgages.

PUBLIC UTILITIES
Auerbach & Nathanson's Cases on Federal Regulation of Transportation, 1223 pages, 1953.

QUIZZERS
Ballantine's Problems.
Burby's Law Refreshers.
Owen's Quizzer.
Smith's How to Answer Law Examinations.
Smith's Reviews for Law Examinations.

REAL PROPERTY
Aigler, Smith & Tefft's Cases on Property, 2 Vols., 1339 pages, 1960.
Burby's Text, 2nd Ed., 758 pages, 1954.
Horack and Nolan's Land Use Controls, 240 pages, 1955.
Jacobs' Cases Landlord and Tenant, 2nd Ed., 815 pages, 1941.
Moynihan's Introduction, 254 pp., 1962.
Smith's Survey, 398 pages, 1956.

REMEDIES
Wright's Cases, 498 pages, 1955.

RESTITUTION
Keeton's Cases, (Fraud and Mistake) 514 pages, 1954.
Thurston's Cases, 964 pages, 1940.

RIGHTS IN LAND
Aigler, Smith and Tefft's Cases on Property, 2 Vols., 1339 pages, 1960

LAW SCHOOL PUBLICATIONS — Continued

SALES

McCurdy's Cases, 727 pages, 1959.
Vold's Cases, 3rd Ed., 860 pages, 1960.
Vold's Text, 2nd Ed., 611 pages, 1959.

STATUTES

Selected Statutes, 5th Ed., 373 pages, 1944.
See Legislation.

SURETYSHIP AND GUARANTY

Osborne's Cases, 65 pages, 1955.
Simpson's Text, 569 pages, 1950.
Simpson's Cases, 538 pages, 1942.
Sturges' Cases Credit Transactions, 4th Ed., 599 pages, 1955.

TAXATION

Bruton and Bradley's Cases, 808 pages, 1955.
Hellerstein's Cases on State and Local Taxation, 2nd Ed., 659 pages, 1961.
Lowndes and Kramer's Text, 911 pages, 1962.

TITLES

Aigler, Bigelow & Tefft's Cases on Property, 2 Vols., 1339 pages, 1960.

TORTS

Green, Malone, Pedrick & Rahl's Cases on Injuries to Relations, about 500 pages, 1959.
Green, Malone, Pedrick & Rahl's Cases, 2nd Ed., 855 pages, 1957.
Hepburn's Cases, 3rd Ed., 540 pages, 1954.

TORTS—Continued

Prosser's Text, 2nd Ed., 952 pp., 1955.
Seavey, Keeton and Keeton's Cases, 768 pages, 1957.

TRADE REGULATION

See Federal Anti-Trust Laws.
See also Unfair Trade Practices.

TRIAL PRACTICE

Karlen's Cases, 436 pages, 1961.
McBaine's Cases, 3rd Ed., 1063 pages, 1952.
Stayton's Cases, Texas Civil and Criminal Trial, 794 pages, 1953.
Stayton's Cases, Texas Appellate Procedure, 796 pages, 1952.

TRUSTS

Bogert's Text, 3rd Ed., 804 pages, 1952.
Powell's Cases, Trusts and Wills, 639 pages, 1960.
Smith's Survey, 167 pages, 1949.

UNFAIR TRADE PRACTICES

Oppenheim's Cases, 1534 pages, 1950.
Oppenheim's Supplement, 389 pages, 1960.

WILLS

Atkinson's Text, 2nd Ed., 975 pages, 1953.
Turrentine's Cases, 2nd Ed., 473 pages, 1962.

*

INTRODUCTION

TO THE

LAW OF REAL PROPERTY

An Historical Background of The
Common Law of Real Property
And Its Modern Application

By

CORNELIUS J. MOYNIHAN
Professor of Law, Boston College Law School

ST. PAUL, MINN.
WEST PUBLISHING CO.
1962

Copyright © 1962
by
WEST PUBLISHING CO.

PREFACE

This book is basically a revised edition of A Preliminary Survey of the Law of Real Property. In the twenty-two years that have elapsed since the publication of the Preliminary Survey, there have been many important changes and developments in real property law. This new edition reflects such changes.

A substantial portion of the text has been re-written and the treatment of such topics as estates and future interests is more extensive than in the earlier edition. The possibility of reverter, the power of termination, the contingent remainder, and the doctrine of worthier title, for example, are discussed more fully. But the scope of the two books is the same and the general arrangement of the subject matter in the earlier work has been retained. And there has been no change in the objective stated in the preface to the Preliminary Survey of providing the beginning student with "a simple, concise text setting forth in outline form the older and the modern law" in selected areas of real property law.

The past few years have witnessed the publication of three great treatises on the law of property—the American Law of Property (Casner ed.), Powell on Real Property, and Simes and Smith on Future Interests. Anyone writing in this field is necessarily indebted to the authors of these works. My frequent citations to these treatises are not only for the purpose of indicating supporting authority for textual statements; they are also used to encourage students to turn to these books for a more comprehensive treatment of the topics under discussion.

I acknowledge with gratitude the kind permission of the following publishers to reproduce copyrighted materials: The American Law Institute, publisher of The Restatement of the Law of Property; Oxford University Press, Inc., publisher of English Historical Documents; Little, Brown and Company, publisher of the fourth edition of Gray, Rule Against Perpetuities; Roland

PREFACE

Gray, Jr., Esq., copyright owner of the latter work; and Cambridge University Press, publisher of The Collected Papers of Frederic William Maitland, Edited by H. A. L. Fisher.

I am especially indebted to my colleague, Professor Emil Slizewski, for reading the manuscript and making valuable suggestions and criticisms.

CORNELIUS J. MOYNIHAN

Boston, Massachusetts
August, 1962

x

SUMMARY OF CONTENTS

Page

Preface _____ IX

Chapter

1. The Background _____ 1

2. Freehold Estates _____ 28

3. Non-freehold Estates _____ 63

4. Seisin and Its Significance _____ 87

5. Common Law Types of Future Interests _____ 93

6. The Rule In Shelley's Case And The Doctrine of
   Worthier Title _____ 138

7. Common Law Methods of Conveyancing _____ 163

8. Uses And The Statute of Uses _____ 173

9. The Effect of The Statute of Uses _____ 185

10. Concurrent Ownership _____ 216

Table Of Cases _____ 237

Index _____ 245

TABLE OF CONTENTS

		Page
Chapter 1. The Background		1
Introduction		1
Section		
1.	The Norman Settlement	2
2.	The Introduction of Feudal Tenure	4
3.	The Creation of Sub-tenures	5
4.	The Domesday Survey	7
5.	Legal Relations of Lord and Tenant	8
6.	The Classification of Tenures	10
7.	The Incidents of Free Tenures	18
8.	Statutes Affecting Tenure	22
9.	Tenure in the United States	25
10.	The Effects of Tenure	27
Chapter 2. Freehold Estates		28
Section		
1.	The Theory of Estates	28
2.	The Fee Simple	29
3.	Modern Law—Creation and Characteristics of a Fee Simple	33
4.	The Qualified or Defeasible Fee Simple	35
5.	The Fee Tail	37
6.	Modern Law—The Fee Tail in the United States	41
7.	Construction Problems—Meaning of Death without Issue	43
8.	Construction Problems—Devise to B and His Children	46
9.	Life Estates	48
10.	Creation of Life Estates by Deed or Will	48
11.	Life Estates Created by Operation of Law	51
12.	Characteristics of a Life Estate	58

TABLE OF CONTENTS

Page

Chapter 3. Nonfreehold Estates _____ 63

Section
1. The Estate for Years—Historical Background and
   Its Consequences _____ 63
2. Creation and Characteristics _____ 65
3. The Modern Lease and Its Covenants _____ 69
4. Transfer of the Interest of Lessor or Lessee _____ 73
5. Distinction Between Assignment and Sublease ____ 76
6. Termination of an Estate for Years _____ 78
7. Periodic Estates _____ 79
8. Estates at Will _____ 83
9. Tenancy at Sufferance _____ 85

Chapter 4. Seisin and Its Significance _____ 87

Section
1. The Meaning of Seisin _____ 87
2. The Significance of Seisin _____ 88
3. The Decline of Seisin _____ 90

Chapter 5. Common Law Types of Future Interests _____ 93

Section
1. The Nature of a Future Interest _____ 93

A. REVERSIONS _____ 94
2. Reversions _____ 94

B. POSSIBILITY OF REVERTER _____ 95
3. The Nature of a Possibility of Reverter _____ 95
4. The Possibility of Reverter and Quia Emptores ____ 96
5. The Possibility of Reverter Distinguished from
   Right of Entry for Condition Broken _____ 97
6. Creation of Possibility of Reverter—Constructional
   Problems _____ 99
7. Characteristics of Possibility of Reverter _____ 101

C. RIGHT OF ENTRY FOR CONDITION BROKEN _____ 103
8. The Nature of the Right of Entry for Condition
   Broken _____ 103
9. Creation of Right of Entry for Condition Broken—
   Constructional Problems _____ 104

TABLE OF CONTENTS

Chapter 5. Common Law Types of Future Interests— Continued

C. RIGHT OF ENTRY FOR CONDITION BROKEN—Continued

Section | Page
10. Enforcement of the Right of Entry _____ 105
11. Alienability of Right of Entry for Condition Broken 107
12. Duration of Right of Entry Arising from Fee Simple
on Condition Subsequent _____ 109

D. REMAINDERS _____ 110
13. The Concept of a Remainder _____ 110
14. Historical Basis of Distinction Between Remainders 112
15. The Classification of Remainders _____ 114
16. The Definition of a Vested Remainder _____ 116
17. The Classification of Vested Remainders _____ 117
18. The Nature of a Contingent Remainder _____ 123
19. Remainders Subject to a Condition Precedent ____ 124
20. Remainders to Unascertained Persons _____ 125
21. Destructibility of Contingent Remainders at Common Law _____ 128
22. The Destructibility Rule Today _____ 134
23. Alienability of Remainders _____ 135

Chapter 6. The Rule in Shelley's Case and the Doctrine of Worthier Title _____ 138

A. THE RULE IN SHELLEY'S CASE _____ 138

Section
1. Statement of the Rule _____ 138
2. Origin and Development of the Rule _____ 139
3. Operation of the Rule _____ 142
4. The Rule in Modern Law _____ 148

B. THE DOCTRINE OF THE WORTHIER TITLE _____ 149
5. Statement of the Doctrine _____ 149
6. Origin of the Doctrine _____ 151
7. The Doctrine in American Law _____ 153
8. The Testamentary Branch of the Doctrine _____ 153
9. The Inter Vivos Branch of the Doctrine _____ 154
10. Statutory Modification of the Doctrine _____ 161

TABLE OF CONTENTS

Page

Chapter 7. Common Law Methods of Conveyancing ------- 163

Section

1. Creation and Transfer of Present Freehold Estates 163
2. Creation of Non-freehold Estates ---------------- 166
3. Creation of Future Interests -------------------- 167
4. Common Law Rules Restricting the Creation of Future Interests -------------------------------------- 169
5. Transfer of Future Estates --------------------- 170

Chapter 8. Uses and the Statute of Uses ------------------- 173

Section

1. The Nature of a Use --------------------------- 173
2. Use Estates and Interests Including Springing and Shifting Uses --------------------------------- 176
3. Methods of Creating or Raising a Use ------------- 179
4. Resulting Uses ------------------------------- 180
5. The Statute of Uses --------------------------- 181

Chapter 9. The Effect of the Statute of Uses -------------- 185

Section

1. The Effect of the Statute on Conveyancing -------- 185
2. Feoffment to Uses ---------------------------- 186
3. Resulting Uses After the Statute ---------------- 186
4. Conveyance by Bargain and Sale ----------------- 188
5. Conveyance by Lease and Release ---------------- 188
6. The Covenant to Stand Seised ------------------- 190
7. The Effect of the Statute on Future Interests—Executory Interests ------------------------------- 192
8. The Statute of Wills and Executory Devises ------- 195
9. Characteristics of Executory Interests ----------- 196
10. Contingent Remainders and Executory Interests -- 199
11. Executory Interests in Modern Law -------------- 205
12. Unexecuted Uses ----------------------------- 207
13. The Statute of Uses in the United States --------- 212

XV

TABLE OF CONTENTS

Page

Chapter 10. Concurrent Ownership _____ 216

Section

1. The Concept of Joint Tenancy _____ 216
2. Creation of a Joint Tenancy _____ 217
3. Characteristics of a Joint Tenancy _____ 220
4. Tenancy in Common _____ 224
5. Relations of Cotenants Inter Se _____ 225
6. Tenancy by the Entirety—The Common Law Concept _____ 229
7. The Tenancy by the Entirety in Modern Law _____ 230
8. Tenancy in Coparcenary _____ 235

Table of Cases _____ 237

Index _____ 245

†

INTRODUCTION TO THE LAW
OF REAL PROPERTY

Chapter 1

THE BACKGROUND

INTRODUCTION

It would be economical in terms of time and effort if we could begin the study of the law of real property by proceeding directly to a consideration of that law as it is in our own day and place. Unfortunately, such a short cut is not practical. A thorough understanding of the modern land law is impossible without a knowledge of its historical background. That law has been a millenium in the making. During this long period great changes have been effected by means of legislation and decisions, as well as by the development of new social systems and customs, but the process of change has been one of evolution, not revolution. The imprint of the past is still discernible in the present. In this branch of the law more than any other we can time and again invoke the often quoted statement of Mr. Justice Holmes: "Upon this point a page of history is worth a volume of logic." [1] And if the aridity of legal history tends to be irksome we might

---

[1] New York Trust Co. v. Eisner, 256 U.S. 345 at 349, 41 S.Ct. 506 at 507, 65 L.Ed. 963 at 983 (1921).

recall Mr. Justice Cardozo's statement that this is a field "where there can be no progress without history." [2]

SECTION 1. THE NORMAN SETTLEMENT

And so we begin with the England of the Norman Conquest (1066). The Norman arrow, shot perhaps at random, that pierced the eye socket of Harold, the Saxon king, decided not only the Battle of Hastings but deflected the course of development of English law for centuries to come. The Conquest, while preserving the frame-work of the Old English state, gave to England a new dynasty, a new ruling class and a new system of land holding.

The Conqueror operated on the principle of political legitimacy. Tenuous as his claim to the English throne may have been, his successes in battle put beyond dispute his assertion that he was the legitimate successor of Edward the Confessor and, therefore, entitled to the rights and prerogatives of an English king.[1] Consequently, those who had opposed him at Hastings and in the later risings forfeited their lands.[2] The Saxon nobility, who had formed the backbone of the opposition, were for the most part wiped out or driven into exile. Their lands became available for distribution to William's men as a reward for services and the distribution itself served as a means of establishing on a solid foundation a new Norman aristocracy.

It is a tribute to the extraordinary administrative ability of William that this vast redistribution of English lands was carried

[2] Cardozo, Nature of the Judicial Process 54 (1921). And see Wyzanski, History and Law, 26 U. of Chi.L.Rev. 236 (1959).

[1] The struggle between Harold and William for the English Crown is vividly and authentically portrayed in Hope Muntz's magnificent historical novel, The Golden Warrior (1949).

[2] See the writ of William I to the Abbot of Bury St. Edmunds ordering the abbot to turn over to the king the lands of the abbey tenants "who stood in battle against me and were slain" at Hastings. The writ is set out in Douglas and Greenaway, 2 English Historical Documents 918 (Oxford Univ. Press, 1953).

out in an orderly manner. The whole process was controlled by the firm hand of the king. Immense holdings were granted, as might be expected, to his kinsmen and to his closest associates in the great project of the Conquest. To ten of his principal followers he gave almost one-fourth of England.[3] To lesser barons he made grants of the smaller fiefs or holdings of English earls and thegns. Normally, the grants were not of a compact territorial unit but consisted of manors scattered through several counties.

The properties granted consisted in part of land for use and occupancy, and in part of a congeries of rights and privileges correlative to customary services and duties owed by the humbler tenants living within the manorial extent. The peasant occupants of village lands were probably left undisturbed for the most part in their little holdings but they acquired new lords to whom they must render the ancient dues. Continuity with the past was preserved through the principle applied by the Conqueror that every earl, bishop, abbot and baron to whom he gave land held it with the same rights and privileges as his English predecessor in title had on the day when King Edward the Confessor "was alive and dead." [4]

The larger baronial estates, or honours as they came to be called, were normally created out of the holdings of numerous Englishmen. As many as eighty English estates, situated in different regions, might be combined to compose a single lord's honour. In the course of the Norman settlement several thousand smaller estates were compressed into fewer than two hundred major honours. The lords of these honours were the men who, with William, established the new English state.

[3] See Douglas and Greenaway, 2 English Historical Documents 22 (Oxford Univ. Press, 1953).

[4] This curious expression comes from Domesday Book, the record of the great survey of England made by William's order in 1086. See infra, § 4.

SECTION 2. THE INTRODUCTION OF FEUDAL TENURE

From the legal standpoint one of the significant aspects of the Norman plantation was the introduction into England of the most highly organized type of feudal tenure—military tenure. Feudalism is a generic term that may be used to describe the social structure of Western Europe in the Middle Ages. It had for its central core the relationship of lord and vassal (not then a word of opprobrium) bound together by a bond of personal loyalty and owing mutual aid and assistance. The relation was usually evidenced by the solemn ceremony of homage wherein the vassal knelt before the lord, acknowledged himself to be his man, and swore fealty to him. It was frequently accompanied by a grant of land from the lord to the vassal, the land to be held of the lord by the vassal as tenant.[1] Normally, by the terms of the grant specific services were imposed on the tenant and these services (*servitia debita*) were considered to be a burden on the land itself.

Military tenure was known in Normandy and the Conqueror used it to build in England a military organization adequate to maintain the Crown against rebellion from within and invasion from without. Most of the lords and barons to whom he granted English lands held them under an obligation to supply a specified quota of knights for the royal host whenever they should be required. The number of knights to be furnished was in each case fixed by the terms of the charter evidencing the grant and, therefore, initially depended on the will and necessities of the king. This number bore no constant relation to the size or value of the honour granted. The lay lords who received grants of the

---

[1] Land was not the only subject matter of a feudal grant. It was custo-mary throughout Western Europe in the Middle Ages for great and petty lords to obtain vassals bound to render military service by granting to such vassals a monetary annuity. The feudal bond was created by the rendition of hom-age by the grantee to the grantor. These grants numbered in the thousands. In the medieval period status performed the function that contract does in the modern law. For a detailed study of feudal annuities see Lyon, From Fief to Indenture (1957).

king [2] were, of course, accustomed in their own countries to the institution of tenure, or land holding, in return for military service to a lord. Not so were the bishops and abbots to whom William gave lands, or confirmed older grants, on condition of knight service. On these ecclesiastical tenants in chief he also imposed the duty of finding a stipulated number of knights for service in the feudal host.[3] This innovation of the Conqueror, induced by the military necessities of the times, yielded an additional 800 knights, in round numbers, for the king's service. In all, the quota of knights demanded of the lay and ecclesiastical baronage amounted to approximately 5000 men.

SECTION 3.   THE CREATION OF SUB-TENURES

The expense to the tenants in chief of maintaining as part of their households the prescribed quota of knights must have been considerable. Moreover, the constant presence in the household of a number of armed men, inclined to be disorderly at times, was a matter of concern particularly to the ecclesiastical tenants. Slowly at first but with increasing frequency the tenants in chief made allotments of lands to their knights who thereupon became tenants of their lords. The amount of land given in return for the obligation to supply the service of one knight (the knight's fee of feudal records) varied. It depended on the bargain made by the lord and his prospective tenant. A particular tract might be made up of a number of knight's fees and, in later times, might be subdivided into fractional parts of a knight's fee. In

---

[2] A person holding land directly under the king was called a tenant in chief (in Latin, tenant *in capite*)

[3] The Constitutions of Clarendon (1164), purporting to embody established feudal customs, provided in Cl. XI: "Archbishops, bishops and all beneficed clergy of the realm, who hold of the king in chief, have their possessions from the lord king by barony and are answerable for them to the king's justices and officers; they observe and perform all royal rights and customs and, like other barons, ought to be present at the judgments of the king's court together with the barons, until a case shall arise of judgment concerning mutilation or death." Douglas & Greenaway, 2 English Historical Documents 721 (Oxford Univ.Press, 1953).

some cases the number of knights enfeoffed, that is, given land, by the tenant in chief exceeded the quota owed for the king's service and in other cases the number was less.[1] This was a matter of the development of the individual honour.

All tenure implied service due from the tenant but the service fixed at the creation of the tenure might be and often was non-military in nature. The king made provision in land for his important administrative and household officials and to such tenures was attached the duty of rendering specific services necessary to the functioning of the royal household. The service prescribed required the performance of such duties as those of marshal, steward, butler or chamberlain. These were tenants of dignity and rank but this type of tenure also embraced tenants who served the king in his chamber, his pantry and his kitchen. The Conqueror, for example, gave half a hide of land (about 60 acres) in Gloucestershire to his cook. The greater tenants in chief, whose households were often royal establishments in miniature, also gave lands to some of their retainers subject to the obligation to render a prescribed personal service to the lord. Such tenures, whether held of the king or of an intermediate lord, became known as serjeanty tenures.[2]

Moreover, many a small landholder found it advisable in an unruly age to place himself under the protection of some powerful earl or abbot by becoming his man. He hoped thereby to

[1] In 1166 Henry II ordered each of his tenants in chief to answer what amounted to a questionnaire on the number of knights enfeoffed on the tenant's estate and the number required by his *servitium debitum*. The purpose of this survey may have been to provide a basis for an increase in the feudal assessment which in most cases had been fixed in the Conqueror's reign. The returns of the tenants in chief (*Cartae Baronum*) show in many cases the enfeoffment of more knights than required for the king's service. The return of the Archbishop of York explains how this came about: "For our predecessors enfeoffed more knights than they owed to the king, and they did this, not for the necessities of the royal service, but because they wished to provide for their relatives and servants." Douglas and Greenaway, 2 English Historical Documents 907 (Oxford Univ.Press, 1953); 3 Holdsworth, History of English Law 42–43 (3rd ed. 1927).

[2] Serjeanty tenure is further described in § 6, infra.

gain as an ally "a mightier friend than the law could be." [3] He surrendered his lands to the lord to be received back from him subject to the duty of rendering military or other service. By this process of commendation the tenurial system was further expanded.

SECTION 4. THE DOMESDAY SURVEY

In the last year of his reign the Conqueror caused to be made a comprehensive and detailed survey of most of the land in England. The primary purpose of the survey was fiscal in nature. The king desired precise, up-to-date information as to contributions made by each estate to the Danegeld, a direct tax levied throughout the country. But in addition he sought an accurate and complete picture of the results of the redistribution of English lands that had taken place in the twenty years that had elapsed since the Norman invasion.

The great survey was carried out through commissioners who were sent into most of the shires to receive the sworn verdicts of selected jurors as to the property holdings of each tenant—the source of his title, the extent and value of his holdings, the composition of the estate, and any changes in the size of the estate since the Conquest. The entire project was accomplished with a ruthless Norman efficiency that shocked the easy going Saxons.[1] The information obtained was rearranged and summarized

---

[3] Maitland, Domesday Book and Beyond 70 (1897).

[1] The Anglo-Saxon Chronicle after relating that William at his Christmas Council in 1085 had "much thought and very deep speech" with his council "about this land, how it was set and by what men" goes on to tell us: "Then he sent his men all over England into every shire and had them find out how many hundred hides there were in the shire, or what land and cattle the king himself had in the country, or what dues he ought to have in twelve months from the shire. Also he had a record made of how much land his archbishops had, and his bishops and his abbots and his earls—and though I relate it at too great length—what or how much everybody had who was occupying land in England, in land or cattle, and how much money it was worth. So very narrowly did he have it investigated, that there was no single hide nor a yard of land, nor indeed (it is a shame to relate but it seemed no shame

according to the holdings in each county of the king's tenants-in-chief and to that extent the survey became a statistical record of feudal tenures. The rearranged summary or digest was compiled in two volumes which became popularly known as Domesday Book.[2] The two volumes, originally kept in the king's treasury, are still preserved in the Public Record Office in London—the finest extant legal record of any medieval kingdom.

Although Domesday Book tells us little of the kinds of tenure and the services due from the tenants, it does make clear that the principle of dependent tenure had been firmly established as the basic form of English land holding.[3] At the end of the Conqueror's reign there was little place in English law for the man who, in the words of Domesday Book, had been free "to go with his land to whatever lord he would."

SECTION 5. LEGAL RELATIONS OF LORD AND TENANT

In addition to the personal relationship arising from the feudal bond between lord and tenant there existed a legal relationship which, to use modern terms, rested partly in contract and partly

to him to do) one ox nor one cow nor one pig was there left out, and not put down in his record: and all those records were brought to him afterwards." Douglas and Greenaway, 2 English Historical Documents 161 (Oxford Univ. Press, 1953).

[2] One explanation of the name of the book is that the records were deemed by the populace to be as conclusive as the day of judgment. See 2 Holdsworth, History of English Law 163 (1927). For a brief description of the Domesday inquisition and translated excerpts from the book, see Douglas and Greenaway, 2 English Historical Documents 847–878 (1953). Maitland's essays on the subject (Domesday Book and Beyond) are a highly specialized treatment.

[3] "The general theory that all land tenure, except indeed the tenure by which the king holds land in demesne, is dependent tenure, seems to be implied, not only by many particular entries, but also by the whole scheme of the book. Every holder of land, except the king, holds it of (*de*) some lord, and therefore every acre of land that is not royal demesne can be arranged under the name of some tenant in chief. Even a church will hold its land, if not of the king, then of some other lord." Maitland, Domesday Book and Beyond 151 (1897).

in property.   The lord owed protection and warranty to the tenant [1] and the tenant owed services to the lord.   But both parties also had rights centered in the land which was the subject of the tenure.   If B holding land under A is in actual occupancy he is said to be tenant in demesne and obviously has property rights consisting of a general right to possess, use and enjoy the land.   But his lord, A, who in turn may hold of the king, also holds the land—not in demesne but in service.   Not only B but the land itself owes the service stipulated when the tenure between A and B was created.   This service attaches to the land and runs with it.   No transfer of the land by B will free it from this obligation.   If B transfers the land to C the parties are free to agree between themselves as to how the service will be discharged but A's right to the service cannot be eliminated.   If the service be not forthcoming A has the remedy of distress (the right to seize any chattels found on the land whether owned by B or C) and in some cases a remedy against the land itself. [2]

So also, the service owing to the king from A as a tenant in chief binds the tenement regardless of the number of sub-tenures created or of the sub-divisions made of the land.

The same piece of land, then, could be the subject of property rights in different persons in the sense that several persons could have proprietary interests centered in the land.   And since a sin-

[1] The doing of homage by a tenant created an implied obligation on the part of the lord to warrant the title to the lands conveyed to the tenant.   If the tenant was later ousted by one having a better title the lord was required to give him a tenement of equal value.   In any proceeding against the tenant by one claiming title to the land the tenant could call upon his lord to defend the title.   The advantage to the tenant of being able to call in (vouch to warranty) a powerful lord to assume the defense of his title helps to explain the creation of tenures by commendation.   See § 3, supra.   In the thirteenth and later century express warranties were commonly inserted in charters of feoffment.

[2] In early feudal times a deliberate refusal on the part of the tenant to render the services due to the lord amounted to felony and the lands on conviction of the tenant reverted or escheated to the lord.   Cessation of services soon ceased to be a felony but the Statute of Gloucester (1278) gave the lord the remedy of forfeiture of the land for wilfully withholding the services.

gle parcel could be the subject of several tenures with a different service attaching to each tenure, the adjustment of the rights of the persons in the feudal hierarchy became an increasingly complex process.[3]

Viewing the system of tenure as a whole it appears as a pyramidal structure. At the top of the pyramid is the king who alone is always lord and never tenant. Directly under him are the tenants in chief; beneath these are tenants of lower social standing holding the smaller parcels into which an honour or barony is sub-divided. At the broad base are the peasants actually tilling the soil (the tenants paravail). All persons having an intermediate place in this structure hold the land in a dual capacity— they are tenants of those above them and lords (mesne lords) with respect to those holding under them.

SECTION 6.   THE CLASSIFICATION OF TENURES

Inasmuch as lord and tenant were free to fix between themselves at the time of the creation of a new tenure the kind and amount of services due from the tenant a wonderful variety of tenures came into existence. But by the thirteenth century the land law was becoming private property law and less a branch of public law involving governmental, military and jurisdictional aspects. The king's courts, administering a centralized legal system, assumed the task of reducing the variety of tenures to a manageable classification and by the time of Edward I's reign (1272–1307) the great division of tenures into free and unfree had been established and the list of free tenures had become fixed under four major headings.[1]

---

[3] "It is no impossibility that Edward should hold in villeinage of Ralph, who holds in free socage of the Prior of Barnwell, who holds in frankalmoin of Earl Alan, who holds by knight's service of the king." 1 Pollock and Maitland, History of English Law 239 (2d ed. 1898) (hereinafter cited as Pollock and Maitland).

[1] For a detailed discussion of the distinction between free and unfree tenure, see 3 Holdsworth, History of English Law 29–34 (3rd ed. 1927) (hereinafter cited as Holdsworth); 1 Pollock & Maitland 368–373.

The distinction between free and unfree tenures indicates the connection between personal status and tenure that obtained in the medieval land law and still existed at the end of the thirteenth century. The principal test applied by the judges in any given case to determine the nature of the tenure as free or unfree was the character of the services required to be rendered by the tenant: were the services definite and certain or were they dependent on the will of the lord as to quantity or manner of performance; were they of a servile nature or worthy of a free man? The legal consequence of the tenure being free or unfree was important. The tenant of land holding in free tenure was protected by the king's courts and had the benefit of the real actions; the unfree tenant had his remedy against those disturbing his possession only in his lord's court.

FREE TENURE

Free tenures were classified under four main divisions:

A. Tenure by knight service;

B. Serjeanty;

C. Frankalmoin;

D. Free and common socage.

A few words may be said about each of these tenures.

A. *Tenure by Knight Service*

This was the typical tenure of feudalism and most of the tenants in chief of the king held their lands by this tenure. Originally the most honorable form of tenure, it gave to the tenant in the twelfth century not only land ownership but a voice in the great council and jurisdiction over his sub-tenants.[2] The obliga-

---

[2] Attendance at the king's court by tenants in chief and at the lord's court by under-tenants was an auxiliary service attaching to most tenures. In medieval times the word "court" was not restricted to a tribunal presided over by a professionally trained judge sitting with or without a jury. As to suit of court, see 1 Pollock & Maitland 586–594.

tion to render military service by supplying the specified quota of properly armed and equipped knights for the king's host meant actual military service in the first century after the Conquest. In theory the required period of service was forty days and then only within the kingdom. But as the art of war developed it was becoming increasingly clear that an army of paid professional soldiers was more efficient than a hastily summoned motley assortment of non-professionals and Henry II (1154–1189) encouraged his tenants in chief to make a monetary payment instead of providing knights. This monetary payment, known as scutage, having been made to the king by the tenants in chief, they in turn proceeded to levy scutage on their own tenants who owed the duty of supplying knights for the king's service. From the middle of the twelfth to the latter part of the thirteenth century military tenure supplied knights, or the money to hire knights, for the royal army but the tendency to treat scutage as merely another form of direct tax became more pronounced. Because of the splitting of knights' fees into fractional parts and the very complexities of tenure itself, it proved an inefficient form of tax and gradually fell into disuse. With the decay of the feudal system military tenure had become inadequate to supply either the men or the money to furnish the sinews of war. As Maitland so well puts it: "But in truth, the whole system is becoming obsolete. If tenure by knight service had been abolished in 1300, the kings of the subsequent ages would have been deprived of the large revenue that they drew from wardships, marriages and so forth; really they would have lost little else." [3]

B. Serjeanty Tenure

Serjeanty means service and is derived from the medieval Latin word "serientia." It designates a type of tenure characterized by the obligation to perform a personal service definite as to time and usually localized as to place of performance. The services were heterogeneous in nature ranging from honorable to

---

[3] 1 Pollock and Maitland 276.

menial. They related to solemn occasions of state, performance of duties in the royal or seignorial household, military service, royal sporting activities, and the rendering at stated times of supplies or specific articles.[4] Many officers of state, members of the royal household, important officials attached to the households of magnates, and humbler tenants held their lands by serjeanty in the twelfth and thirteenth centuries.

The wide variety of services due from serjeanty tenants and the similarity of some of the services to those due from other classes of tenants made it difficult to distinguish this tenure in many cases from knight service or socage tenure.[5] The element of personal service seems to have been its one distinguishing feature. When the practise of retaining hired servants developed in the fourteenth century the services due from serjeanty tenants were in many cases commuted to a payment of rent and the tenure was converted into socage.

Eventually, serjeanty tenure became divided into grand serjeanty and petty serjeanty. The former name was reserved for serjeanty tenures held directly of the king and requiring the performance of some honorary ceremonial service. Petty serjeanty became socage tenure in effect and involved services of a humbler nature—such as to provide military supplies or articles of small value.[6] A few vestiges of grand serjeanty remain to the present day in England in connection with coronation ceremonies but as

---

[4] For a description of the services due from different serjeanty tenants, see Kimball, Serjeanty Tenure in Medieval England (1936) 69–129. 3 Holdsworth, History of English Law (3rd ed. 1927) 46–51.

[5] It has been suggested that the classification of many holdings involving different services under the single heading of serjeanty tenure was made by royal officials in the twelfth century for administrative convenience in collecting the revenues due the king. See Kimball, op. cit., 15–16; 1 Pollock and Maitland 287.

[6] Although serjeanty tenures were held of the crown and of mesne lords in the twelfth and thirteenth centuries, yet by the latter part of the fifteenth century serjeanty tenure could be held only of the king. Since wardship was incident to grand serjeanty but not to petit serjeanty, Littleton writing about 1481 could describe the latter class as "socage in effect." Littleton, Tenures § 160. As to wardship, see § 7, infra.

a whole this form of tenure had no important impact on the land law.

C.   Frankalmoin Tenure

Frankalmoin, meaning free alms, was a tenure arising from a gift of lands to a church, religious body or ecclesiastical official in return for services of a religious nature, such as saying Masses or prayers, but with no secular obligation. No lay person could hold by frankalmoin. The mere fact that land was held by an ecclesiastical tenant, such as a bishop or abbot, did not make the tenure frankalmoin. Many prelates and ecclesiastics held lands by knight service, as we have seen. The strictly religious nature of the service and the absence of any secular duty was the characteristic quality of frankalmoin.

Grants of land to be held in frankalmoin could not be made, except by the king or with his permission, after the Statute Quia Emptores (1290); hence, this form of tenure became of slight importance.

D.   Free and Common Socage

The services due from a man holding by socage tenure were normally of an agricultural or monetary nature. He was bound to perform specified agricultural work on the lord's own lands, or to render annually to the lord a definite quantity of agricultural products, or, more often, to pay in money a periodic rent. This money rent might be nominal or substantial. But whatever service was due it was fixed and definite, not dependent on the will of the lord as to amount or quantity. For in this quality of definiteness lay the distinguishing feature between socage tenure and unfree tenure. Eventually, this form of tenure became the great residual tenure. A free tenant who did not hold by military service or by serjeanty or by frankalmoin was deemed to hold in socage. Originally it was not as dignified a form of holding as military tenure but because it was freer from oppressive financial burdens than the more aristocratic tenures it had distinct advantages for the tenant when knighthood ceased to be in flower.   It was destined to become, as we shall see later, the one surviving form of tenure.[7]

UNFREE TENURE

Unfree tenure has for its background the manorial organization that dominated so much of life in medieval England.   The manor was an agricultural, governmental and fiscal unit, usually co-extensive in territory with the ancient village, composed of lands held by the lord and by tenants of different classes.   A portion of the manorial lands were held of the lord by free tenants in socage or by knight service.   The remaining lands (demesne lands) were retained by the lord in his own possession and enjoyment and consisted of the manor house with its appurtenances, scattered strips of arable land in the open fields, and the pasturage and waste lands.   The labor force required to work these demesne lands of the lord was supplied by a servile class of manorial inhabitants, called villeins.   The villein was a serf but not a slave.   Against his lord he had no rights save security of life and limb but against third persons he had the rights of a free man.   He could not leave the manor and his time and his labor were at the arbitrary command of the lord; his humble cottage or hovel, as well as his little strip in the common fields, he held at the will of the lord.

Not only did the lord supervise the agricultural economy of the manor; he also, through the manorial courts over which he presided in person or through his bailiff, adjudicated controversies among his tenants and regulated much of their daily lives.[8]

---

[7] Two special varieties of socage tenure, both of them influenced by local custom, were gavelkind tenure and burgage, or borough English, tenure. Gavelkind prevailed in the county of Kent and was subject to special rules, the most important being that on the death of the tenant the land descended to all of the sons equally. Burgage tenure existed in a few places (such as in a portion of Nottingham) by special custom. On the death of the tenant the land descended to the youngest son—the precise opposite of the general common law rule of primogeniture.

[8] The lord's rights of jurisdiction were exercised by means of two courts: the Court Baron for free tenants and the Court Customary for villein tenants.

Such protection as the villein tenant received as tenant he obtained from the manorial and not the royal courts.

Such was the manor in thirteenth century England. But in the next century began the evolutionary process that in time was to change the personal status of the villein into that of a free man, and to convert his precarious tenure into that of a substantial property owner. A growing scarcity of agricultural labor, greatly accentuated by the plague of the Black Death (1348–1349), forced most lords to substitute a money rent for labor service by the villein tenants.[9] And gradually, the obligations of the villein tenants became fixed by manorial customs so that their land holding became a definite type of customary tenure, no longer dependent on the lord's will.[10]

In most manors the court exercised not only civil jurisdiction but also criminal jurisdiction of minor offenses. Actions of detinue, debt, covenant and tort for defamation were common. As proof that the age of chivalry was over, consider this case from one of the Courts Baron: "It is found by inquest (the jury of tenants) that Rohese (Rose) Bindebere called Ralph Bolay thief, and he called her whore. Therefore both in mercy 3d. (fined three pence each). And for that the trespass done to the said Ralph exceeds the trespass done to the said Rohese, as has been found, therefore, it is considered that the said Ralph do recover from the said Rohese 12 d. for his taxed damages." And sad to relate, a manorial court found it necessary to issue the following rule: "It is ordered that all women in the vill hold their tongues and not scold or defame anyone." See 2 Holdsworth 383.

[9] The decline in the value of money which resulted from the importation to Europe of gold and silver from the new world inured to the benefit of the fourteenth century villein tenants' successors. In Maitland's striking phrase, the increase in the value of the land during the seventeenth century was "an unearned increment, the product of the American mines." See 3 Holdsworth 212.

[10] Brief mention may be made of a peculiar form of manorial tenure known as tenure in ancient demesne. This was restricted to tenants of manors which had belonged to the Crown in the time of Edward the Confessor and William the Conqueror. These tenants stood midway between free and villein tenants and had special privileges and obligations. Traces of this tenure persisted into the twentieth century. See Mertenns v. Hill, (1901) 1 Ch. 842. It was converted into socage tenure in 1926. Law of Property Acts, 1922 and 1925. Proof that a particular parcel of land was held in ancient demesne was established by resort to Domesday Book and the records of that book were conclusive.

This customary tenure evolved into a unique type of land holding which later became known as copyhold tenure. The rights of such tenants were evidenced by the records of the manorial courts. They had the right to transfer their lands upon payment of a fine to the lord but such transfers could not be made by the common law methods of feoffment and grant available to tenants holding by a free tenure. Copyhold lands were transferable only by surrender and admittance. The tenant could, by custom, surrender the lands to the lord of the manor to the use of a person designated by the tenant and the lord was bound to admit such person into the tenancy. The surrender and admittance were recorded on the rolls of the manorial court and a copy of the rolls delivered to the new tenant as evidence of his title. Hence, the tenant was said to hold by copy of court roll and the form of holding was labelled copyhold tenure.

The freehold of lands originally held by an unfree tenure was in the lord, not the tenant, hence a copyhold tenant could not maintain a real action in the royal courts to protect his interest. In fact, until the fifteenth and sixteenth centuries the tenant's only remedy was in the manorial courts. But the courts of equity, and later the common law courts, became active in regulating and supervising the manorial courts and the customary tenant was given protection against the lord of the manor and against third persons. Yet copyhold tenure continued to bear the marks of its origin even at the period of its ultimate development, and because of its unsuitability to modern life it was the subject of considerable legislation in the nineteenth century. Statutes were enacted providing for compulsory enfranchisement of the land at the option of either lord or tenant.[11] It was finally abolished as of January 1, 1926 by the Law of Property Act, 1922, which converted it into free and common socage.[12]

---

[11] For a detailed treatment of the history of copyhold tenure, see 7 Holdsworth 296–312.

[12] For a brief explanation of the scope of the Law of Property Act, 1922, 1925 see Cheshire, Modern Real Property Law (8th ed. 1958) 7, 82–84. A few incidents, e. g., the tenants' rights of common of pasturage of beasts, continue to attach to lands formerly copyhold unless lord and tenant agree to their extinction.

SECTION 7. THE INCIDENTS OF FREE TENURES

In addition to the particular services required to be rendered by the tenant to his lord in accordance with the terms stipulated at the creation of the tenure, there were further rights given to the lord, and obligations imposed on the tenant, known as incidents of tenure. These incidents derived from the feudal relationship, apart from any express agreement of the tenant. By the fifteenth century the services due from the various tenants had for the most part been commuted into fixed money rents which decreased in value as the purchasing power of money declined. But some of the profitable incidents of tenure were tied to the land itself and, therefore, became more valuable as land values increased. As a consequence, such incidents had a more significant effect on the development of the land law than the ancient tenurial services or their monetary equivalents.

The principal incidents were homage and fealty, relief and primer seisin, wardship and marriage, aids, fines for alienation, and escheat.

Homage and Fealty

Homage was the feudal ceremony whereby the tenant, kneeling unarmed before the lord, solemnly acknowledged himself to be the man of the lord. It was a necessary incident to tenure by knight service and became obsolete when that tenure ceased to be military in fact. Fealty was the oath sworn by the tenant to be faithful to his lord. Like homage it fell into disuse and was no longer exacted in practise after the end of the feudal period. The duty of allegiance owed to the king as supreme lord overshadowed and eventually eliminated the fealty owed to other lords.

Relief and Primer Seisin

A relief was a sum payable to the lord by the heir of a deceased tenant for the privilege of succeeding to his ancestor's lands. Inheritance was a privilege to be paid for, not an unconditional right.   Originally incident only to tenure by military service, it was later extended to socage and serjeanty tenures. In the case of socage tenure the amount of the relief became fixed at one year's rent and in that of serjeanty tenure at one year's value of the land.   As early as Magna Carta (1215) the relief payable by the heir of a military tenant was set at 100 shillings for a knight's fee.   Payment of the relief by the heir of a subtenant entitled him to immediate possession but on the death of a tenant in chief the king by royal prerogative was entitled to first seisin (*primer seisin*) of all the deceased tenant's lands, not only those held directly of the king but also those held of mesne lords.   Only after an official inquest to determine heirship, the doing of homage, and the payment of the relief was the heir admitted to seisin or possession.

Wardship and Marriage

Upon the death of a tenant holding by knight service or grand serjeanty leaving as his heir a male under 21 or a female under 14, the lord was entitled to wardship of both the person and the lands of the heir.   The lord had a right to the rents and profits of the lands with no duty to account at any time to the heir and this profitable guardianship continued during the male heir's minority or until the female heir married or attained the age of 16.   The custody of the ward's person imposed on the lord a duty to maintain and educate the ward but also gave him the right to arrange a suitable marriage for the ward and to pocket the profit from the arrangement.   The heir might refuse the tendered marriage but in that event the lord had a right to the value of the marriage, that is, to that sum which the prospective spouse's family was willing to pay for the match.   If the heir married without the consent of the lord, the lord was entitled to double the value of the marriage.   In early feudal times the lord had a legitimate interest in the marriage of his female ward to insure that she did not marry an enemy of his but the extension of this right of marriage to male wards indicates that both wardship and marriage soon found the real basis for their continued existence in their pecuniary value to the king and the mesne lords.

As early as the thirteenth century they were looked upon as valuable rights to be bought and sold and as late as the seventeenth century they were an important source of royal revenue.[1]

Socage tenure was free from the burdensome aspects of wardship and marriage that applied to military tenures. Guardianship of the infant socage tenant was given to his nearest relative who was incapable of inheriting the land, and the guardian in socage was accountable at the end of the guardianship to his ward for the profits derived from the land as well as for any profits accruing from the ward's marriage.[2]

Aids

Aids were originally financial contributions made to the lord by the tenant to assist the lord in times of emergency and arose out of the close personal bond inherent in the early tenures. But what had been once a matter of benevolence on the part of the tenant crystallized into an obligation. The chief aids due from a military tenant were to ransom the lord's person if taken prisoner, to help in the expense of making his eldest son a knight, and to assist in providing a dowry for his eldest daughter on her marriage. Statutes in the thirteenth and fourteenth century fixed the amounts of the latter two aids and tenants in socage were subject to these statutory aids. Aids were abolished in 1660.

---

[1] So important to the Crown were the revenues from feudal dues that in 1540 a special administrative and judicial tribunal, the Court of Wards and Liveries, was set up by Parliament (32 Henry VIII C. 46) to supervise the collection of those dues. The records of this Court show that in the period 1610–1613 sales of wardships averaged about one hundred and twenty-three per year and that by 1640 the average annual revenue from sales of wardships and marriages was over 39,000£. Bell, The Court of Wards and Liveries 57, 114 (1953).

[2] Oddly enough, the term "guardian in socage" still appears in the New York statutes (McKinney's N.Y.Dom.Rel.Law, § 80) although tenure has long ceased to exist in that state. In Combs v. Jackson, 2 Wend. 153 (N.Y.1828), common law guardianship in socage was recognized with respect to lands granted in socage prior to the American Revolution.

Fines for Alienation

Prior to 1290 the tenant could not alienate or transfer his fee without a license from the lord of the fee who exacted a fine or monetary payment for the license. By the beginning of the thirteenth century tenants other than tenants in chief had the power, within rather vague limits, to convey their lands to others, but seignorial rights in the land were still sufficiently strong to preserve to the lord a financial return on the transaction.³ The Statute Quia Emptores, enacted in 1290, granted to "every freeman" the right to alienate without paying a fine to his lord. This statute was construed as not affecting the rights of the king, hence tenants *in capite* continued to be subject to fines for alienation until 1660 when legislation was adopted abrogating most of the tenurial incidents.

Escheat

On the death of the tenant without heirs the land returned or escheated to the lord of the fee. Moreover, if the tenant was convicted of felony the land in that case also escheated or fell back to the lord on the theory that the tenant's blood had been so corrupted as to lose its inheritable quality.⁴ In the event of escheat for felony the Crown was entitled to hold the felon's

---

3 The Great Charter of 1217 provided; "No free man shall henceforth give or sell so much of his land as that out of the residue he may not sufficiently do to the lord of the fee the service which pertains to that fee." Although the Charter did not distinguish between tenants in chief and mesne tenants, in fact such a distinction was drawn in the thirteenth century and the king's right to prohibit tenants in chief and serjeanty tenants from alienating was recognized. In 1327 it was provided by statute that where lands held directly of the king were alienated without his license they would not be held forfeited but the transfer would be subject to a reasonable fine. 3 Holdsworth 78–87.

4 Felony originally meant a serious breach of the feudal bond created by the tenant's homage. Only later did it come to include grave crimes of various kinds. Magna Carta (1215) settled the right of the feudal lord to escheat for felony. c. 32. But if the tenant committed high treason the lands of the traitor were forfeited to the Crown. This right of forfeiture was based on royal prerogative, not on tenure, and it undercut the feudal lord's right of escheat in high treason cases.

lands for a year and a day and to waste them—a right which the lord of the fee usually bought off or compounded for in later times. Escheat for felony was abolished by statute in 1870 and escheat for failure of heirs was abrogated in 1925.

SECTION 8. STATUTES AFFECTING TENURE

After it had become established that a mesne tenant could alienate or transfer his interest in the land, subject to the payment of a fine to the lord of the fee, the alienation might be made by substitution or by sub-infeudation. If B holds land under A and conveys his entire interest in the land to C, C now holds as tenant under A and B drops out of the tenurial picture. It is true that so long as the services required of the tenant were of some importance the lord of the fee would have a personal interest in the identity of the tenant but in time the incidents of tenure became much more valuable than the particular services so that it made no practical difference to the lord whether B or C was his tenant. Hence, the lords had no strong objection to alienation by substitution. But the practice of alienation by sub-infeudation was definitely objectionable from the viewpoint of the lords. By sub-infeudation a new tenure was created. Thus, B, holding lands under A, conveys to C the whole or a portion of his holding so that C holds the land so conveyed under B. B has now become a mesne lord and a new tenure has been created between B and C. This will have little effect on the services due to A since the latter can still look to the land for their rendition, but it may seriously minimize the value of the incidents of tenure due to A. For example, suppose that in making the conveyance to C, B reserved as the only services to be performed by C the payment of a penny a year rent. In the event of B dying without heirs, A's right of escheat would only entitle him to the annual rent of a penny. B's seignory would escheat to A, not the land itself; and B's seignory is almost valueless. Again, if B died leaving an infant heir A's right of wardship and marriage would be of inconsequential value.

To protect the interests of the lords against alienations by sub-infeudation the Statute Quia Emptores was enacted in 1290.[1] This statute gave mesne tenants the right to alien their lands without payment of a fine to the overlord but the transferee would hold not under the transferor but under the transferor's lord. The statute provided that "from henceforth it shall be lawful to every free man to sell at his own pleasure his lands and tenements or part of them, so that the feoffee shall hold the same lands or tenements of the chief lord of the same fee, by such service and customs as his feoffor held before." [2] Free alienation by substitution was granted but alienation by sub-infeudation was forbidden. The important result of this statute was to prevent the creation of new tenures. Over a period of time, as mesne lordships fell in and as existing tenures were dissolved by death of the tenant without heirs, by escheat for felony, or by forfeiture for treason, the cumulative effect was to break down the pyramid of tenures and bring them directly under the king. This process was further aided by the presumption applied by the courts that in the absence of proof to the contrary a tenant is deemed to hold directly of the king. If a tenant holds land in fee simple under a mesne lord in England today the tenure must have been created prior to 1290. It is to be noted that the statute was applicable only to conveyances of an estate in fee simple. And since the statute did not purport to bind the king, freedom of alienation was not given to his tenants in capite. The king continued to exact a fine for alienation from his tenants in capite until his right was abolished in 1660.

It is not profitable to discuss in detail the steps by which the strictly feudal system of tenure evolved into the present type of land ownership. Some of the changes have already been men-

---

1 18 Edw. I, c. 1. The name of the statute derives from its two opening Latin words, meaning "Because purchasers. . . ." English statutes were written in Latin or French until the fifteenth century.

2 The statute also provided that where the tenant conveyed only a part of the land the feoffee (transferee) must render to the lord of the fee a proportionate part of the services attached to the tenure. Inevitably, this led to a fragmentation of the services among numerous landholders.

tioned. Many of the services required to be rendered by the tenant were commuted into money payments. With the decline in the value of money, many rents became so insignificant as not to be worth collecting. Homage and fealty became meaningless formalities never observed in practice. But the incidents of marriage, wardship, aids and fines for alienation were burdensome exactions still imposed on many landholders to the benefit of the king. These incidents were not unfair under feudal conditions but when feudalism disappeared and a strong central government was able to give adequate protection to life and property their continuation served only the purpose of increasing the royal revenue. In the seventeenth century they were felt to be intolerable and Parliament afforded relief by enacting the Statute of Tenures in 1660.[3] This statute converted tenure by knight service into tenure of free and common socage. It abolished the incidents of wardship, marriage, aids, primer seisin, fines for alienation, homage and scutage. It did not affect in any way frankalmoin or copyhold tenure. It did not abolish the honorary services attached to grand serjeanty. As a result of the statute, practically all lay free tenure became socage tenure. The obligations of that tenure were usually to pay a rent and a relief amounting to one year's rent. (It will be recalled that a relief was a sum payable by an heir of full age on succeeding to his ancestor's lands.) In place of the revenues of which the Crown was deprived by the Statute of Tenures, there was granted to the king an hereditary tax on beer. Thus, the landholders were enabled to unload their burden onto the people at large.

At the beginning of the twentieth century the situation with respect to tenure in England may be summarized thus: most land

---

[3] 12 Charles II, c. 24. The statute was retroactive to 1645. The abolition of military tenures and the Court of Wards and Liveries had long been an issue between king and parliament. Negotiations between the contending parties had broken down in 1610 over the question of the amount of annual revenue to be granted to the king as compensation for giving up wardships and marriages. James I's price of 200,000 pounds per annum was unacceptable to the House of Commons. Bell, The Court of Wards and Liveries 133–149 (1953).

was held in common socage, a substantial part was held by copyhold, and a small amount in frankalmoin. The peculiar customs applicable to gavelkind and borough English affected the law of descent in some localities. The incidents of relief and escheat still remained. But by the end of the first quarter of the century a series of sweeping reform statutes completed the process of simplification that had begun with Quia Emptores in 1290.[4] All tenure was reduced to a single form—common socage. Copyhold, frankalmoin and the customary tenures of gavelkind, borough English and ancient demesne were abolished. Escheat was replaced by a right of the Crown to take the property of a deceased tenant who died intestate and without heirs. Of the incidents of tenure only the right of relief remains to a mesne lord and as a practical matter relief would be payable at the present time only in the very rare case of an existing intermediate tenure. In England today land is still theoretically held in tenure, not owned absolutely, but, with respect to the tenant's enjoyment of the land, tenure is an innocuous theory.

SECTION 9.   TENURE IN THE UNITED STATES

There can be no doubt that lands in the original American colonies were held in tenure. Some of the early royal grants of lands specified that the lands should be held in free and common socage and reserved nominal services, such as the annual render of "two beaver skins" stipulated in the grant to William Penn. Since Quia Emptores did not bind the king he could grant to his tenants in chief the right to sub-infeudate and this power was expressly given to some of the proprietaries. The Penns, for example, made grants of lands to be held of them in free and common socage. The service reserved was usually the payment

---

4 This reform legislation consisted of nine acts beginning with the Law of Property Act, 1922 (12 & 13 Geo. 5, c. 16) and went into effect for the most part on January 1, 1926. The principal statutes are set out in 20 Halsbury, Statutes of England (2d ed. 1950) 331 et seq.

of a small sum of money annually and was called a quit rent.[1] In New England, quit rents were exceptional and long before the Revolution land was held completely free of any feudal service or incidents. After the Revolution, lands were deemed to be held in tenure of the state as sovereign in place of the Crown. Several states passed statutes, or enacted constitutional provisions, declaring lands to be owned allodially and abolishing tenure.[2] In the remaining states it would seem that lands are still held in tenure of the state as overlord. In those states in which tenure exists Quia Emptores is in force, except in South Carolina and, perhaps, in Pennsylvania.[3]

From the practical standpoint it is not important today whether lands are owned allodially or are held in tenure. If tenure exists in a particular state and Quia Emptores is deemed to be in force there can be no sub-infeudation. If tenure exists and Quia Emptores is not in force a rare question might conceivably arise as to the nature of the rent reserved on a convey-

[1] In the charters granted to Lord Baltimore and to Penn they were given the right to erect manors and to hold therein courts-baron and courts-leet. Perhaps the closest approach to a successful attempt to set up a manorial system took place in New York. Some of the grants made by Colonial governors to the great proprietors purported to confer manorial privileges. The proprietors in turn made to settlers numerous conveyances in fee reserving in the deeds a perpetual rent payable in wheat, "fat hens" and a day's service "with carriage and horses" and a fine for alienation. These perpetual rents resulted in the 1840s in resentment, rioting, litigation and legislation. The story is told briefly and well in Sutherland, Tenantry on the New York Manors, 41 Corn.L.Q. 620 (1956).

[2] See e. g. Conn.Gen.Stat. (1958) T. 28 § 47–1; N.Y.Const. Art. I, § 10. Prior to 1938 the New York constitution (Art. I, Sec. 11) expressly provided: "All feudal tenures of every description, with all their incidents, are declared to be abolished, saving however, all rents and services certain which at any time heretofore have been lawfully created or reserved." The New York State Constitutional Convention of 1938 dropped the provision on the ground it was obsolete. One of the delegates asked reproachfully: "We are a people in a hurry. . . . Have we no space for four lines on one page reminding us that we are a people with a history?" Sutherland, id. at 620.

[3] As to Pennsylvania, see Chestnut, Effect of Quia Emptores on Pennsylvania and Maryland Ground Rents, 91 U. of Pa.L.Rev. 137 (1942); Gray, Rule Against Perpetuities, (4th ed. 1942) §§ 24–28.

ance in fee.[4] The right of escheat was in its origin a consequence of feudal tenure but in all states there are statutes to the effect that title to lands of a person dying intestate and without heirs shall vest in the state or a political subdivision thereof. Escheat has become an incident of sovereignty in place of an incident of tenure.

SECTION 10. THE EFFECTS OF TENURE

If the doctrine of tenure had ceased to have vitality at the close of the medieval period its long range effects would probably not have been significant.[1] But due to the lack of an adequate tax structure the incidents of tenure continued to exist as a primary source of royal revenue and the attempts of land owners to circumvent these burdens, and the counter-moves to prevent such evasions, had a profound effect on the development of real property law. The Statute of Uses,[2] perhaps the most important single statute in the long history of the land law, was directed at attempts to evade the feudal dues by conveyances to uses. The Rule in Shelley's Case [3] and the Doctrine of the Worthier Title [4] were judicial responses to attempts by landowners to escape the incidents of tenure. In this struggle over tenurial incidents the law of real property became distorted and tortured. The medieval doctrine of tenure left to later ages a legacy of complexity and confusion. Modern legislatures and courts have had the task of cutting away the rank growth accumulated through the centuries.

[4] The old distinction between a rent service and a rent seck turned on the question of tenure. For an explanation of their different consequences see 1 American Law of Property (1952) § 1.41.

[1] This statement is subject to the qualification that the theory that all land is ultimately derived from the sovereign is a product of the institution of tenure. This theory was transplanted to American law and even today in some states the original source of a good record title to land must be a grant or patent from the sovereign. See 3 American Law of Property §§ 12.15, 12.16 (1952).

[2] See c. 8, infra

[3] See c. 6, infra

[4] See c. 6, infra.

Chapter 2

FREEHOLD ESTATES

SECTION 1. THE THEORY OF ESTATES

Thus far we have considered the various kinds of tenure or landholding, the services that characterized them and the feudal incidents attaching to them. We now consider the system of classification that was developed to mark out the different interests that tenants might have in land. By the end of the thirteenth century English land law had begun to work out the doctrine of estates as the primary basis of classification of interests. The word estate is of feudal origin and is derived from the Latin word *status*. It speaks to us of a time when landholding was inseparably connected with a man's political and personal status in the community.

The theory of estates, a peculiarity of Anglo-American law, is based on the concept of ownership measured in terms of time. "Proprietary rights in land are, we may say, projected upon the plane of time. The category of quantity, of duration, is applied to them." [1] The maximum allowable interest, the estate in fee simple, is of potentially infinite duration; a life estate or an estate for years is of finite duration. Out of the maximum estate, the fee simple, the owner may carve out smaller estates of lesser duration.

In medieval times the only estates fully recognized by the law and given protection in the King's courts were the freehold estates: the fee simple, the fee tail and the life estate. The later common law recognized the existence of nonfreehold estates, the most important of these being the term of years. When the common law had fully developed, an estate could be defined as an

---

[1] 2 Pollock and Maitland 10.

interest in land which is presently possessory or would be possessory were it not for the existence of a prior possessory interest in some other person.[2]

The catalogue of estates as finally evolved by the common law was as follows: the fee simple, fee tail, life estate, estate for years, periodic estate, estate at will and estate at sufferance. Since these estates are the principal basis for the classification of rights in land under the modern law they will be discussed in some detail.

SECTION 2. THE FEE SIMPLE

An estate in fee simple was, and still is, the largest estate known to the law: it denotes the maximum of legal ownership, the greatest possible aggregate of rights, powers, privileges and immunities which a person may have in land. Littleton, in his famous treatise "Of Tenures" written in the fifteenth century began his book by defining the estate thus: "Tenant in fee simple is he which hath lands or tenements to hold to him and his heirs forever." [1] This definition is still valid. It contains

[2] The Restatement of the Law of Property adopts a broader definition of the word "estate." It describes it as "an interest in land which (a) is or may become possessory; and (b) is ownership measured in terms of duration." § 9. (Copyright 1936. Reprinted with the permission of The American Law Institute.)

[1] The student should have at least a bowing acquaintance with the great figures of English legal literature who helped to shape the development of Anglo-American law. The principal treatises are: Glanvill, *De Legibus et Consuetudinibus Regni Angliae* (c. 1187; the first treatise on the common law; Woodbine's ed. 1932; the book was written in Glanvill's time but probably not by Glanvill); Bracton, *De Legibus et Consuetudinibus Angliae* (c. 1260; Woodbine's ed. 1915–1942); Littleton, Tenures (c. 1481; Wambaugh's ed. 1903); Coke on Littleton (1628; the formal title is "The First Part of the Institutes of the Laws of England; or A Commentary on Littleton"; commonly cited as Co.Litt.; first American edition, 1812); Blackstone, Commentaries on the Laws of England (1765); there are numerous American editions. For an excellent brief discussion of the influence of these works, see Plucknett, Concise History of the Common Law 255–289 (5th ed. 1956). Citations to and quotations from Blackstone and Coke are not uncommon in modern re-

the two essential elements of the estate; potentially infinite duration, and inheritability by collaterals as well as by lineal descendants of the owner of the estate.

The concept of the estate in fee simple was developed in the period between the Conquest and the enactment of the Statute Quia Emptores (1290). In the era immediately after the Conquest a gift of land to a tenant conferred on the donee only a life estate and the land would revert to the lord of the fee upon the tenant's death. Whether the heir of the deceased tenant would be permitted to succeed to the land depended on the will of the lord. In any event the heir had to make a monetary payment before being granted the privilege. By the late 1100s, it would seem, succession by the heir had become the usual situation and the lord was entitled to exact from the heir only a reasonable relief. Where the donor intended that the land descend to the donee's heir the form of the gift specified that the grant was to the donee and his heirs. Such expression of intention was effective to insure the right of the heir to inherit the land.

The right of the tenant to alienate or transfer the land during his lifetime was slowly established.[2] Restrictions on alienation had a two-fold source: in the rights of the lord of the fee, and also in the rights of the tenant's heirs. Since gifts of land were feudal in nature the lord had, especially in the case of military tenures, a legitimate interest in the identity of the tenant. Until the thirteenth century the lord had a right of control over alienations by his tenant but the law was changing. In the middle 1200s the consent of the lord was no longer needed for an alienation by the tenant who held land to himself and his heirs but the lord could still exact a fine for the alienation. Quia Emptores (1290) eliminated this seignorial incident in the case

ports but only rarely is a reference to Bracton found. For one such instance, see Foot v. Baumann, 333 Mass. 214, 217, 129 N.E.2d 916, 918, 55 A.L.R.2d 1139 (1955).

[2] For a scholarly discussion of the development of the alienability and inheritability of the fee simple, see Thorne, English Feudalism and Estates in Land, 1959 Camb.L.J. 198. Cf. Simpson, Introduction to the History of the Land Law 46–48 (1961).

of the mesne tenant by granting him the right "to sell at his own pleasure his lands or tenements or part of them." But tenants in chief of the Crown continued to be subject to the requirements of the payment of a fine for alienation until 1660 when this last vestige of feudal restraint on alienation of free tenures was removed by the Statute of Tenures.[3]

When the principle of inheritability was admitted, a gift to a man and his heirs clearly gave the donee an estate that would endure during the donee's life and would continue after his death by descent to his heir. But the form of the gift "to B and his heirs" seemed to give the heir also an interest in the land. Could B convey to a third person and thereby defeat the expectancy of his heir apparent? The law of the twelfth century hesitated over this question. But by 1225 it was decided that at least where the ancestor had conveyed with warranty for himself and his heirs the heir could not after the ancestor's death upset the conveyance.[4] And from the thirteenth century on, the words "and his heirs" in a conveyance "to B and his heirs" merely indicated that B was given an estate in fee simple; B's heirs took no interest by virtue of the gift.

We would explain this today by saying that the words "and his heirs" are words of limitation, not words of purchase. Words of limitation are those marking or defining the quantum of interest given to the grantee; words of purchase indicate the grantee. Put another way, words of purchase indicate him who takes; words of limitation indicate what is taken. A purchaser is any person acquiring an estate in any way other than by descent. The term is not restricted to a grantee who pays value for the conveyance. A donee or a devisee takes by pur-

---

[3] 12 Charles II, c. 24. For a discussion of the tenant's power of alienation in the medieval period, see 3 Holdsworth 73–87.

[4] D'Arundel's Case, Bracton's Note Book, case 1054. Since the heir was bound by the ancestor's warranty made to the grantee he was debarred from claiming the land. Although the doctrine of warranty thus contributed to the formulation of a rule of free alienability, other factors, such as the rule of primogeniture (descent to the eldest son) and a growing policy in favor of free alienation, also influenced the final result.

chase; an heir who inherits land does not acquire by purchase.[5]

Since an estate in fee simple was an estate of general inheritance it was necessary at common law for the creation of such an estate that the conveyance use words of general inheritance. And with the verbal ritualism so characteristic of the period only the words "his heirs" were sufficient for this purpose. As stated by Littleton: "If a man would purchase lands or tenements in fee simple, it behoveth him to have these words in his purchase, To have and to hold to him and to his heirs: for these words, his heirs, make the estate of inheritance." [6] Substitute words were not effective. A conveyance by A "to B and his heirs" gave B a fee simple (assuming, of course, that A had a fee simple to convey); a conveyance "to B forever" or "to B and his assigns" or "to B in fee simple" gave B a life estate.[7]

A few exceptions to this general rule were admitted by the common law. The rule never applied to wills, hence a devise passed an estate in fee simple to the devisee without the use of the magic word "heirs" if the will manifested an intent to give a fee simple. A similar relaxation was applicable to a conveyance to trustees: the trustee got a legal estate of such quantum as would enable him to carry out his duties as trustee despite the absence of the word "heirs" in the conveyance to him. And since a corporation can have no heirs a conveyance to it gave it a fee simple unless a contrary intention was expressed. Finally, where joint tenants held in fee simple a release of his interest by one tenant to his co-tenant was effective to pass the interest in fee without the use of the word "heirs." [8]

[5] The distinction between words of purchase and words of limitation is a constantly recurring problem in the construction of wills and trusts. See e. g. Smith v. Groton, 160 A.2d 262 (Conn.1960); Fatheree v. Gregg, 20 Ill.2d 620, 170 N.E.2d 600 (1960).

[6] Co.Litt. § 1.

[7] Id.; Restatement, Property, § 27, Comment b (1936). This Restatement is hereafter cited as Restat.Prop.

[8] Restat.Prop., § 29, Comment e. But a conveyance by one tenant in common to his cotenant required the use of the word "heirs" to carry the fee.

SECTION 3.   MODERN LAW—CREATION AND CHARAC-TERISTICS OF A FEE SIMPLE

The common law rule requiring words of inheritance to create a fee simple has been abolished in all but a few jurisdictions, usually by statute [1] but occasionally by decision.[2] But the ancient rule retains its vitality with respect to conveyances made before the effective date of any abrogating statute in the particular jurisdiction [3] and it is sometimes applied in those states having no statute or prior decision affecting it.[4]

Modern deeds usually follow a standardized form and when properly drafted rarely raise a question of the class of estate created. But deeds and wills drafted by laymen (and sometimes by lawyers) not infrequently present a problem of construction because of a failure to use language clearly defining the estate intended to be given. If, for example, A devises land "to B for his own use and enjoyment forever, whatever is left on B's death to go to C" does B get a fee simple or a life estate? Most courts have held in this and similar situations that B gets a life estate

---

[1] The usual statute provides in substance that a conveyance passes to the conveyee the entire estate of the conveyor unless an intent is expressed in the conveyance to create a lesser estate. For a list of these statutes, see 1 American Law of Property, § 2.4, n. 1 (1952); 2 Powell, Real Property, § 184, n. 65 (1950).

[2] See e. g. Cole v. Lake, 54 N.H. 242 (1874); Dennen v. Searle, 176 A.2d 561 (Conn.1961).

[3] Ivey v. Peacock, 56 Fla. 440, 47 So. 481 (1908); Elwell v. Miner, 174 N.E.2d 43 (Mass.1961).

[4] See Cole v. Steinlauf, 144 Conn. 629, 136 A.2d 744 (1957) (dictum that deed "to B and his assigns forever" gives B only a life estate); Grainger v. Hamilton, 228 S.C. 318, 90 S.E.2d 209 (1955). The dictum in Cole v. Steinlauf, supra, was repudiated in Dennen v. Searle, 176 A.2d 561 (Conn.1961). The Restatement, despite some criticism, takes the position that in the absence of statute the common law rule applies. Restat.Prop. § 27. For the Reporter's justification of this position see 2 Powell, Real Property, § 180 (1950); compare 1 American Law of Property, § 2.4 (1952). The Restatement (§ 27, Comm. c, d and f) states that the following limitations are effective to create a fee simple in the conveyee: "to B and heir"; "to B or his heirs"; "to B and his eldest heirs."

because of the gift over to C.[5] Basically, the question is one of the intention of the grantor or testator as manifested by the language of the deed or will viewed in its entirety.[6]

The estate in fee simple today has the same formal characteristics that it had in the common law period: it is an estate of general inheritance and it is of potentially infinite duration. Attempts by transferors of land to curtail the inheritability of the fee simple have been struck down by the courts. Littleton stated: "A man cannot create a new kind of inheritance"[7] and modern courts have agreed with him. Thus, if A devises land "to B and her heirs on her father's side" B takes an estate in fee simple absolute and the attempt to restrict the descent to the paternal side of the family is ineffective.[8] And the strong policy developed by the common law in favor of free alienability of land has coincided with modern concepts of public policy so as generally to invalidate attempted restraints on the alienation of a fee simple.[9] In one important respect the modern fee owner has an increased power of disposition of his property. At common law lands were not devisable except by special custom in certain localities in England. It was not until the first Stat-

[5] Mitchell v. Bagot, 48 Cal.App.2d 281, 119 P.2d 758 (1941); Matter of Kramer, 114 N.Y.S.2d 15 (1952). So also, if one clause of a will purports to give B a fee simple and a subsequent clause provides for a gift over to another devisee on B's death it is usually held that B takes a life estate. Morris v. Smith, 332 Mass. 34, 123 N.E.2d 212 (1954); cf. In re Wadsworth's Estate, 176 Minn. 445, 223 N.W. 783 (1929). A similar rule is applied to the construction of deeds. Moore v. Stanfill, 313 S.W.2d 486 (Tenn.App.1957).

[6] Chestnut v. Chestnut, 300 Pa. 146, 151 A. 339, 75 A.L.R. 66 (1930); Restat. Prop., § 108, Comment b, f, g.

[7] Co.Litt. 27.

[8] Johnson v. Whiton, 159 Mass. 424, 34 N.E. 542 (1893); and see Beeman v. Stillwell, 194 Iowa 231, 189 N.W. 969 (1922).

[9] Cf. Gale v. York Center Community Cooperative, Inc., 21 Ill.2d 86, 171 N.E.2d 30 (1960) (Partial restraint in favor of co-operative housing association upheld). For a thorough treatment of restraints on alienation of estates, see 6 American Law of Property, §§ 26.1–26.47; 6 Powell, Real Property §§ 839–843.

ute of Wills was enacted in 1540 that a limited power to devise was granted land owners.[10]

While the estate in fee simple absolute still represents the ultimate in ownership of land, the right of an owner in fee simple to make such use of his land as he pleases, subject to the rights of adjacent owners, is in modern times considerably curtailed by governmental controls in the form of zoning and subdivision laws, and urban redevelopment programs. Moreover, in many cases, by reason of restrictive covenants imposed by a former owner of the land, the uses to which the land can be put are limited.[11]

SECTION 4.   THE QUALIFIED OR DEFEASIBLE FEE SIMPLE

Thus far we have spoken only of the fee simple absolute but an estate in fee simple may also be qualified or defeasible. A qualified fee simple is one subject to a special limitation, or a condition subsequent, or an executory limitation, or any combination of these.

A fee simple subject to a special limitation is usually called a fee simple determinable. A fee simple normally comes to an end upon the death of the owner thereof intestate and leaving no heirs but a fee simple determinable is also limited to expire automatically upon the happening or non-happening of an event

---

[10] 32 Hen. VIII, c. 1. This statute permitted the owner in fee simple to devise all his lands held in socage tenure and two-thirds of his lands held by knight service. When the Statute of Tenures (1660) converted tenure by knight service into free and common socage this restriction on the privilege to devise was automatically removed.

[11] It is obvious that ownership of land in the urban areas of twentieth century America is substantially different from ownership in the nineteenth century. The topics of planning and land use control are beyond the scope of this book. For a sample of the rapidly expanding literature in this field see Williams, Planning Law and Democratic Living, 20 Law and Contemp. Problems 317; Cross, The Diminishing Fee, Id. 517 (1955); Consigny and Zile, Use of Restrictive Covenants in a Rapidly Urbanizing Area, 1958 Wis. L.Rev. 612.

stated in the conveyance or will creating the estate. Thus, A owning land in fee simple absolute, conveys it to B "to have and to hold to B and his heirs so long as the land is used for residential purposes and when the land is no longer so used it shall revert to A and his heirs." B has a fee simple determinable. The estate granted is a fee because it is generally inheritable and it may last forever. Yet it is a determinable fee because it will expire on the non-occurrence of the stated contingency, namely, the use of the land for residential purposes. The estate conveyed to B automatically ends if and when the land is used for non-residential purposes and A again owns an estate in fee simple absolute. During the existence of B's estate A retains a future interest in the land called a possibility, or right, of reverter.

A fee simple subject to a condition subsequent exists when the fee simple is subject to a power in the grantor to terminate the estate granted on the happening of a specified event. Thus, A conveys to B "to have and to hold to B and his heirs on the express condition that if the land shall not be used for residential purposes A or his heirs shall have a right to re-enter and possess the land as of his former estate." B has a fee simple on condition subsequent and A has a right of entry or power of termination. On the happening of the stated event, that is, on breach of the condition, the granted estate continues in existence until A effectively exercises his option to terminate by making an entry or bringing an action to recover the land.[1] The breach of the condition does not cause an automatic termination of the granted estate. The basic difference, therefore, between the fee simple determinable and the fee simple on condition subsequent is that the former automatically expires by force of the special limitation, contained in the instrument creating the estate, when the stated contingency occurs, whereas the fee simple on condition

---

[1] At common law it was necessary for the grantor to make an actual entry on the land in order to terminate the granted estate. At the present time the grantor may bring an action to recover the land without first making an entry although in some jurisdictions he must give notice of his election to terminate before bringing the action. But see Storke v. Penn. Mutual Life Ins. Co., 390 Ill. 619, 61 N.E.2d 552 (1945).

subsequent continues despite the breach of the specified condition until it is divested or cut short by the exercise by the grantor of his power to terminate.

The third type of qualified fee simple, the fee simple subject to an executory limitation, exists when the fee simple is subject to divestment in favor of a person other than the conveyor upon the happening of a specified event. Thus, A conveys "to B and his heirs but if B die leaving no children him surviving, then to C and his heirs." B has a fee simple subject to an executory interest in C. This type of defeasible fee could not exist at law prior to the Statute of Uses (1536). The nature of an executory interest will be discussed in a later chapter.[2]

The qualified or defeasible fee simple in one of the forms above described is found fairly frequently in modern practise and is, therefore, of current importance. It is treated briefly at this point in our discussion of the nature of an estate in fee simple but will be examined again in connection with the topic of Future Interests.[3]

SECTION 5.   THE FEE TAIL

Prior to the year 1285 a gift of land to a man and the heirs of his body created a fee simple conditional. The courts con-

[2] c. 9, §§ 7–11, infra. The fee simple subject to an executory limitation is sometimes called a fee simple on conditional limitation. See e. g. Brattle Square Church v. Grant, 3 Gray (Mass.) 142 (1855); 1 American Law of Property, § 2.10. Unfortunately, courts sometimes refer to a special limitation (the clause creating a determinable estate) as a "conditional limitation" thereby adding to the confusion. See e. g. Storke v. Penn. Mut. Life Ins. Co., 390 Ill. 619, 61 N.E.2d 552 (1945); Markey v. Smith, 301 Mass. 64, 16 N.E.2d 20 (1938); Board of Chosen Freeholders v. Buck, 79 N.J.Eq. 472, 82 A. 418 (1912). It should be noted that a fee simple conditional is a substantially different interest from a fee simple on conditional limitation. See § 5, infra.

[3] c. 5, §§ 3–10, infra. The Restatement of Property gives an excellent exposition of the several types of defeasible fees and the forms of limitations sufficient to create them. §§ 44–58. It should be mentioned that there can be a defeasible estate other than in fee simple. An estate in fee tail, a life estate and an estate for years can be subject to a special limitation, a condition subsequent or an executory limitation.

strued such a conveyance as though it were to a man and his heirs on condition that he have an heir of his body. They held that upon the birth of issue the condition had been fulfilled and the donee had power to alienate the land in fee simple. They did not go so far as to hold that the donee himself thereby acquired for all purposes an estate in fee. If the donee had issue who predeceased him and the land had not been alienated it reverted on the death of the donee to the donor, even though the donee left surviving collateral relations. This construction of a gift to a man and the heirs of his body was undoubtedly influenced by the judges' bias in favor of free alienability but it ran counter to the intention of the donors. Such gifts were commonly made to subsidize marriages and it was the intention of the donors that upon failure of issue the lands should revert. By the construction of the gift as one of a fee simple conditional, the donee was able in most instances to defeat the rights of the issue and of the donor.

In 1285 Parliament afforded relief to donors by enacting the statute De Donis Conditionalibus.[1] The statute, after reciting the grievances of donors by reason of the courts' construction of a gift to a man and the heirs of his body as a conditional fee simple, provided: " * * * that the will of the giver according to the form in the deed of gift manifestly expressed shall be from henceforth observed, so that they to whom the land was given under such condition shall have no power to aliene the land so given, but that it shall remain unto the issue of them to whom it was given after their death, or shall revert unto the giver or his heirs if issue fail * * *." The effect of this statute was to abolish the old common law estate of fee simple conditional and to create a new kind of estate of inheritance—the estate in fee tail. The estate in fee tail was so called because it was an estate of inheritance the descent of which was cut down (in Latin, "talliatum"; in French, "taille") to the heirs of the body of the donee.

---

[1] 13 Edw. I, c. 1. The opening Latin words of the statute may be translated: "Concerning gifts of land made upon condition" etc.

After the statute De Donis a gift of land to B and the heirs of his body created in B an estate in fee tail. The estate would last so long as there were any lineal descendants of B and upon the failure of such issue the land would revert to the donor or his heirs. B, the tenant in tail, could convey the land to a third person but the transferee acquired only an estate for B's life. The restrictions imposed by the statute prevented B from making any conveyance effective to cut off the rights of the issue or the reversioner. These restrictions were burdensome and Parliament was petitioned to repeal the statute but refused. We find the reason for such refusal in the fact that the estate in fee tail was not subject (beyond the tenant's lifetime) to forfeiture for treason or attainder for felony and was not liable for the debts of former tenants in tail. But the courts sanctioned methods to evade the statute. In 1472 [2] it was indicated that by means of the fictitious real action called a common recovery the rights of the issue could be barred; in the next century it was decided that not only the issue but also the reversioner or remainderman would be barred by a common recovery. Also, in the sixteenth century by means of the fictitious action known as a fine the rights of the issue alone could be barred and a "base" fee created in the person in whose favor the fine was levied. The process of converting the estate tail into a fee simple was known as docking or barring the entail. In 1833 fines and recoveries were abolished by statute and a tenant in tail in possession was permitted by the statute completely to dock the entail by a deed recorded in the Court of Chancery.[3]

---

[2] Taltarum's Case, Y.B. (Year Book) 12 Edw. IV 19. Familiarity with the esoteric learning of fines and recoveries is not necessary for the modern student. For a brief description of these two forms of conveyance by judicial proceeding see Plucknett, Concise History of the Common Law 613–615, 617–622 (5th ed. 1956); Simpson, An Introduction to the History of the Land Law 121–129 (1961). It may be mentioned that in 1739 one Mr. Pigott wrote a book entitled "Common Recoveries." Chief Justice Willes complained: "Mr. Pigott has confounded himself and everybody else who reads his book." Plucknett, op. cit. supra at 621.

[3] Fines and Recoveries Act, §§ 15, 40. The estate tail can no longer be created in England as a *legal* estate. Under the sweeping reform legislation of 1925

Since a fee tail was an estate of inheritance it could not be created by an inter vivos conveyance at common law without the use of the word "heirs" in the limitation.[4] This strict rule did not apply to limitations in a will. The intention of the testator, if clearly expressed in the will, would be given effect despite the absence of the word "heirs." The words "of the body" were those commonly used in both deeds and wills to show the intention to create a fee tail rather than a fee simple but other words having the same meaning were equally effective.

It was permissible for the grantor of a fee tail to restrict the inheritance (by proper words in the limitation) to a particular group of the lineal descendants of the grantee. There could be an estate in tail male or in tail female, and either one of these could be a fee tail general or a fee tail special. A grant to a man and the heirs male of his body created a fee tail male. A grant to a man and the heirs female of his body created a fee tail female. If the grant was to a donee and the heirs of his body by a particular spouse the estate was a fee tail special; if no particular spouse was designated it was a fee tail general. Estates in tail female were, in fact, rarely created but estates in tail male were an integral part of the English family settlement and were, therefore, very numerous in the eighteenth and nineteenth centuries.

the only estates capable of being created as *legal* estates are the fee simple absolute in possession and the term of years absolute. The estate in tail and the life estate can exist only as *equitable* estates. A tenant in tail may nevertheless disentail and enlarge his equitable interest into a legal fee simple. Cheshire, Modern Law of Real Property (8th ed. 1958) 184–191.

[4] Co.Litt. 20 a. b. A conveyance to "B and his issue" gave B a life estate. As to modern law, see § 6, infra. The problem arising from a gift of land by will (devise) to "B and his issue" is also treated in § 6.

SECTION 6.   MODERN LAW—THE FEE TAIL IN THE UNITED STATES

The estate in fee tail received a hostile reception in the United States. It was recognized at an earlier date in the great majority of jurisdictions but opposition to it developed in the post-revolutionary era on the ground that it was incompatible with American social conditions.[1] This opposition arose partly from the association of the fee tail with the rule of primogeniture (descent of land to the eldest son to the exclusion of all other children) and partly from the employment of the fee tail in England as a legal device to keep ancestral lands in the family for use as a basis of social and political power.[2]

Beginning in the late eighteenth century and extending into the twentieth, state after state enacted legislation abrogating the fee tail and creating a statutory substitute so that at the present time only four jurisdictions, Delaware, Maine, Massachusetts, and Rhode Island (as to deeds only), recognize the estate as it existed at common law.[3] The statutory provisions dealing with the fee tail are not uniform but they may be grouped under three main headings:

A. The most common form of statute converts what would have been a fee tail at common law into a fee simple in the

[1] See Morris, Primogeniture and Entailed Estates in America, 27 Col.L.Rev. 24 (1927) (treating of the Colonial period).

[2] Why could not the entail be docked by having the tenant in tail suffer a common recovery? Because this could be done only by the tenant in tail in possession and under the typical English family settlement the lands were limited to B for life, then to B's eldest son in fee tail male, remainder in succession to the other sons, according to seniority, in tail male. Neither B nor his eldest son could alone dock the entail although it could be done by both together when the eldest son attained his majority. For a brief description of the English "settlement" of lands see Cheshire, Modern Real Property 69 (8th ed. 1958).

[3] The Restatement of Property lists and classifies the statutory and nonstatutory material relating to the fee tail. c. 5, Introductory Note, pp. 201–211; Restatement of the Law, 1948 Supp. pp. 379–385.

grantee or devisee. Thus, a limitation "to B and the heirs of his body" will give B a fee simple. This result is reached in twenty-seven jurisdictions.[4]

B. In the next largest group of states (eight in all) the statutes substitute for the fee tail a life estate in the grantee or devisee and a remainder in fee simple in his issue.[5] Thus, in these states a limitation "to B and the heirs of his body" will give B a life estate and on B's death his issue will take in fee simple.[6]

C. In three states, Connecticut, Ohio and Rhode Island (as to wills only) statutes provide that an estate given in fee tail shall be an estate in fee simple absolute to the issue of the donee in tail. These statutes have the effect of giving the donee a fee tail for his lifetime only and on his death his issue take in fee simple. Thus, in these states a limitation "to B and the heirs of his body" gives B an estate in fee tail for his life and on his death his children take in fee simple. B's estate has the same characteristics as a normal fee tail but, except in Rhode Island, he cannot convey an estate greater than for his own life.[7]

---

[4] The California statute is fairly typical: "Estates tail are abolished, and every estate which would be at common law adjudged to be a fee-tail is a fee simple; and if no valid remainder is limited thereon, is a fee simple absolute." West's Ann.Cal.Civ.Code, § 763. Statutes of this kind, or statutes so construed as to reach the same result, exist in the following jurisdictions: Alabama, Arizona, District of Columbia, Georgia, Indiana, Kentucky, Maryland, Michigan, Minnesota, Mississippi, Montana, Nebraska, New Hampshire, New Jersey, New York, North Carolina, North Dakota, Oklahoma, Pennsylvania, South Dakota, Tennessee, Vermont, Virginia, West Virginia, Wisconsin and Wyoming. The Texas constitution forbids recognition of the fee tail (Art. 1, § 26) and in Hawaii the estate has been held not to exist. See Restat.Prop. § 104.

[5] Statutes of this type exist in Arkansas, Colorado, Florida, Illinois, Kansas, Missouri, and New Mexico. Georgia is also included in this group as to limitations which would under English law create a fee tail by implication.

[6] On the question of the necessity of the issue surviving the donee in order to take, see 2 Powell, Real Property § 199 (1950).

[7] St. John, Adm'r v. Dann, 66 Conn. 401, 34 A. 110 (1895); Guido v. Thompson, 160 N.E.2d 153 (Ohio Com.Pl.1957). See Restat.Prop. §§ 88–96.

In the four states which still recognize the fee tail in its common law form, Delaware, Maine, Massachusetts and Rhode Island (when created by deed) a tenant in tail in possession has the power to convey in fee simple by an ordinary deed and thereby bar the entail and all reversions, remainders or executory interests expectant thereon. A creditor of a tenant in tail in possession can, except in Delaware, subject the estate to his claim as though it were owned by the debtor in fee simple.[8] But the tenant in tail has no power to dispose of the estate by will. Oddly enough, it is not clear whether on the tenant's death the estate will descend to all of his children equally or the rule of primogeniture will apply so as to give it exclusively to the eldest son.[9]

In the states of Iowa, Oregon and South Carolina the statute De Donis is not deemed to be in force, hence a limitation to a man and the heirs of his body (or an equivalent limitation) will in those states create a fee simple conditional.[10]

SECTION 7.   CONSTRUCTION PROBLEMS—MEANING OF DEATH WITHOUT ISSUE

It is not unusual to find in a will a gift of property to a person with a further gift over to a second person if the first

[8] In Delaware the creditor of the tenant in tail can cause to be sold on execution only an estate for the life of the tenant in tail. Hazzard v. Hazzard, 29 Del. 91, 97 A. 233 (1916).

[9] The laws generally governing the descent of lands in England before 1925 were called Canons of Descent. Two of these rules were: 1. Males exclude females of equal degree; 2. Among males of equal degree only the eldest inherits. The latter was the rule of primogeniture. Females inherited equally. Lands held in gavelkind tenure and in burgage tenure were subject to special customs. Gavelkind lands descended to all sons equally; burgage lands to the youngest son only (the exact reverse of primogeniture). In the United States the law of intestate succession is governed by a statute of descent and distribution in each state. These statutes provide that all of the children share equally. But in Massachusetts the statute in terms applies only to the descent of lands in fee simple or for the life of another. Mass.Gen. Laws Ann. c. 190, § 3.

[10] See 1 American Law of Property §§ 2.11–2.12, Restat.Prop. §§ 68–77.

named person dies without issue. Thus, A devises land "to B and his heirs but if B die without issue then to C and his heirs." Occasionally, a disposition of this type is also found in a gift by deed. The words "die without issue" are ambiguous. They may mean that C is to take only when the whole line of B's descendants (children, grandchildren, etc.) runs out, whenever that occurs. Or they may mean that C is to take if, and only if, at the time of B's death he leaves no issue surviving him. Put another way, the problem is whether the words "die without issue" should be construed to mean indefinite failure of issue or definite failure of issue—failure of issue at an undefined point of time or failure of issue at a definite point of time. If the indefinite failure of issue construction is adopted B has a fee tail and C has a remainder in fee simple. Although in form the limitation to B and his heirs appears to give B a fee simple yet the additional phrase "if he die without issue" cuts down B's interest to one which will last only as long as he has lineal descendants—a period which marks the duration of a fee tail. Thus, the indefinite failure of issue construction of the words "die without issue" gives the limitation the same legal effect as if it read "to B and the heirs of his body, then to C and his heirs." But if the words "die without issue" are given the definite failure of issue construction, that is, if they are taken to mean failure of issue at the time of B's death only, then B has a fee simple subject to an executory interest in C. C will take only in the event that B dies leaving no lineal descendant surviving him.[1] If B dies leaving a child C will not take even if the child should die a month later leaving no issue.

At a relatively early date the English courts established a preference for the indefinite failure of issue construction with the result that in the limitation under discussion B would get a

---

[1] The question may also arise whether the phrase "die without issue" means "die without ever having had issue" or "die without leaving issue surviving." The courts have usually assumed or held that it means death without leaving issue surviving. But cf. Bullock v. Seymour, 33 Conn. 289 (1866); Tolley v. Wilson, 371 Ill. 124, 20 N.E.2d 68 (1939).

fee tail by implication and C would have a remainder in fee simple.[2]   At the time, this construction was reasonable because until the Statute of Uses (1536)[3] executory interests were not recognized as valid and if C were to take at all he would have to take by way of remainder on the expiration of B's interest.[4] After executory interests became valid the same constructional policy was continued.   But since the preference for the indefinite failure of issue construction amounted only to a rebuttable presumption, language in the will indicating that the testator intended that the gift over should take effect at the death of the first taker or on the death of another named person or within a designated period was given controlling weight.[5]

Influenced by the English precedents, a considerable number of American courts at an earlier date adopted the preference for the indefinite failure of issue construction.   But in about thirty states there are statutes [6] establishing a preference for the definite failure of issue construction and a similar result has

---

[2] So also a limitation by devise to "B for life but if B shall die without issue then to C and his heirs" would give B a fee tail with a remainder in C in fee.   Machell v. Weeding, 8 Sim. 4, 59 Eng.Rep. 2 (1836).   In this case Shadwell, V. C. stated: "I consider it to be a settled point that, whether an estate be given in fee or for life, or generally, without any particular limit as to its duration, if it be followed by a devise over in case of the devisee dying without issue, the devisee will take an estate tail."   But a similar limitation in a deed would give B a life estate since in a conveyance by deed the word "heirs" was at English common law necessary to create a fee tail.   See 1 Simes & Smith, Future Interests § 522 (1956).

[3] 27 Hen. VIII, c. 10.   This statute is discussed in detail in c. 8 and 9, infra.

[4] There could be no remainder after a fee simple.   The subject of remainders is treated in c. 5, infra.   For a thorough discussion of the English common law preference, see 1 Simes & Smith, Future Interests (2d ed. 1956) § 522 ; Warren, Gifts Over on Death Without Issue, 39 Yale L.J. 332 (1930).

[5] The often cited case of Pells v. Brown, Cro.Jac. 590, 79 Eng.Rep. 504 (1620) affords a good illustration.   There A devised land to "Thomas and his heirs forever, and if Thomas died without issue, living William his brother, then to William and his heirs."   The court held that definite failure of issue was intended by the testator and, therefore, Thomas took a fee simple subject to an executory interest in William.

[6] For a list of these statutes, see 5 American Law of Property § 21.50 (1952); 1 Simes & Smith, Future Interests (2d ed.) § 526.

been reached in a few jurisdictions without the aid of statute. At the present time, therefore, in most jurisdictions there is a constructional preference for definite failure of issue.[7] It would not be accurate, however, to say that the constructional problem no longer exists since the statutes do not apply to deeds or wills taking effect prior to the statutes so that as to such instruments the former rule in the particular jurisdiction will govern.[8] And the fact that the fee tail has been abrogated by statute in a state does not necessarily prevent a court from applying the indefinite failure of issue construction to a limitation even though its application will result in B taking a statutorily substituted estate in place of a fee tail.[9]

SECTION 8. CONSTRUCTION PROBLEMS—DEVISE TO B AND HIS CHILDREN

If A by will makes a gift of land "to B and his children" and at the testator's death B has no children what interest does B take, and what interest, if any, do B's after-born children take? Basically, the problem is whether the words "and his children" are to be taken as words of limitation indicating the size of the estate given to B or as words of purchase indicating a gift also to the after born children themselves. The English courts, and a number of American courts, have held that, in the absence of an expressed contrary intent by the testator, the words are words of limitation and B takes a fee tail. This rule of construc-

---

[7] The Restatement of Property rejects the common law presumption of indefinite failure of issue. § 266. The common law presumption also applied to dispositions of personal property even though there can be no fee tail in personalty. See Simes & Smith, op. cit. n. 6, supra, § 523.

[8] For example, in Hayes v. Hammond, 336 Mass. 233, 143 N.E.2d 693 (1957) the indefinite failure of issue construction was applied to a limitation in a will executed before 1888, the effective date of the Massachusetts statute establishing a preference for the definite failure of issue construction.

[9] For a comprehensive treatment of this topic and related problems, see 5 American Law of Property §§ 21.49–21.57 (1952); 3 Powell, Real Property §§ 340–344 (1952); 1 Simes & Smith, Future Interests §§ 521–551 (1956).

tion is the so-called first Rule in Wild's Case.[1]   It stems from a dictum in that case: "If A devises his lands to B and to his children or issues (sic), and he hath not any issue at the time of the devise, that the same is an estate tail." [2]   This peculiar construction of the word "children" (which normally means issue in the first generation only) was in part due to the popularity of the fee tail in England at the time, and in part due to a desire to have the children take more than the life estate which would have been the maximum they could have taken as purchasers by way of remainder, because of the absence of words of inheritance or their equivalent.

In modern America there is no sound reason for applying a rule of construction that the testator is presumed to have intended to create a fee tail.   Therefore, the first resolution in Wild's Case has been generally repudiated although there are cases in some jurisdictions which adopt it even though a local statute converts the fee tail into some other estate.[3]   The preferable view, and the one most frequently held, is that B takes a life estate and the children a remainder.[4]   The first resolution in Wild's Case applied only to devises of land since in a conveyance by deed it was at common law necessary to use words of inheritance in order to create a fee tail.   Although a fee tail or its statutory equivalent can today be created by deed without the use of the

---

[1] 6 Co. 16 b, 1 Eq.Cas.Abr. 181 (1599).

[2] A second rule or resolution is derived from a second dictum in Wild's Case. The second resolution was that if at the time of the devise to B and his children B had living children then B and his children take concurrent interests as joint tenants for life. This second resolution has been generally adopted in the United States as a rule of construction in so far as it presumes that the testator intended that B and the children take as co-tenants but today they would usually be held to take as tenants in common in fee simple. Restat.Prop. § 283. A few states, notably Kentucky and Pennsylvania, adopt the view that B takes a life estate and the children take a remainder. See 5 American Law of Property §§ 22.22–22.26 ; 2 Simes & Smith, Future Interests §§ 691–702.

[3] See 5 American Law of Property § 22.20 ; 2 Simes & Smith, Future Interests § 696.

[4] Restat.Prop. § 283.

word "heirs," an inter vivos conveyance to B and his children (B having no children at the time) would rarely be construed to give B a fee tail which would be converted by the local statute into some other estate.[5]

SECTION 9.   LIFE ESTATES

An estate for life is an estate which is not terminable at any fixed or computable period of time and has its duration measured by the life or lives of one or more persons. Unlike the fee simple and fee tail it is not an estate of inheritance but like these two estates it was classified at common law as a freehold estate. Life estates may be created by act of the parties, that is, by deed or by will (under the older terminology these were called conventional life estates); or they may be created by operation of law, in which case they were called legal life estates. Whether a particular life estate is a conventional or a legal one makes no difference other than in the mode of creation, but the distinction does provide convenience of classification for purposes of our discussion.

SECTION 10.   CREATION OF LIFE ESTATES BY DEED OR WILL

A life estate arises when the conveyance or will expressly limits the duration of the created estate in terms of the life or lives of one or more persons, or when the instrument, viewed as a whole, manifests the intent of the transferor to create an estate measured by the life or lives of one or more persons. The simplest and most common form of limitation is "to B during his life", but no words of art are necessary and a life estate results from other limitations of a similar nature. Thus, if A, owner in fee simple, conveys "to B until he dies," or "to B for his use during his natural life," or "to B and at his death to go to B's children,"

---

[5] But see Sewell v. Thrailkill, 209 Ark. 393, 194 S.W.2d 202 (1945); cf. Herrick v. Lain, 375 Ill. 569, 32 N.E.2d 154 (1941).

in each case B will get an estate for his own life. At common law a conveyance "to B" without more gave B a life estate but under modern law B would normally take a fee simple because of the widespread existence of statutes creating a presumption that a conveyor intends to pass his entire estate to the conveyee.[1]

It is not unusual to find in a will, in addition to the language giving an interest to the designated beneficiary, further provisions specifying the powers of disposition the beneficiary shall have or restricting his powers of disposition. These additional provisions raise a problem of construction as to the estate intended to be given to the beneficiary. Thus, if A devises "to B with the right to use or dispose of as he sees fit" B will be held to have a fee simple in the absence of other language in the will indicating a contrary intent.[2] But if A devises "to B with power to sell or mortgage if he finds it necessary" B has only a life estate.[3] Here the restricted power of disposition, being inconsistent with a fee simple, indicates the testator's intent to limit B's interest to a life estate. If the estate given to the beneficiary is expressed to be for life, the addition of a power to convey in fee will not, by the weight of authority, enlarge the estate into a fee simple. Thus, A devises "to my wife, B, all my property to have and to hold and use same as she sees fit during her lifetime. I give my wife power to sell any part or all of my real estate, also power to mortgage, assign as she sees fit or deems proper." B takes a life estate with a super-added power to sell or mortgage.[4] This is not the equivalent of a fee simple since B has no power to devise the land and it is not inheritable by her heirs.

---

[1] See § 3, n. 1, supra.

[2] Benz v. Fabian, 54 N.J.Eq. 615, 35 A. 760 (1896).

[3] See Restat.Prop., § 108, Comm. e.

[4] Langlois v. Langlois, 326 Mass. 85, 93 N.E.2d 264 (1950). It should be noted that this was a "home-made" will. In some states there are statutes providing that when a life tenant is given a power to dispose of the fee the estate is to be regarded as a fee simple in favor of creditors, purchasers and mortgagees. For a list of these statutes, see 2 Powell, Real Property, § 204, n. 75.

An estate which is measured by the life of the grantee is called simply a life estate. An estate which is measured by the life of a person other than the grantee is called an estate pur autre vie. Thus, A conveys to B "to have and to hold during the life of C." B has an estate pur autre vie. At common law if B died before C the property was regarded, until C died, as without an owner, hence the first person to take possession (called the common occupant) was entitled to the estate. This conclusion resulted from the fact that the estate pur autre vie was not an estate of inheritance and could not descend to the heirs of the life tenant, and not being personal property it could not pass to the administrator. But if the conveyance was to "B and his heirs for the life of C," then on the death of B during C's lifetime the heir of B took, not by descent but as "special occupant." This common law rule was abolished in England by statute and is the subject today of statutory regulation in most states.

An estate pur autre vie may be created with more than one measuring life. Thus, A conveys "to B to have and to hold for the lives of A, B and C." B gets a life estate which will endure until the death of the survivor of the three in the absence of an expressed intent that B should take during the joint lives of the three.[5]

A life estate, as well as a fee simple, may be one on special limitation (that is, determinable),[6] or subject to a condition subsequent[7] or executory limitation.[8] Whether a devise by a testator to his wife "so long as she remains a widow" (there being no gift over on the wife's death) creates a defeasible fee simple

---

[5] In a few states there are statutes limiting the number of the measuring lives to two when the life estate is followed by a remainder. See 6 American Law of Property, §§ 25.92–25.98.

[6] Bekins v. Smith, 37 Cal.App. 222, 174 P. 96 (1918) (to B so long as she lives and conducts religious services).

[7] Knowles v. South County Hospital, 87 R.I. 303, 140 A.2d 499 (1958) (to B for life provided he lives on the farm at least three months each year, and "grows at least a peck of Indian maize, or Rhode Island Johnycake corn, on the ear.")

[8] In re Audley's Estate, 256 Wis. 433, 41 N.W.2d 378 (1950).

or a defeasible life estate presents a difficult problem of construction in many cases. The Restatement favors the determinable life estate construction,[9] but recent cases indicate a trend towards holding that the devisee takes a fee simple defeasible on her marriage.[10]

SECTION 11. LIFE ESTATES CREATED BY OPERATION OF LAW

Legal life estates, or life estates created by operation of law, arose out of the marital relationship. The various kinds of legal life estates were: A. Tenancy in fee tail after possibility of issue extinct; B. The husband's estate by the marital right; C. Curtesy; D. Dower.

A. *Tenancy In Fee Tail After Possibility of Issue Extinct*

A tenant in fee tail special, upon death of the designated spouse without issue, has only a life estate in the land. Thus, A conveys land to B and the heirs of his body by his wife, Mary. Mary dies leaving no issue, B surviving. It is obvious that there can never be issue capable of inheriting the estate. On B's death the land must, by virtue of De Donis, revert to A. Hence, B may be properly said to have, after the death of Mary, only a life estate. But if the original conveyance had created a fee tail general, instead of a fee tail special, there could not be tenant in tail after possibility of issue extinct. Since the fee tail estate exists today in only a few jurisdictions, a life estate

---

9 Restat.Prop. § 108, Comm. bb (Supp.1948).

10 See e. g. Dickson v. Alexandria Hospital, Inc., 177 F.2d 876 (C.A.4th 1949); Ramsey v. Holder, 291 S.W.2d 556 (Ky.1956); Kautz v. Kautz, 365 Pa. 450, 76 A.2d 398 (1950); In Re Mattison's Estate, 177 A.2d 230 (Vt.1962). Cf. Bowman v. Brown, 394 Pa. 647, 149 A.2d 56 (1959) ("to my wife as long as she sees fit to remain on the premises and keep said premises in repair and pay taxes on same" held to give wife determinable life estate). A gift to a woman "during widowhood" is usually held to create a determinable life estate and the Restatement takes the position that a devise to a wife defeasible on her remarriage is normally an equivalent limitation. Restatement, n. 9 supra. Cf. Taylor v. Farrow, 239 S.W.2d 73 (Ky.1951).

resulting from a tenancy in tail after possibility of issue extinct is rarely found in modern law.[1]

B. Estate by The Marital Right

At common law the husband had, by right of marriage, a life estate in all lands of which his wife was seised of a freehold estate (an estate of inheritance or for life) at any time during the marriage and prior to birth of issue. This estate, also known as the husband's estate jure uxoris, was probably a product of the concept that the husband was guardian of the wife. It entitled the husband to the use and occupation of the land, as well as the rents and profits, free from any claim of the wife. He could convey the land without her consent and it was liable to execution for his debts, but the purchaser obtained an estate that could not outlast the marriage. Actually, the estate was not measured by the life of the husband but was one which continued until the marriage was dissolved by death or divorce, or until issue was born alive of the marriage. Upon the birth of issue alive, the husband acquired in his wife's inheritable estates an estate by the curtesy initiate which lasted until his death.[2] If he survived his wife, this estate by the curtesy initiate became, on his wife's death, an estate by the curtesy consummate. The estate by the curtesy initiate differed from the estate by the marital right in that the husband now held for his own life and had sole seisin in himself whereas prior to birth of issue his estate was substantially an estate during the joint lives of husband and wife, and both were jointly seised.

---

[1] It will be recalled that in some states statutes abrogating the fee tail have the effect of substituting a life estate in the conveyee for the common law fee tail. See § 2.6, supra. In a sense, a life estate so created can be said to be a life estate created by operation of law although the phrase is not usually applied to this situation.

[2] Technically, the estate by the curtesy initiate existed only in the wife's estates of inheritance which the issue of the marriage were capable of inheriting. Thus, it would exist in the wife's estate in fee simple or in fee tail general but not in a fee tail special if the husband was not the named spouse. The estate by the marital right, but not an estate by the curtesy initiate, could exist in lands in which the wife had only a life estate.

Although the husband had rights in his wife's equitable estates similar to those given to him in her legal estates, it was through courts of equity that married women first obtained some amelioration of the harsh rules of the common law. This result was achieved through two devices—the doctrine of the wife's equity to a settlement, and the recognition of the validity of a trust for the wife's sole and separate use. At the end of the seventeenth century it became established that if the husband sought to reach his wife's equitable assets he would be allowed to do so only if he consented to an adequate settlement out of those assets for her separate use and benefit. This settlement usually took the form of a new trust for the separate use of the wife and the issue; the terms of this new trust being determined by the Court of Chancery. This doctrine of the wife's equity to a settlement was supplemented in the eighteenth century by rulings that property could be conveyed or devised to third persons as trustees for the benefit of a married woman for her separate and exclusive use free from the control of her husband. Later it was held that lands could be conveyed directly to a married woman, without the intervention of trustees, for her "sole and separate use" and in such case equity would protect the property from the claims of her husband and his creditors. Although at law the husband in such a case acquired a life estate in the land, in equity he was treated as a trustee for his wife. Property interests of the wife so protected in equity were called a married woman's separate equitable estate or her "sole and separate" estate.[3]

The reforms thus inaugurated by the chancellors in the seventeenth century were carried to completion in the nineteenth century by legislation abolishing the husband's estate by the marital right and the estate by the curtesy initiate. These statutes, commonly called Married Woman's Property Acts, generally give to married women the same rights in their real and personal property which they would have if unmarried, subject in some jurisdictions to the husband's estate by the cur-

[3] See 1 American Law of Property, §§ 5.50–5.56.

tesy consummate or to a requirement that the husband must join in a conveyance of the wife's lands to make the transfer fully effective.[4]

C. Tenancy by the Curtesy

A tenancy by the curtesy was, at common law, a life estate to which the husband was entitled in all lands of which his wife was seised in fee simple or in fee tail at any time during the marriage provided that there was issue born alive capable of inheriting the estate.[5] On the birth of such qualified issue the husband's tenancy by the marital right was enlarged to an estate for his own life which he held "by curtesy of the law of England."[6] Although, as pointed out above, the husband's estate for his life was called curtesy initiate prior to his wife's death and curtesy consummate after her death, he had a present life estate in both situations and there was no substantial difference between the two types of curtesy.[7]

In modern American law curtesy is obsolescent as a source of life estates. Curtesy initiate was swept away by the Married Women's Property Acts. Curtesy consummate, or more simply curtesy, has been completely abolished in a majority of the

---

[4] The Massachusetts statute is illustrative: "The real and personal property of a woman shall upon her marriage remain her separate property, and a married woman may receive, receipt for, hold, manage and dispose of property, real and personal, in the same manner as if she were sole." Mass.Gen.Laws Ann. c. 209, § 1. The statute further provides that any conveyance of real property by a married woman is subject to the husband's statutory estate by the curtesy unless waived by him. Cf. McKinney's N.Y.Dom.Rel.Law, §§ 50, 51.

[5] "The time when the issue was born is immaterial, provided it were during the coverture; for, whether it were born before or after the wife's seisin of the lands, whether it be living or dead at the time of the seisin, or at the time of the wife's decease, the husband shall be tenant by the curtesy." Blackstone, Comm. 128.

[6] In contrast to the more restricted rights of a husband in his wife's lands under Norman and French law. For the historical development of curtesy, see 1 American Law of Property, §§ 5.58–5.59.

[7] Curtesy attached to the wife's equitable estates in fee, at least where not excluded by the terms of the conveyance to the wife.

states.[8] Generally, the husband is given instead a statutory distributive share in the wife's estate.[9] In the remaining states curtesy survives in a modified form, usually as a protected expectancy during the lifetime of the wife although the statutes vary greatly as to the power of the wife to bar curtesy by deed or by will and as to the share the husband takes.[10]

D. Dower

At common law a widow was entitled on the death of her husband to a life estate in one-third of the lands of which he had been seised at any time during the marriage of an estate in fee simple or in fee tail, provided that the estate was one capable of being inherited by issue of the marriage.[11] During the husband's lifetime the wife had a protected expectancy, called inchoate dower. No conveyance by the husband, even to a bona fide purchaser for value, would be effective to defeat the wife's right to dower, nor could creditors of the husband impair her right. On the husband's death the widow was entitled to have assigned or set off to her the specific lands to be held in dower and her dower then became consummate.[12] Once dower had become consum-

---

8 See 2 Powell, Real Property, § 218.

9 See e. g. McKinney's N.Y.Dec.Est.Law, §§ 18, 82, 83; McKinney's N.Y. Real Property Law, § 89.

10 Even in a state which retains curtesy in a modified form it may be seldom claimed because of the surviving husband's right to elect, in lieu thereof, a larger distributive share of the wife's estate. See Opinion of the Justices, 337 Mass. 786, 151 N.E.2d 475 (1958).

11 If the husband's estate was one in fee simple or in fee tail general there would be no problem of the capacity of the issue to inherit. But if lands were given in fee tail special to a man and a named wife, his second wife would not be entitled to dower because no issue of the second marriage could inherit the estate.

12 In comparing curtesy and dower it should be noted that: 1. birth of issue was a pre-requisite to curtesy but not to dower—the widow was entitled to dower even if no issue resulted from the marriage; 2. the husband's estate by the curtesy was a life estate in *all* of the lands of which the wife was seised of an appropriate estate during the marriage but the widow's estate in dower was a life estate in only one-third of the husband's lands; 3. the husband's estate by the curtesy initiate commenced on the birth of issue, but the wife's right to dower became an estate only on the assignment

mate her status was the same as that of any other life tenant.

Since seisin by the husband of an estate of inheritance was a pre-requisite to dower, his widow was not entitled to dower in lands in which he had a reversion or remainder expectant upon an estate of freehold. And since the concept of seisin applied only to legal estates, dower did not attach to equitable interests.[13] Moreover, the husband's seisin must have amounted to beneficial ownership. If he held legal title as trustee for another, his widow had no dower in the lands thus held.[14]

At a time when land was the principal source of wealth dower was a fairly adequate device for assuring to the widow some measure of support after the death of her husband.[15] In an agrarian economy it was an acceptable form of social and economic security for the widow. Partly for this reason and partly because it was a familiar institution, common law dower obtained generally in the United States in the colonial and post-Revolutionary period. In the nineteenth century it was frequently broadened to include equitable estates. But in the twentieth century dower has become of diminishing importance and it has been abolished in more than one-half of the states.[16] The statutes frequently give to the widow, as a substitute for dower, a fractional share in fee simple in the realty owned by the hus-

of her dower lands to her; 4. unlike the husband's estate by the curtesy initiate, the wife's inchoate right of dower could not be independently transferred to a third person although it could be released to a conveyee of the husband's estate.

[13] This rule was changed by the Dower Act in 1833. 3 & 4 Will. IV, c. 105, § 3. Dower was abolished in England in 1925 by the Law of Property Act, 15 Geo. V, c. 23, § 45(c).

[14] For a thorough discussion of dower, see 2 American Law of Property, §§ 5.1 to 5.49.

[15] It should be remembered that at common law the wife was not an heir of her husband and that a land owner had no power of devise (except by custom in a few localities) prior to 1540.

[16] See e. g. McKinney's N.Y.Real Property Law, § 190 (as to realty acquired by the husband since 1930).

band at his death as well as a share of the personal property. Further protection is given to the widow by making her a forced heir, that is, allowing her to take a distributive share in her husband's estate despite the provisions of his will. In other states, the widow may elect to take in lieu of dower a distributive share in the husband's estate. This distributive share, since it is an absolute rather than a life interest in the assets, and extends to personalty as well as realty, is usually more valuable than a dower estate.[17] In the minority of states retaining dower there are found statutes establishing procedures for claiming dower and sometimes modifying its common law incidents.[18]

In most situations both dower and curtesy are treated as derivative estates and, therefore, the interest of the surviving spouse cannot outlast the basic estate from which the dower or curtesy derived. Thus, if the husband acquires a title in fee simple which is defective because of a superior title in a third person, the wife's dower rights are subject to the same infirmity.[19] So also, if the basic estate is a fee simple determinable or a fee simple on condition subsequent, the fact that it is a fee simple defeasible will not initially prevent dower or curtesy, but the happening of the specified event which causes the expiration or termination of the fee simple will also end the dower or curtesy interest.[20] Whether the same result follows when the fee simple is defeasible because subject to an executory interest [21]

[17] In Massachusetts, for example, the widow may elect to take either dower or a distributive share of her deceased husband's realty but as a practical matter dower is seldom claimed.

[18] See Petta v. Host, 1 Ill.2d 293, 115 N.E.2d 881 (1953).

[19] If the husband acquires the fee simple subject to an option in a third person to buy the land, the wife's dower interest is also subject to the option. Forte v. Caruso, 336 Mass. 476, 146 N.E.2d 501 (1957); Matlack v. Arend, 2 N.J.Super. 319, 63 A.2d 812 (1949).

[20] See 1 Restat.Prop., § 54 and Monograph on Dower and Curtesy as Derivative Estates, Appendix to volume 1.

[21] Thus, if A conveys "to B and his heirs but if B die leaving no issue surviving at his death then to C and his heirs", B has a fee simple subject

is the subject of dispute. The *Restatement* takes the flat position that dower and curtesy are derivative estates and, therefore, come to an end when the estate of the spouse acquiring the fee simple defeasible would have ended under the terms of the creating limitation.[22] In this respect the *Restatement* adopts the view of the minority of the courts which have passed on the question.[23]

Under English law the surviving spouse of a tenant in tail was entitled to dower or curtesy despite the failure of issue at the tenant's death. There is slight American authority on the point, but the *Restatement,* adhering to the view of the derivative nature of dower and curtesy, takes the position that dower and curtesy are not allowed when no issue survive.[24]

SECTION 12. CHARACTERISTICS OF A LIFE ESTATE

A tenant for life of a possessory estate has a right to the undisturbed possession of the land [1] and to the income and profits

---

to an executory interest in C. The problem is whether B's widow is allowed dower if B dies leaving no issue surviving him. If B does leave issue surviving, his widow will get dower in those states which still recognize it.

[22] 1 Restat.Prop., § 54. Compare 1 American Law of Property, §§ 5.26–5.29.

[23] For the reasons in support of the Restatement position, see 2 Powell, Real Property, § 215.

[24] Restat.Prop., § 84 (fee tail); § 93 (fee tail preserved as such for a single lifetime only). See 1 American Law of Property, § 5.27.

[1] The prevailing view is that the life tenant can recover from a third party wrongdoer only the damages sustained as to his life estate and not full damages to the fee. Zimmerman v. Shreeve, 59 Md. 357 (1882); Tinkham v. Wind, 319 Mass. 158, 65 N.E.2d 14 (1946); Contra, Rogers v. Atlantic, Gulf & Pacific Co., 213 N.Y. 246, 107 N.E. 661 (1915). The matter is now regulated by statute in New York so as to allow the life tenant to recover for all damage done to the realty only if all living persons having an interest in the land are made parties to the action. McKinney's N.Y.Real Property Law, § 538; N.Y.Civ.Pr.Act, § 193(c). The Restatement adopts the view that the life tenant is restricted to recovery of damages to his life estate, the damages being measured by the difference between the value of the life estate before the trespass or other wrongful conduct and its value after the wrongful conduct. § 118.

thereof. His use and enjoyment of the premises is limited by the law of waste, that is, he is under a duty to refrain from any act which will diminish the value of the reversion or the remainder if such act is also, under all of the circumstances, an unreasonable use of the premises.[2] On the termination of the life estate for a reason other than the tenant's own act or default, he, or his executor or administrator, is entitled to emblements, that is, to cultivate and harvest annual crops previously planted.[3]

A life estate has the quality of alienability, hence, the life tenant can convey his estate to a third person. But he cannot (apart from the now obsolete common law doctrine of tortious feoffment) convey a greater estate than his own.[4] Sometimes the deed or will creating the life estate contains language purporting to restrict the life tenant's power to convey his estate. The validity of the restraint on alienation depends largely on the type of the restriction. In most jurisdictions a direct or disabling restraint on alienation of the life estate (to B for life "but without power to convey") is void. But a restraint in the form of a forfeiture of the estate on attempted alienation (to B for life "but if B ceases to live on the land or conveys it, then to C") is held valid in nearly all states. The forfeiture restraint is less objectionable since, apart from its deterrent effect on the life

---

2 The above statement is admittedly a broad generalization. It is intended primarily as a caveat that the rights of the owner of a possessory life estate must be balanced with the rights of the owner of a future estate in the same land. For a discussion of the law of waste, see 5 American Law of Property, §§ 20.1–20.14; 5 Powell, Real Property, §§ 636–646.

3 A life tenant also has the privilege of taking estovers, that is, to cut timber reasonably necessary for repairs to fences and structures and as fuel for fires. Zimmerman v. Shreeve, 59 Md. 357 (1882).

4 If A has an estate for his life and he conveys to B "for life" does B get an estate measured by A's life or one measured by B's life (provided that B does not outlive A)? If A dies first there is no problem since B's estate will necessarily fall with A's death. But if B dies before A and B had an estate for the life of A it will not end on B's death. Normally, B will take an estate for A's life but the extrinsic facts may indicate that A intended to transfer to B an estate that would in no event outlast B's life. See Restat.Prop., § 108, Comm. a.

tenant, it does not render the land unmarketable in the hands of the reversioner or remainderman.[5]

Since a life tenant has a limited interest in the land, he owes certain duties to the owner of the future interest in the land, the remainderman or the reversioner. He is obligated to preserve the land and structures in a reasonable state of repair, but he is not bound to make expenditures for that purpose in excess of the profits, rent or income received by him. Failure to discharge this duty amounts to permissive waste for which the life tenant is liable to the owner of the future interest.[6] But the life tenant is under no duty to make extraordinary repairs, or to rebuild structures damaged or destroyed without his fault, or to make improvements. If he voluntarily makes improvements he cannot call on the owner of the future interest to contribute to the cost. The life tenant must pay the carrying charges on the property to the extent of the gross income, or the fair rental value if he personally occupies the property. Therefore, he must pay the interest on any mortgage or other incumbrance to which the life estate and the future interest are subject but he is not personally obligated to make payments on the principal.[7] He has a duty to pay current taxes levied on

---

[5] Conger v. Lowe, 124 Ind. 368, 24 N.E. 889, 9 L.R.A. 165 (1890) ; 6 American Law of Property, §§ 26.48–26.50. It should be noted that we are here discussing restraints on alienation of a legal life estate only. The question of restraints on alienation of equitable interests is part of the problem of spendthrift trusts, a topic beyond the scope of this book.

[6] Beliveau v. Beliveau, 217 Minn. 235, 14 N.W.2d 360 (1944). As to the remedies available to the owner of the future interest, see 1 American Law of Property, § 2.24; 1 Restat.Prop., §§ 129, 131.

[7] However, if both the life estate and the future interest are subject to a mortgage and the principal of the mortgage debt becomes due and is paid by the owner of the future interest, the latter has a lien on the life estate to enforce payment out of that estate of a proportionate part of the sum paid. The burden of payment should be apportioned between the life estate and the future interest in accordance with their respective values, under the view taken by the Restatement. § 132, Accord, Matter of Colligan, 202 Misc. 728, 110 N.Y.S.2d 638 (1952) (under New York statute).

the property.[8] Assessments by a municipality or other public authority (frequently called betterment assessments) for public improvements specially benefiting the property must be borne wholly by the life tenant where the life of the improvement does not exceed the probable duration of the life estate. But where the special assessment is one for an improvement of a permanent or quasi-permanent nature, it must be apportioned between the owner of the life estate and the owner of the future interest in accordance with the respective values of the two estates.[9]

Although a life tenant is free, in the absence of a valid restraint in the creating instrument, to sell his interest, a life estate is not as a practical matter a marketable commodity. The life tenant, therefore, is faced with a difficult situation when the land is unproductive or the carrying charges exceed or substantially diminish the income. Can the life tenant maintain judicial proceedings to compel a sale of the fee simple over the objections of the owner of the future interest, or when the owner of the future interest is unascertained or a minor? In approximately one-half of the states there are statutes which, under specified conditions, authorize a court to order a sale of the complete ownership of the land for reinvestment.[10] Apart from

---

[8] Taxes are normally assessed on the realty as a unit and not on the basis of the separate estates of the life tenant and the reversioner or remainderman. An unpaid tax usually constitutes a lien on the entire property and this lien is enforceable by a sale of the fee simple, thus destroying both the life estate and the future interest.

[9] The problem of valuation of a life estate may arise in a number of other situations: e. g. apportionment of damages recovered for an injury to the land by a third person; apportionment of the award when the property has been taken by eminent domain proceedings; valuation for estate or inheritance tax purposes. The basic problem of valuation is that of determining the present value of an annuity equal to the expected annual net income of the property to be received by the life tenant. The process involves the use of mortality tables to determine the life expectancy of the life tenant, an estimate of future annual earning capacity expressed in terms of a percentage of the value of the fee simple (e. g. 4% by statute in New York), and the use of a "discount rate" to obtain the present value of the future earning capacity. As to the details, see 5 Powell, Real Property, § 666.

[10] For a detailed break-down of the statutes, see 2 Restat.Prop., § 179, Note on Statutory Sale for Reinvestment (Supp.1948).

statute, the present trend of judicial authority recognizes a power to order a sale when necessary for the protection of the persons interested, particularly when the owners of the future interest are minors or unascertained.[11]

[11] See e. g. Cauffiel v. Cauffiel, 161 A.2d 432 (Del.Ch.1960). For a thorough discussion, see Simes & Smith, Future Interests, §§ 1941–1946.

Chapter 3

NONFREEHOLD ESTATES

The estate for years, the periodic estate, and the estate at will have a common legal characteristic in that they are all classified under the general heading of "nonfreehold" estates. And since each of these estates normally involves a duty on the part of the estate holder to make a periodic payment for the use of the land (rent) they comprise the core of the landlord-tenant relationship. Hence, they are grouped together in this chapter.

SECTION 1. THE ESTATE FOR YEARS—HISTORICAL BACKGROUND AND ITS CONSEQUENCES

The estate for years—an estate of fixed duration expressed in terms of a multiple or fraction of a year—originally performed a social and economic function different from that of the fee simple, the fee tail, and the life estate. These three estates were family estates in the sense that they provided the necessary economic support for the family unit. By contrast, the term for years was used in the thirteenth century principally as a money lending device designed to evade the Church's prohibition of usury. The borrower, rich in land but short of cash, would give the lender a long term lease of a portion of his lands and out of the lands the lender would recoup both principal and profit. Probably because of this difference of function, the common law set the term of years apart from the older estates and denied that the lessee for years was seised of a free tenement.[1] Thus, the fee simple, the fee tail and the life estate were "freehold" estates but the estate for years was "nonfreehold."

---

[1] Plucknett, Concise History of the Common Law 570–574 (5th ed. 1956). Cf. Simpson, Introduction to the History of the Land Law 68–73 (1961).

The consequence of this refusal to view the tenant for years as seised of a free tenement was that he was denied the benefit of the real actions (in which the successful plaintiff recovered a judgment for possession of the land) and his only remedy against a stranger to the title who dispossessed him was an action for damages. But the rise of the agricultural or husbandry lease in the fourteenth and fifteenth centuries made imperative additional protection for the lessee and in 1499 he was given the judicially moulded remedy of ejectment by which he could recover possession from one who ousted him.[2] Although the action of ejectment finally gave the lowly termor or tenant for years a better remedy than the real actions available to the owners of freehold estates, the common law had already classified the estate for years as personal property. To distinguish it from other chattel interests it was called a chattel real. Since it was personal property, on the death of a tenant for years the unexpired term passed not to the tenant's heir but to his executor or administrator.[3]

In modern law the term for years is an interest in land, an estate, but it has not completely outlived its peculiar history and its common law classification as personal property.[4] Statutes which use the words "real property," "real estate," or "lands, tenements and hereditaments" without indicating their intended applicability to leaseholds invite litigation over the question whether an estate for years is included within the statutory coverage. The answers given in the decisions have not been uniform since policy considerations in a particular case may outweigh legal history.[5]

---

[2] The action of ejectment, originally available only to lessees, was later extended to holders of freehold estates and by the seventeenth century had become the standard action to try title.

[3] Under modern statutes real and personal property normally pass to the same persons when the owner dies intestate.

[4] The Restatement of Property, for example, in the definition of "real property" excludes estates for years, periodic estates and tenancies at will. § 8, Comment c.

[5] E. g. Stagecrafters' Club, Inc. v. District of Columbia Div. of American Legion, 110 F.Supp. 481 (D.C.1953) (leasehold subject to sale on execution as

SECTION 2.   CREATION AND CHARACTERISTICS

It has been orthodox doctrine since the days of Littleton that an estate for years must have a fixed and certain period of duration. This requirement of definiteness of duration is satisfied if the estate has a certain ending even though its commencement in possession is stated to depend on the happening of a stipulated event.[1] But if the termination date is indefinite the estate does not meet the traditional requirement for a term of years.[2] This requirement of certainty of duration relates to the maximum period of duration. The estate for years may, like an estate in fee simple or a life estate, be subject to a special limitation,[3] or a condition subsequent,[4] or an executory limitation. In fact, the

personal property); Harbel Oil Co. v. Steele, 83 Ariz. 181, 318 P.2d 359 (1957) (mortgage of leasehold held mortgage of real property); Hutchinson v. Bramhall, Deane & Co., 42 N.J.Eq. 372, 7 A. 873 (1886) (mortgage of leasehold need not be recorded as real estate mortgage); Pierce v. Pierce, 4 Ill.2d 494, 123 N.E.2d 511 (1954) (partition available to joint owner of leasehold although partition statute referred to "lands, tenements and hereditaments"). Cf. Mayor etc. of New York v. Mabie, 13 N.Y. 151 (1855). See Comment, 25 N.C.L. Rev. 516 (1947).

[1] See e. g. Wunsch v. Donnelly, 302 Mass. 286, 19 N.E.2d 70 (1939) (lease of roof for advertising purposes for "term of five years beginning with date of erection of sign"). But cf. Haggerty v. City of Oakland, 161 Cal.App.2d 407, 326 P.2d 957, 66 A.L.R.2d 718 (1958).

[2] Farris v. Hershfield, 325 Mass. 176, 89 N.E.2d 636 (1950); Idalia Realty and Development Co. v. Norman, 232 Mo. 663, 135 S.W. 47, 34 L.R.A.,N.S., 1069 (1911); Restat.Prop., § 19. Cf. Elm Farm Foods Co. v. Cifrino, 328 Mass. 549, 105 N.E.2d 366 (1952). Leases "for the duration" of the war, or until the cessation of hostilities have caused a split in the courts as to their effectiveness in creating an estate for years. Holding to the traditional view are: Lace v. Chantler, (1944) 1 K.B. 368, 1 All.Eng.L.Rep. 305; Stanmeyer v. Davis, 321 Ill.App. 227, 53 N.E.2d 22 (1944). Contra, Rupp Hotel Operating Co. v. Donn, 158 Fla. 541, 29 So.2d 441 (1947); Watkins v. Cohen, 91 N.E.2d 708 (Ohio Com.Pl.1949). See 32 Calif.L.Rev. 199 (1944).

[3] See e. g. Gunsenhiser v. Binder, 206 Mass. 434, 92 N.E. 705 (1910); Haskins v. Kelly, 192 Misc. 366, 78 N.Y.S.2d 912 (1948).

[4] At times a lease may contain both a special limitation and a power of termination. See e. g. Ghoti Estates, Inc. v. Freda's Capri Restaurant, Inc. 332 Mass. 17, 123 N.E.2d 232 (1955).

great majority of leases create estates for years on condition subsequent by reason of the presence in the instrument of a clause giving the lessor a right of re-entry or power of termination on breach by the lessee of any of the specified conditions.

No particular form of words is necessary to create an estate for years. "Any language by which the possession and enjoyment of land is granted for a specified term at a stipulated rental creates a tenancy, and is in effect a lease." [5] At common law an estate for years could be created by oral agreement but the original Statute of Frauds (1677) provided, in effect, that leases for more than three years "from the making thereof" must be in writing to be enforceable as such.[6] American jurisdictions have followed the general pattern of this statute but most of them authorize oral leases for not more than a year.[7] Normally, these statutes do not in terms restrict the period to one year "from the making" of the lease, but another section of the Statute of Frauds, which required contracts not to be performed within one year to be in writing in order to be enforceable, has been widely adopted. Considerable controversy has arisen, therefore, as to the validity of an oral lease for one year when

[5] F. H. Stoltze Land Co. v. Westberg, 63 Mont. 38, 44, 206 P. 407, 408 (1922). Since a lease is normally a commercial transfer of an estate in land, rent is a usual incident of the transaction; but an estate for years can be created without obligation of the tenant to pay rent.

[6] 29 Car. II, c. 3. If the lease for more than three years was not in writing it was to be given the effect of a tenancy at will, thereby making it terminable by either party without notice.

[7] In a few states oral leases for not more than three years are enforceable. In most of the New England states an oral lease for any period creates a tenancy at will. Me.Rev.Stat. c. 168, § 16 (1954); Mass.Gen.Laws Ann. c. 183, § 3; N.H.Rev.Stat.Ann. c. 506:1 (1955); Vt.Stat.Ann.Tit. 27, § 302 (1959).

An oral lease for longer than the permissible statutory period is not void for all purposes. Only the agreement as to duration is invalidated and all other provisions of the lease, such as amount and time of payment of rent, and termination, are given effect. Ferri v. Liberatoscioli, 338 Pa. 454, 13 A.2d 45 (1940); Creech v. Crockett, 59 Mass. (5 Cush.) 133 (1849); see Coudert v. Cohn, 118 N.Y. 309, 23 N.E. 298, 7 L.R.A. 69 (1890). Cf. Darling Shops Delaware Corp. v. Baltimore Center Corp., 191 Md. 289, 60 A.2d 669, 6 A.L R.2d 677 (1948).

the term is to commence at a future date. The authorities are about evenly divided on the point.[8]

The period of duration of the estate may vary from one day to a thousand years or more. At common law the length of the term was immaterial but in many jurisdictions, due to statutory provisions, the length of the term has certain legal consequences. In nearly all states there are statutes requiring leases for more than a specified period (usually ranging from one to seven years) to be recorded.[9] And in a few states leases for agricultural purposes and leases of specified kinds of property are limited to a prescribed number of years.[10]

The common law drew a distinction between the status of the lessee prior to his entry into possession under the lease and after his entry. Prior to his entry the lessee had a contract right to an estate for years but not an estate. Until actual entry the lessee's interest, known as an *interesse termini* (interest in a term) would not enable him to maintain an action of trespass against a third party. In modern law, the concept of *interesse termini* serves no useful purpose and is frequently ignored by the courts although traces of the doctrine may be found in an occasional case.[11]

[8] See 1 American Law of Property, § 3.18; 19 Univ. of Chi.L.Rev. 529 (1950).

[9] A list of these statutes may be found in 4 American Law of Property, § 17.8, nn. 9, 10.

[10] See e. g. West's Ann.Cal.Civ.Code, § 717 (lease of land for agricultural purposes restricted to 15 years); § 718 (lease "of any town or city lot" restricted to 99 years); § 718f (oil and gas leases limited to 99 years). In Massachusetts a term for 100 years or more, having 50 years unexpired, is treated as a fee simple for purposes of dower and curtesy, descent and distribution, levy on execution, and sale by executors and administrators. Mass.Gen.Laws Ann. c. 186, § 1.

[11] See e. g. Simon v. Kirkpatrick, 141 S.C. 251, 139 S.E. 614, 54 A.L.R. 1348 (1927). The doctrine of *interesse termini* was abolished in England by the Law of Property Act, 1925, 15 Geo. V, c. 20, § 149(1) (2) and a term of years takes effect without entry into possession by the lessee.

Speaking of entry by the lessee, suppose that at the time fixed for the commencement of the lessee's estate the premises are in the possession of a

It often becomes necessary to distinguish between leasehold interests and other interests having similar aspects but different legal consequences. Thus, a particular transaction may, arguably, create an estate for years or a license or an easement.[12] Depending on how the transaction is classified, different legal incidents attach to the relationship. If, for example, A, owner of a building, gives to B for a specified term the exclusive right to erect and maintain an advertising sign on the roof or the wall of the building, the nature of B's interest determines whether the privilege given to B is revocable, whether possessory remedies are available to B, and the tort liability of A and B to third persons for the condition of the premises.[13] In this and analogous situations, the test usually applied by the courts in determining

former tenant who is wrongfully holding over? The lessee can normally recover possession in an action against the holdover tenant but this involves delay and expense. Can he hold the lessor liable for damages? This depends on whether the court is willing to imply a covenant on the part of the lessor to deliver possession to the lessee. The courts are about evenly split on the question. The so-called American rule (applied in California, Illinois, Maryland, Massachusetts, Mississippi, New Hampshire, New York and Virginia) denies recovery against the lessor. The opposite, or English rule, holds the lessor liable. Coe v. Clay, 5 Bing. 440, 130 Eng.Rep. 1131 (1829) ("he who lets, agrees to give possession, and not merely to give a chance of a law suit.") The English rule is followed in Alabama, Arkansas, Connecticut, Indiana, Iowa, Kentucky, Missouri, Nebraska, North Carolina, Oregon and Tennessee. The advisability, from the lessee's standpoint, of an express covenant in the lease that the lessor will deliver possession to the lessee at the commencement of the term is apparent.

12 A license is usually defined as a revocable privilege to do an act or series of acts on land in the possession of another. Cf. 4 Restat.Prop., §§ 512, 514, 519. An easement is an interest in land in the possession of another consisting of the privilege of making a limited use of the land. An easement is not revocable at the will of the grantor. See 4 Restat.Prop., § 450; Baseball Pub. Co. v. Bruton, 302 Mass. 54, 18 N.E.2d 362, 119 A.L.R. 1518 (1938). A common type of easement is a right of way across the land of another.

13 The advertising sign cases are fairly numerous. See e. g. Gaertner v. Donnelly, 296 Mass. 260, 5 N.E.2d 419 (1936); Lewis v. Baxter Laundries, Inc., 254 Mich. 216, 236 N.W. 239 (1931); Bridge Hardware Co. Inc. v. Disosway & Fisher, Inc., 199 Misc. 259, 101 N.Y.S.2d 863 (1950). Absent a clearly expressed intention to create a tenancy, the courts usually hold that the arrangement amounts to a license. Occasionally, the transaction is held to create an easement. Baseball Pub. Co. v. Bruton, n. 12, supra

the nature of the interest created is the intention of the parties with respect to conferring a possessory right on the recipient of the interest. The distinctive feature of an estate for years is the right of the tenant to exclusive possession of a defined physical area for the duration of the specified term.[14] Whether such a right of possession has been given to the transferee is often not a matter of easy determination because of ambiguous language in the creating instrument, or the restricted rights imposed on the transferee by the terms of the agreement, or the circumstances of the transaction.[15]

SECTION 3.   THE MODERN LEASE AND ITS COVENANTS

The modern lease is both a conveyance and a contract. It is a conveyance inasmuch as it creates in the lessee an estate for years but it is also a contract because of the covenants or promises made by the respective parties. The lessor covenants either expressly or impliedly (by the prevailing view) that the lessee will have quiet enjoyment of the demised premises. He will frequently make additional express covenants, depending on the nature of the property, with respect to repairs, furnishing of heat and other services, non-competition with the lessee, and many other matters. The lessee in turn will normally covenant to pay the rent, to use the premises in a specified manner and only for the specified purpose, not to assign or sub-let without the lessor's consent, and to surrender the premises at the end of the term in good condition. Covenants relating to taxes, insurance, repairs and improvements, as well as provisions concerning acci-

[14] Willett v. Pilotte, 329 Mass. 610, 109 N.E.2d 840 (1953); Tips v. United States, 70 F.2d 525 (C.C.A.5th 1934).

[15] It may, for example, be difficult to determine whether a non-transient occupant of furnished rooms is a tenant or a lodger. See Roberts v. Casey, 36 Cal.App.2d 767, 93 P.2d 654 (1939); Davis v. Francis Scott Key Apartments, Inc., 140 A.2d 188 (Mun.App.D.C.1958); Comment, Tenant, Lodger, and Guest: Questionable Categories for Modern Rental Occupants, 64 Yale L.J. 391 (1955). For a thorough discussion of the distinction between leases and other arrangements, see 2 American Law of Property, §§ 3.3–3.10.

dental destruction of the premises, condemnation proceedings against the property, and defaults by the lessee are usually found in leases of business properties.[1] Thus, the modern lease is a highly complex instrument in which the contract element is a substantial, if not the predominant, ingredient.

Yet courts, for the most part, have refused to apply modern principles of contract law to leases. The law as to leases is still to a large extent "a matter of history that has not forgotten Lord Coke."[2] Thus, the principle of the mutual dependency of promises that is normally applicable to bilateral contracts is not applied to leases. If the lessor covenants in the lease to make repairs, a breach of this covenant will not relieve the tenant of his obligation to pay rent although it will give rise to a cause of action for breach of contract. So also, a breach by the lessee of his covenant to pay rent or a breach by him of any other covenant in the lease will not give the lessor the right to terminate the lease, in the absence of a statutory provision, or of a clause in the lease, conferring such right.[3]

[1] For a discussion of the running of the benefit and burden of covenants in leases, see 2 American Law of Property, §§ 9.1–9.7; 2 Powell, Real Property, § 246.

[2] Holmes, J. in Gardiner v. William S. Butler & Co., 245 U.S. 603, 38 S.Ct. 214, 62 L.Ed. 505 (1918). Coke (1552–1634) deserves more than a footnote in any property book. Sir Edward (commonly called Lord Coke but actually not a lord) was successively Solicitor-General, Attorney-General, Chief Justice of the Common Pleas, Chief Justice of the King's Bench, and parliamentary leader. Master of the common law and expert on the Year Books, his famous work on Real Property (Coke on Littleton) is still the authoritative exposition of post-feudal land law. On his death his widow, after thirty-six years of stormy married life, wrote: "We shall never see his like again, praises be to God." The thousands of law students in America who, until the middle 1800s, were forced to master the technicalities of Coke on Littleton, were inclined to agree. For a full scale treatment, see Bowen, The Lion and the Throne (1956).

[3] At common law the landlord had the right of distress, that is, the right to seize any chattels of the tenant or of others on the land and hold them as security for payment of the overdue rent. The right of distress exists today in only a few states although in several states the landlord is given a statutory lien on the tenant's goods on the land. The most common form of protection for the landlord against the tenant's non-payment of rent is through a clause

The emphasis on the real property aspect of a lease is most evident in the cases dealing with the lessee's liability to pay rent after the accidental destruction of a building on the leased premises.   With few exceptions the courts have held that the lessee, in the absence of a so-called "fire clause" in the lease, continues to be liable to pay the reserved rent despite the destruction or damage.   The lease is viewed as a sale of the term of years and the rent is regarded as the purchase price.[4]   On this theory there has been no failure of consideration even though the lessee has lost the expected benefit of the transaction.   The harshness of this result has led to the enactment in many jurisdictions of statutes relieving the tenant of liability for future rent in the event of accidental destruction or injury to a leased building.[5]   And an exception to the common law rule has been made where the subject matter of the lease is space or rooms in a building, such as an apartment or suite of offices, as distinguished from a lease of land and building.

An exception to the rule of the independency of covenants in leases is made in cases of actual or constructive eviction of the tenant by the lessor.   The unfairness of allowing the lessor to collect rent after he has wrongfully ousted the tenant has impelled the courts to resort to the contract doctrine of failure of consideration.[6]   An actual eviction takes place whenever the lessor wrongfully deprives the lessee of possession of the whole or a part of the demised premises.   If the eviction is total the lessee's obligation to pay rent is suspended during the period he is deprived of possession.   He may sue to recover possession or he

in the lease reserving to the landlord the power to terminate the tenancy in the event of the tenant's default.   In some states the lessor is given a statutory right to forfeit the lease for non-payment of rent.   See e. g. Mass.Gen.Laws Ann. c. 186, § 11.

4 A leading case is Fowler v. Bott, 6 Mass. 63 (1809).

5 See e. g. McKinney's N.Y.Real Property Law, § 227. In Suydam v. Jackson, 54 N.Y. 450 (1873), the statute was construed so as not to relieve the tenant where the injury to the leased building was due to gradual deterioration.

6 Morse v. Goddard, 54 Mass. (13 Metc.) 177 (1847); Fifth Avenue Building Co. v. Kernochan, 221 N.Y. 370, 117 N.E. 579 (1917).

may treat the lease as terminated and sue for damages for breach of the lessor's covenant of quiet enjoyment. If the eviction is partial only, he may continue in possession of the remainder of the leased premises without liability to pay any rent although he is still liable on other covenants of the lease.[7] Where the partial eviction is not by act of the lessor but by paramount title (a title in a third person superior to that of the landlord) the rent is apportioned and the tenant is liable for the rental value of the retained land.

In the case of a constructive eviction, that is, conduct of the lessor which deprives the tenant of the beneficial enjoyment of the property although there is no physical dispossession, the tenant may terminate the lease and extinguish his liability for future rent. But in order to avail himself of the defense of constructive eviction the tenant must abandon possession of the premises within a reasonable time after the wrongful act, or omission to act, on the part of the landlord.[8] A typical case of constructive eviction is the failure of the lessor to furnish heat or other services in breach of a covenant in the lease undertaking to do so.[9] The present trend is to broaden the doctrine of constructive eviction so as to include within its scope diverse situations wherein the lessor in breach of his covenants has substantially impaired the beneficial enjoyment of the lessee.[10]

[7] The reason assigned for the suspension of the entire rent is that the landlord may not apportion his own wrong. Smith v. McEnany, 170 Mass. 26, 48 N.E. 781 (1897).

[8] What is a reasonable time is usually a question of fact. The Automobile Supply Co. v. The Scene-in-Action Corp., 340 Ill. 196, 172 N.E. 35, 69 A.L.R. 1085 (1930); Westland Housing Corp. v. Scott, 312 Mass. 375, 44 N.E.2d 959 (1942).

[9] The Automobile Supply Co. v. The Scene-in-Action Corp., supra, n. 8; Shindler v. Milden, 282 Mass. 32, 184 N.E. 673 (1933) (failure to install heating system as covenanted).

[10] Kulawitz v. Pacific Woodenware and Paper Co., 25 Cal.2d 664, 155 P.2d 24 (1944) (breach of covenant not to lease other space in same building for competing business); Barnard Realty Co. v. Bonwit, 155 App.Div. 182, 139 N.Y.S. 1050 (1913) (plague of rats in walls of apartment house); Bruckner v. Helfaer, 197 Wis. 582, 222 N.W. 790 (1929) (noise from adjoining apartment).

In effect, the doctrine of constructive eviction is used as a substitute for the contract rule of the mutual dependency of covenants.[11]

On the whole, it may be said that the present trend is in the direction of giving greater recognition to principles of contract law in dealing with the rights and duties of lessor and lessee. Thus, the doctrine of anticipatory breach is usually applied so as to allow the lessor to recover full damages without waiting until the end of the term when the lessee repudiates the lease.[12] The defense of "frustration" may be conceded to the lessee where unforeseeable events completely defeat the purpose of the lease.[13] And a few decisions frankly adopt the contract approach of the mutual dependency of the covenants by the lessor and lessee.[14]

SECTION 4. TRANSFER OF THE INTEREST OF LESSOR OR LESSEE

Usually, the lessor is the owner of an estate in fee simple in the premises prior to the execution of the lease. The effect of the lease is to carve an estate for years out of this fee and to leave in the lessor a reversion in fee simple. This reversion is freely transferable. A transfer of the reversion normally carries with

The disturbance of the tenant, in order to amount to a constructive eviction, must be attributable to fault of the landlord or his agents. Compare with the last cited case, Hughes v. Westchester Development Corp., 64 App.D.C. 292, 77 F.2d 550 (1935).

[11] See Bennett, The Modern Lease, 16 Tex.L.Rev. 47 (1937).

[12] See e. g. In re Edgewood Park Junior College, Inc., 123 Conn. 74, 192 A. 561 (1937). Cf. Hermitage Co. v. Levine, 248 N.Y. 333, 162 N.E. 97, 59 A.L.R. 1015 (1928).

[13] Lloyd v. Murphy, 25 Cal.2d 48, 153 P.2d 47 (1944); 119 Fifth Ave. Inc. v. Taiyo Trading Co., 190 Misc. 123, 73 N.Y.S.2d 774, affirmed 275 App.Div. 695, 87 N.Y.S.2d 430 (1949). Contra, Leonard v. Autocar Sales & Service Co., 392 Ill. 182, 64 N.E.2d 477, 163 A.L.R. 670 (1945).

[14] Medico-Dental Bldg. Co. v. Horton & Converse, 21 Cal.2d 411, 132 P.2d 457 (1942); University Club v. Deakin, 265 Ill. 257, 106 N.E. 790, L.R.A.1915C 854 (1914).

it the right to future rents as an incident although there can be an assignment of rent without an assignment of the reversion, as well as an assignment of the reversion without the rent.[1] Moreover, an assignment of the reversion transfers to the assignee the benefit of the lessee's covenants which run with the land as well as the burden of the lessor's covenants of the same nature.[2] At common law attornment by the tenant, that is, assent to the transfer, was necessary to make the assignment effective but the requirement of attornment no longer exists.

The interest of the lessee, being an estate for years, is normally transferable in the absence of a restrictive clause in the lease or a statutory provision forbidding transfer without the lessor's assent.[3] Most leases, in fact, contain a provision forbidding the lessee to assign or sublet without the written consent of the lessor. Such provisions, since they are restraints on alienation, are

---

[1] Where the lessor transfers "the within lease" to a third person the question arises whether the transfer is an assignment of the rent alone or also an assignment of the reversion. It is usually held that an assignment by the lessor of the "lease" without mention of the reversion operates as an assignment of the rent only. United States v. Shafto, 246 F.2d 838 (C.A. 4th 1957); Hunt v. Thompson, 2 Allen (Mass.) 341 (1861). Cf. Masury v. Southworth, 9 Ohio St. 340 (1859). See 2 American Law of Property, § 9.45.

The common law view is that rent due in the future is not a chose in action but an incorporeal interest in real property. The rent is deemed to issue out of the land. Accrued rent, however, is personal property, a chose in action.

[2] At earlier common law an assignee of the reversion could not enforce against the lessee the covenants and conditions in the lease. A remedy was given to transferees of the reversion by the statute 32 Henry VIII, c. 34 (1540). In some states this statute is deemed to be in force as part of the common law and in other states statutes having the same effect have been enacted. See e. g. West's Ann.Cal.Civ.Code Ann. § 821; McKinney's N.Y.Real Prop. Law, § 223.

[3] Statutes forbidding transfers by the lessee without the lessor's assent are found in only a few states, e. g. Missouri and Texas. Occasionally, the interest of the lessee is held to be non-transferable, even in the absence of statutory provision or express restriction in the lease, on the ground that the lessor relied on the personal qualities or business efficiency of the lessee, the rent being fixed at a percentage of profits or sales. Nassau Hotel Co. v. Barnett & Barse Corp., 162 App.Div. 381, 147 N.Y.S. 283, affirmed 212 N.Y. 568, 106 N.E. 1036 (1914). See Marcelle, Inc. v. Sol & S. Marcus Co., 274 Mass. 469, 175 N.E. 83, 74 A.L.R. 1012 (1931).

strictly construed by the courts. Thus, a provision against assignment without the lessor's consent does not prevent a subletting without his consent. An assignment made in violation of a restrictive clause is not void; the estate for years vests in the assignee until effective action is taken by the lessor to avoid the transfer.[4] Usually, the lease will contain a clause giving the lessor the power to terminate the estate granted for breach of any covenant or condition and this forfeiture provision gives the lessor an effective remedy in case of an unauthorized assignment. The lessor may waive a breach of the nonassignment covenant and acceptance of rent from the assignee with knowledge of the assignment will normally be held to amount to a waiver.

If the lessor does assent to an assignment by the lessee in a particular instance, it would seem that this would not deprive him of the right to refuse assent to any further assignment by the assignee. Yet in Dumpor's Case[5] it was held that a single license to assign operates to extinguish the condition against unauthorized assignments as to all future assignments. The reason given was that "the condition could not be divided or apportioned by the act of the parties." The highly artificial nature of the reason assigned for the rule is apparent. Although the rule of Dumpor's Case was abrogated by statute in England in 1859 and has been criticized by some courts and many writers, it has found acceptance in several American jurisdictions.[6]

4 People v. Klopstock, 24 Cal.2d 897, 151 P.2d 641 (1944).

5 4 Coke Rep. 119b, 76 Eng.Rep. 1110 (1603).

6 Reid v. Wiessner Brewing Co., 88 Md. 234, 40 A. 877 (1898); Aste v. Putnam's Hotel Co., 247 Mass. 147, 141 N.E. 666, 31 A.L.R. 149 (1923). Contra, Leibowitz v. 18 East 41st Corp., 89 N.Y.S.2d 160 (1949). The rule has been held inapplicable where the lessor in assenting to a specific assignment has expressly reserved the right to require that no further assignment be made except with his consent. Rothrock v. Sanborn, 178 Cal. 693, 174 P. 314 (1918). Cf. Crowell v. City of Riverside, 26 Cal.App.2d 566, 80 P.2d 120 (1938). It has also been held inapplicable to a condition against subletting without the lessor's consent. Seaver v. Coburn, 64 Mass. (10 Cush.) 324 (1852).

SECTION 5. DISTINCTION BETWEEN ASSIGNMENT
AND SUBLEASE

A transfer by the lessee may be either an assignment or a sub-lease. Since different legal consequences flow from the nature of the transfer, it becomes important to distinguish between the two types. An assignment is a transfer by the lessee of his estate for the entire balance of the unexpired residue of the term. There is no reversion left in the lessee. A sublease is a transfer of the leasehold for a shorter period than the unexpired residue of the term. Even if the difference in time between the lessee's unexpired term and the transferee's term is as short as one day the transfer is classified as a sublease. If the transfer is of a physical portion of the leased premises for the entire balance of the lessee's term it is usually classed as a partial assignment. Where the transfer is an assignment the assignee becomes liable on those covenants in the lease made by the lessee which run with the land. The basis of this liability is the privity of estate arising from the landlord-tenant relation between the lessor and the assignee. The lessee continues to be liable on the covenants on the basis of privity of contract but as between lessee and assignee the latter is primarily liable.[1] Thus, the assignee is liable to the landlord for the rent reserved in the main lease and this liability continues for the balance of the term unless and until the assignee makes a further assignment to some one else.[2] But if the transfer by the lessee is a sublease there is

---

[1] Samuels v. Ottinger, 169 Cal. 209, 146 P. 638 (1915). The position of the lessee is to some extent that of a surety for the assignee. Hence, if the lessor without the consent of the lessee assents to substantial alterations of the premises by the assignee and such changes are of no benefit to the lessee the effect is to discharge the lessee from his obligations under the lease. Walker v. Rednalloh Co., 299 Mass. 591, 13 N.E.2d 394 (1938).

[2] Reid v. Wiessner Brewing Co., 88 Md. 234, 40 A. 877 (1898). It is immaterial that the assignee makes the further assignment for the purpose of ridding himself of liability on the lease and that the second assignee is financially irresponsible. Shoolman v. Wales Mfg. Co., 331 Mass. 211, 118 N.E.2d 71 (1954).

neither privity of estate nor of contract between the main lessor and the sublessee.   The lessor, therefore, has no direct action against the sublessee on the covenants in the lease.[3]

Much of the litigation over the nature of the transfer by the lessee has arisen in the situation where the transfer has been for the entire unexpired balance of the term but in the instrument of transfer the lessee has reserved a different rent than in the main lease and has also reserved a right of re-entry in the event of non-payment by the transferee.   It is commonly said that a reversion is necessary for the landlord-tenant relation.   Even though the transfer by the lessee is for the full balance of the term does the reservation of the right of re-entry amount to a retention of a reversionary interest in the lessee?   If so, the transfer is a sublease because of the landlord-tenant relationship between lessee and transferee.   Most courts have taken the view that the reservation of a right of re-entry in the instrument of transfer leaves no part of his former estate in the transferor, and conclude that the transfer operates as an assignment.[4]   The right of re-entry is regarded as a new interest created by the instrument of transfer rather than part of the original estate of the lessee.[5]   A minority of courts hold that the reservation of a right of re-entry leaves in the lessee a "contingent reversionary interest" and that the transfer is, therefore, a sublease.[6]   And an occasional decision, rejecting the formalistic test of the presence or absence of a reversionary interest remaining in the lessee, gives effect to the intention of the parties.[7]   The intention

[3] In a few states there are statutes allowing the lessor to recover the rent from the sublessee. See e. g. Ky.Rev.Stat. § 383.010(5).

[4] See e. g. Sexton v. Chicago Storage Co., 129 Ill. 318, 21 N.E. 920 (1889).

[5] The Restatement on Property takes the position that a right of re-entry (power of termination) is not a reversionary interest.   § 154, Comment a.

[6] The leading case is Davis v. Vidal, 105 Tex. 444, 151 S.W. 290 (1912) which applied the so-called Massachusetts rule.   Dunlap v. Bullard, 131 Mass. 161 (1881).

[7] Jaber v. Miller, 219 Ark. 59, 239 S.W.2d 760 (1951).

test, moreover, is given considerable weight when the litigation is between the lessee and his transferee.[8]

SECTION 6.   TERMINATION OF AN ESTATE FOR YEARS

An estate for years may terminate by reason of the happening of a specified contingency, if the estate is one on special limitation; or by the proper exercise by the lessor of a power of termination, where such power has been reserved in the lease; or by the expiration of the stipulated time; or by surrender.[1]   A few words may be said about surrender.   A surrender is, in essence, an ending of the landlord-tenant relation by mutual agreement.   It was broadly defined by Coke as a yielding up of an estate for years or for life to the reversioner or remainderman by mutual agreement.[2]   The English Statute of Frauds[3] required all surrenders to be in writing unless "by act and operation of law" and the American statutes are substantially similar. Since a surrender requires mutual agreement the unilateral action of the tenant cannot effectuate a surrender.   If the tenant abandons possession and refuses to pay any further rent the landlord can, in most states, allow the premises to remain idle

---

[8] Davidson v. Minnesota Loan & Trust Co., 158 Minn. 411, 197 N.W. 833, 32 A.L.R. 1418 (1924).

[1] These are the usual reasons for termination but the enumeration is not exhaustive.   A lease will also terminate where the fee simple in the premises is taken by governmental authority under the eminent domain power.   And if the lessee becomes bankrupt his trustee in bankruptcy may reject the lease thereby terminating it.   So also, if the lessor's estate was subject to a prior mortgage and the mortgage is foreclosed the lessee's estate will come to an end.

[2] Co.Litt. 337b.   And see Kulawitz v. Pacific Woodenware & Paper Co., 25 Cal.2d 664, 155 P.2d 24 (1944).

[3] 29 Car.II, c. 3, § 3 (1677).   The language of the American Statutes of Frauds varies but most of them deal with surrenders.   In a few states surrenders for short terms are expressly excepted from the statute.   See e. g. McKinney's N.Y.Real Prop.Law, § 242 ("other than a lease for a term not exceeding one year").

and sue the tenant for rent as it falls due. In a few jurisdictions the landlord is obligated to mitigate the damages by making a reasonable effort to relet to a new tenant. But if the landlord unqualifiedly resumes possession for his own benefit he has by his conduct accepted a surrender.[4] Whether there has been an acceptance of a surrender is usually a question of fact as to the intention of the parties as shown by their statements and actions.[5] Considerable litigation has resulted from the action of the lessor in reletting to a new tenant after abandonment of the premises by the original lessee. If a clause in the lease authorizes the lessor to do this on behalf of the lessee and the reletting is done pursuant to this power there is no surrender and the original lessee is liable for the differential in rent. Even in the absence of such a clause in the lease, a majority of courts permit the lessor to relet, after notice to the lessee of such intended action, for the purpose of reducing the lessee's damages even though the lessor was not under a legal duty to mitigate damages.[6] A few courts take the flat position that any reletting without the assent of the lessee operates as an acceptance of a surrender unless by the terms of the lease the lessor has reserved such right.[7]

SECTION 7. PERIODIC ESTATES

A periodic estate is a tenancy which will continue for a year or a fraction of a year and for successive similar periods unless

---

[4] "Any acts which are equivalent to an agreement on the part of a tenant to abandon and on the part of the landlord to resume possession of demised premises amount to a surrender of a term by operation of law." Carlton Chambers Co. v. Trask, 261 Mass. 264, 267–268, 158 N.E. 786 (1927).

[5] Bandera v. Donahue, 326 Mass. 563, 95 N.E.2d 654 (1950).

[6] See e. g. DeHart v. Allen, 26 Cal.2d 829, 161 P.2d 453 (1945); McGrath v. Shalett, 114 Conn. 622, 159 A. 633 (1932); Cassidy v. Welsh, 319 Mass. 615, 67 N.E.2d 226 (1946).

[7] Gray v. Kaufman Dairy & Ice Cream Co., 162 N.Y. 388, 56 N.E. 903, 49 L.R.A. 580 (1900).

terminated by either party by proper notice.[1] There are various kinds of periodic tenancies but the most common are those from year to year and from month to month. By its nature, the periodic tenancy is continuous and of indefinite duration. Thus, if the tenancy is from month to month it is a single, continuous tenancy until terminated, not a tenancy for one month which comes to an end at the expiration of the month and is renewed for the following month.[2]

Although historically the periodic estate was derived from the tenancy at will, its general characteristics are similar to those of the estate for years. The interest of the tenant is assignable, he is liable for permissive waste, and the death of either landlord or tenant leaves the estate unaffected. But unlike the estate for years which terminates without notice at the end of the specified term, the periodic estate continues until terminated by the giving of proper notice by either party. The common law required a six months' notice to terminate a tenancy from year to year, and for lesser periods a notice equal to the period. Thus, in a tenancy from month to month the notice of termination must be a month's notice. In all cases the notice must terminate the estate at the end of a period, not at some intermediate day. Occasionally, the parties by agreement specify the period of notice and their agreement will be given effect.[3] At the present time, there are statutes in most states regulating the length of notice required to terminate such tenancies.[4]

---

[1] Restat.Prop. § 20.

[2] Wagner v. Kepler, 411 Ill. 368, 104 N.E.2d 231 (1951). Accord, Spiritwood Grain Co. v. Northern Pac. Ry. Co., 179 F.2d 338 (C.A.8th 1950) (tenancy from year to year). Occasionally, a statute eliminates the continuity factor and converts what would normally be a periodic estate into one for a fixed period. See e. g. Conn.Gen.Stat. § 47–22 (oral lease for indefinite term at monthly rental creates tenancy for one month only).

[3] See e. g. Israel v. Beale, 270 Mass. 61, 169 N.E. 777, 68 A.L.R. 588 (1930) (tenancy from year to year terminable on two months' notice prior to end of a year).

[4] For a collection of these statutes, see 1 American Law of Property, § 3.90 (1952); 2 Powell, Real Property, § 255 (1950).

A periodic tenancy may be created by express agreement of the parties, or by a letting for an indefinite time with rent payable at periodic intervals, or by holding over with the assent of the lessor after the expiration of an estate for years, or by entry into possession under an invalid lease. The creation of such tenancies by express agreement seems to be relatively uncommon although in some areas there is a practise of leasing housing accommodations for a term certain (one year, for example) followed by a tenancy from year to year.[5]

A more common method of creating such tenancies is by inference on a general letting when the rent is payable periodically. In earlier times if A let premises to B and no duration of the tenancy was expressed but an annual rent was reserved and paid, the English law treated the tenancy as one at will. But in the seventeenth century the courts began to infer an intention of the parties to such a transaction to create a tenancy from year to year.[6] Since the latter tenancy, unlike a tenancy at will, could not be terminated by either party without proper notice it gave protection to both parties against a sudden determination of the tenancy.[7] Since no definite term was specified, the reservation and payment of a periodic rent afforded the basis for the conclusion that a periodic tenancy was intended. Most American courts have adopted this view.[8] In modern times rent is usually paid on a monthly basis when the subject of the tenancy is residential property, and, therefore, a letting on an indefinite basis with the rent payable monthly will, in the absence

[5] This practice is fairly widespread in Massachusetts. See e. g. Israel v. Beale, n. 3, supra; Wheeler v. Boston Housing Authority, 341 Mass. 510, 170 N.E.2d 465 (1960) (lease for one month, then month to month).

[6] 7 Holdsworth, History of English Law 243–245 (1926).

[7] Blackstone remarked that "courts of law have of late years leaned as much as possible against construing demises where no certain term is mentioned to be tenancies at will; but have rather held them to be tenancies from year to year so long as both parties please, especially where an annual rent is reserved." Bl.Com.II, 147.

[8] See e. g. Elliott v. Birrell, 127 Va. 166, 102 S.E. 762 (1920).

of statute, result in a tenancy from month to month.[9]   In a number of states, however, statutes prevent the normal inference from being made and create an estate for a definite period or a tenancy at will.[10]

Periodic tenancies frequently result from a holding over by a tenant after the expiration of an estate for years.   If, after the expiration of the term fixed by the lease, the tenant remains in possession the landlord may elect to treat him as a trespasser [11] and have him ejected by summary process or recognize him as a tenant.   If the landlord elects to recognize the occupant as a tenant, as by accepting rent from him, most courts hold that the new tenancy is from year to year if the original term was for one year or longer.[12]   Some courts take the view that the new periodic tenancy is governed by the manner in which rent was payable under the original lease.   Thus, if a monthly rental was reserved the holdover tenancy is from month to month.

Where a lease for years is unenforceable (usually because of failure to comply with the Statute of Frauds) but the lessee enters into possession and pays rent on a periodic basis in accordance with the terms of the lease agreement a periodic tenancy results.   The provisions of the lease, except as to duration, are normally held to be applicable to the periodic tenancy and

9 See e. g. Bhar Realty Corp. v. Becker, 49 N.J.Super. 585, 140 A.2d 756 (1958).

10 For a collection of these statutes see 2 Powell, Real Property, § 254, n. 20.   In Maine and Massachusetts the Statute of Frauds has been construed as permitting the creation of periodic estates only by written agreement.   In those two states an oral letting for an indefinite time, even though the rent is paid periodically, creates a tenancy at will.   Davis v. Thompson, 13 Me. 209 (1836); Ellis v. Paige, 1 Pick. 43 (Mass.1822).

11 More accurately, the former tenant is a tenant at sufferance, not a trespasser.   As to the effect of rent control legislation, see 2 Powell, Real Property, § 252.

12 See e. g. Fetting Mfg. Jewelry Co. v. Waltz, 160 Md. 50, 152 A. 434 (1930). For an excellent discussion of the holdover problem, see 1 American Law of Property, §§ 3.33–3.36.   In Maine and Massachusetts the tenant holding over with the landlord's consent is a tenant at will.   See n. 10, supra.

regulate the amount and time of payment of rent as well as the other obligations of the parties.

SECTION 8. ESTATES AT WILL

An estate at will is an estate which is terminable at the will of either landlord or tenant and has no other specified period of duration.[1] Such a tenancy is properly an estate since the tenant has an exclusive right to possession and may maintain an action of trespass or ejectment against persons interfering with his possessory interest. Its duration is dependent on the will of both parties and, unlike the periodic estate, no formal notice of a prescribed length of time is required for its termination at common law.

A tenancy at will may be created by an express agreement between the landlord and tenant that the tenant shall hold possession so long as both parties agree.[2] Such explicit agreements are relatively infrequent and more often a tenancy at will is inferred in situations where the holding is indefinite and a periodic tenancy cannot be presumed.[3] Thus, if the premises are let for an indefinite time and no rent is reserved the natural inference is that the parties intended a tenancy at will.[4] An agreement that the tenant shall hold possession at the will of the landlord creates a tenancy at will since it is implied that the tenancy is also terminable at the will of the tenant. Does an agreement that the premises shall be held at the will of the tenant create only a tenancy at will? Thus, if A conveys to B "for as many

---

1 Restat.Prop., § 21.

2 Say v. Stoddard, 27 Ohio St. 478 (1875).

3 See e. g. Farris v. Hershfield, 325 Mass. 176, 89 N.E.2d 636 (1950) (written agreement for letting at $25.00 a month, no duration specified). In Massachusetts an oral letting on a monthly rental basis creates a tenancy at will. In most other states the facts of the case would normally require the inference of a tenancy from month to month.

4 Lepsch v. Lepsch, 275 App.Div. 412, 90 N.Y.S.2d 157 (1949) (divorced wife given right and privilege of occupying former husband's home rent free until parties otherwise mutually agreed).

years as desired by B" does B get a tenancy at will or a determinable life estate? Lord Coke stated that "when the lease is made to have and to hold at the will of the lessee, this must also be at the will of the lessor" [5] and his pronouncement has influenced some courts to hold that a tenancy at will results from such a transfer.[6] Other courts have taken the view that the transferee receives a determinable life estate or a determinable fee simple depending on the language of the instrument.[7]

At common law a tenancy at will could be terminated by either party, without formal notice, by expressing an intention to treat the tenancy as ended. In the event of termination by the landlord, the tenant was allowed a reasonable time to remove his personal property and was entitled to emblements. Since the relation assumes the assent of both parties to a continuance of the tenancy the death of either landlord or tenant terminates the estate. So also, a conveyance of the reversion by the landlord ends the tenancy at will. A lease for years made by the landlord to a third person has the same effect and it is immaterial that the lease was made for the purpose of putting an immediate end to the tenancy.[8] An assignment by the tenant terminates his estate but, according to the modern view, a sublease by the tenant is effective between the parties thereto.[9] Because the common law liability of the estate at will to abrupt termination gave security to neither landlord nor tenant, statutes in most states require that either party desiring to terminate shall give

[5] Co.Litt. § 55a.

[6] Foley v. Gamester, 271 Mass. 55, 170 N.E. 799 (1930); Shorter v. Shelton, 183 Va. 819, 33 S.E.2d 643 (1945).

[7] Thompson v. Baxter, 107 Minn. 122, 119 N.W. 797 (1909); Putnam v. Davis, 166 A.2d 469 (N.H.1960). The Restatement is in accord with this position. Restat.Prop. § 21, Comment a. The fact that a lease for a definite period is subject to termination at the option of the lessor or of the lessee, either conditionally or unconditionally, does not necessarily cause the estate to be a tenancy at will.

[8] Curtis v. Galvin, 1 Allen 215 (Mass.1861).

[9] Anderson v. Ries, 222 Minn. 408, 24 N.W.2d 717 (1946), 31 Minn.L.Rev. 620 (1947); Public Service Co. v. Voudoumas, 84 N.H. 387, 151 A. 81 (1930).

the other written notice of a specified length of time, usually thirty days or a period equal to the interval between rent days. These statutes have generally been construed as not prescribing an exclusive mode of termination and the estate, therefore, comes to an end on the death of either party and on conveyance or lease by the landlord.[10] Hence, the estate at will even as modified by statute is not the equivalent of a periodic estate.

SECTION 9.   TENANCY AT SUFFERANCE

A tenancy at sufferance is a possessory interest in land which exists when a person who had an estate in land wrongfully continues in possession after the termination of such estate. "There is a great diversity between a tenant at will and a tenant at sufferance; for tenant at will is always by right, and tenant at sufferance entreth by a lawful lease, and holdeth over by wrong. A tenant at sufferance is he that at the first came in by lawful demise, and after his estate ended continueth in possession and wrongfully holdeth over."[1] A tenant for the life of another, a periodic tenant, or one for years or at will who wrongfully retains possession after the expiration of his estate becomes a tenant at sufferance. Since his original entry was rightful, a tenant at sufferance is not liable in an action of trespass until after entry by the landlord.

The position of the tenant at sufferance is well summarized in the opinion in Benton v. Williams:[2] "A tenant at sufferance has no estate or title, but only a naked possession, without right and wrongfully, stands in no privity to the landlord, at common

---

[10] Chester A. Baker, Inc. v. Shea Dry Cleaners, Inc., 322 Mass. 311, 77 N.E. 2d 223 (1948); Seavey v. Cloudman, 90 Me. 536, 38 A. 540 (1897). Contra, Gretkowski v. Wojciechowski, 26 N.J.Super. 245, 97 A.2d 701 (1953) (statutory requirement of notice held to prevent termination of estate on death of landlord).

[1] Co.Litt. § 57b.

[2] 202 Mass. 189, 88 N.E. 843 (1909). Accord, Margosian v. Markarian, 288 Mass. 197, 192 N.E. 612 (1934) (landlord not liable to tenant at sufferance for personal injuries caused by defective condition of premises.)

law is not liable for rent, is not entitled to notice to quit, and has no action against his landlord or other person entitled to possession, if himself, his family and goods are ejected without unnecessary force. He differs from a trespasser or disseisor only in that his entry upon the premises is not unlawful. His continued occupancy is due wholly to the laches or forbearance of the person entitled to possession in not evicting him. He may leave at any time without notice or liability. No contractual relation (apart from statute) arises out of a possession of such a character."

In view of the minimal interest of the tenant at sufferance, one may inquire why in modern law that interest is still included in the catalogue of estates. The main justification seems to be that it lends support to the doctrine that the landlord may at his election convert the tenancy at sufferance of the holdover tenant into a periodic tenancy, or, in some states, into a tenancy for a definite period.[3] In a few jurisdictions the interest of the tenant at sufferance has been enlarged by statutes requiring that the landlord give written notice, usually thirty days, before commencing an action against the tenant to recover possession.[4] And an occasional statute makes the tenant liable for "rent" in order to broaden the basis of common law liability for use and occupation which required at least an implied contract to pay.[5]

[3] See § 7, supra.

[4] See e. g. Mich.Comp.Laws, § 554.134 (1948); Mass.Gen.Laws Ann. c. 186, § 13; N.J.Stat.Ann. § 2.58:22. The Massachusetts statute is restricted to a tenancy at sufferance of residential property resulting from a tenancy at will being determined by operation of law or by act of the landlord other than by the statutory notice to quit. The purpose of the statute is to prevent the landlord from evicting the tenant immediately after he has terminated the tenancy at will by leasing to a third person.

[5] See e. g. Mass.Gen.Laws Ann. c. 186, § 3; Merrill v. Bullock, 105 Mass. 486 (1870).

Chapter 4

SEISIN AND ITS SIGNIFICANCE

SECTION 1. THE MEANING OF SEISIN

Seisin was a word of vast importance in the medieval land law. Most of that law concerned itself with seisin, remedies to recover seisin, and the consequences of loss of seisin. The concept of seisin affected the law of descent, the doctrine of estates, modes of conveyancing, the forms of action, and principles of the law of future interests. It later became of diminishing importance and nineteenth century legislation, both in England and in the United States, abolished many of its consequences. But its influence has been too pervasive to be ignored; it explains much of the old law and some of the modern. For example, a widow's right to dower depended at common law on seisin of the lands by the husband during coverture. This is still the law in some states.[1] A brief discussion of seisin is, therefore, necessary.

The word "seisin" has in it an implication of seizure and violence but more properly it connotes peaceful possession. "The man who is seized is the man who is sitting on land; when he was put in seisin he was set there and made to sit there."[2] Originally, seisin meant simply possession and the word was applicable to both land and chattels. Prior to the fourteenth century it was proper to speak of a man as being seised of land or seised of a horse. Gradually, seisin and possession became distinct concepts. A man could be said to be in possession of chattels, or of lands wherein he had an estate for years, but he could not be said to be seised of them. Seisin came finally to mean, in relation to land, possession under claim of a freehold estate there-

---

[1] Mass.Gen.Laws Ann. c. 189, § 1: "A wife shall upon the death of her husband, hold her dower at common law in her deceased husband's land."

[2] 2 Poll. & Mait. 30.

in.[3] The tenant for years had possession but not seisin; seisin
was in the reversioner who had the fee.

SECTION 2. THE SIGNIFICANCE OF SEISIN

It is a familiar process in our legal thinking of today to distinguish sharply between possession and ownership.   Ownership, we say, is a legal concept, a bundle of legal relations; but
possession is a matter of physical fact.   A may own a parcel of
land but B may be in possession of it, even in adverse possession.
We do not assume that B's adverse possession is of such legal importance as to divest A's ownership, apart from the operation of
a statute of limitations.   But in the medieval common law ownership and possession were not so sharply distinguished.   Rather
they blended into each other and merged in the concept of seisin.
Seisin is possession but a peculiar possession—possession of land
by a man holding a freehold estate therein.   Hence, it is much
more than possession—it is the basis of ownership in so far as
the common law admits of ownership of land.[1]

Much of the law of the period was concerned with remedies to
protect seisin.   If A was seised of Blackacre in fee simple and
B entered and ousted A, claiming a freehold estate therein, B
now had seisin and A was disseised.   A could recover seisin by
making a peaceable entry for that purpose.[2]   If such self-help
was not practical he could, as early as 1166, bring an assize of

---

[3] The concept of seisin was also extended to some kinds of intangible rights.
The lord of the fee was said to be seised in service while the feudal tenant
was seised in demesne.   And a man could be seised of an advowson, that is,
the right to present a clergyman to a benefice.   This illustrates the early
common law process of reification of rights—"thing-making."

[1] See Maitland, The Mystery of Seisin, 3 Select Essays in Anglo-American
Legal History 591 (1909).

[2] Prior to 1381 a disseisee could have made a forcible entry in order to recover seisin but a statute enacted in that year made such an entry a crime.
The statute was the forerunner of American statutes forbidding a forcible
entry and detainer of land.   See e. g. Ill.Smith-Hurd Stat.Ann. c. 57, § 1;
Mass.Gen.Laws Ann. c. 184, § 18.

novel disseisin against his disseisor to recover seisin. This action was summary in nature and judgment was entered in the King's court on a verdict returned by a jury of neighbors summoned by the sheriff as directed by the writ. No question of ownership could be litigated, the sole issue being whether the defendant had ousted the plaintiff wrongfully and without judgment. The action would lie only between disseisee and disseisor. If A's ancestor had been seised of the land and on his death and before A entered as heir B wrongfully took possession, A could not use the remedy of novel disseisin. But a new remedy was fashioned to take care of this situation—the action known as the assize of mort d'ancestor. And in the thirteenth century numerous forms of writs of entry were provided to deal with various fact situations—such as descent of the seisin from the disseisor to his heir, the death of the disseisee, and a transfer of seisin by the disseisor to a third person. Finally, the highest and most solemn form of action was the writ of right, an action proprietary in nature but actually deciding the question of the older and better seisin between the demandant and the tenant (plaintiff and defendant).[3]

This system of real actions amounted to "a graduated hierarchy of actions" which reflected the relativity of right to seisin.[4] A's seisin may be better than B's but inferior to that of C and C in turn may have to yield to a stronger claim of D. The judgment in a particular action binds only the parties and stands only until someone else in another action establishes a better

[3] For a good summary of the development of the real actions, see Plucknett, Concise History of the Common Law 354–362 (5th ed. 1956).

[4] 2 Poll. & Mait. 74: " 'Possessoriness' has become a matter of degree. At the bottom stands the novel disseisin, possessory in every sense, summary and punitive. Above it rises the mort d'ancestor, summary but not so summary, going back to the seisin of one who is already dead. Above this again are writs of entry. . . . The writs of entry are not so summary as are the assizes, but they are rapid when compared with the writ of right; the most dilatory of the essoins (excuses for a continuance) is precluded; there can be no battle (trial by battle) or grand assize. Ultimately we ascend to the writ of right. Actions are higher or lower, some lie 'more in the right' than others."

claim.   Thus, the right to seisin is relative—just as in the modern law title or ownership is relative, not absolute.

If we compare the position of the disseisee with that of the disseisor the contrast is striking.   Since B, the disseisor, has seisin (even though wrongfully) he can convey an estate in fee simple to a third person which will be valid against everyone except A, the disseisee.   On the other hand, A is no longer the tenant and he has no estate; he has merely a right of entry which in time will be turned into a right of action and this right, like a chose in action, is non-assignable although it can be released to the disseisee.   A has nothing which he can alienate.   Until A re-enters or recovers seisin after judgment in a real action B is more "owner" than A.   On B's death the fee will descend to his heir and his widow will be entitled to dower.   If B dies without an heir there will be an escheat to the lord of the fee.   If A dies leaving an heir the right of entry will descend to the heir but if A dies without an heir there will be no escheat because there is a tenant (B) who can render the feudal services due to the lord.

So fundamental was the concept of seisin that it was a strict rule that seisin could never be in abeyance or suspended.   There must always be a person seised to whom the lord of the fee can look to the discharge of the feudal obligations and on whom the demandant in a real action may have his writ served.   If a freehold estate in land is to be conveyed it is to be done by a transfer of the seisin; if land is to descend it must descend to the heir of the last person seised, for seisin is the stock of descent.   And no limitation of an estate will be allowed if the effect would be to put the seisin in abeyance.

SECTION 3.   THE DECLINE OF SEISIN

The development of the action of ejectment in the latter part of the fifteenth century eventually made obsolete the real actions and the technicalities of seisin with which they were inextricably bound.[1] In ejectment the emphasis was on possession and although the right to possession ultimately depended on title, seisin became more and more an incident of ownership. By the time of Elizabeth ejectment had displaced the real actions as the standard action to try title.[2] The rout of seisin as a cardinal doctrine in English land law was completed by the reform legislation of the nineteenth century. The Dower Act (1833)[3] provided that a widow should have dower even though her husband was not seised during coverture. The Inheritance Act (1833)[4] changed the rule that descent of land must be traced from the person last seised. In 1837 the right of entry of a disseisee was made devisable[5] and in 1845 it was made transferable by deed.[6]

In the United States the doctrine of seisin, although of some importance in the post-Revolutionary period, was never in force to the same extent as in England.[7] Statutes regulating the law of descent and the effectiveness of future interests, as well as those abolishing dower and curtesy, reduced its area of retained vitality. The rule that an owner who has been disseised has no title which he can convey to a third person has, except in a handful of jurisdictions, been rejected by the courts or abrogated by

---

[1] Although the successful plaintiff in ejectment recovered a judgment for possession of the land, ejectment was classified as a personal, not a real, action because it originated as a special form of the action of trespass. Plucknett, Concise History of the Common Law 573 (5th ed. 1956); 1 Walsh, Commentaries on Law of Real Property § 5(f) (1946).

[2] In contrast with the real actions, ejectment was a safe, simple and expeditious remedy. In a real action the plaintiff proceeded at his peril: if he selected the wrong writ from among the numerous writs of entry or if there was a variance between writ and pleading or pleading and proof the mistake was fatal.

[3] 3 & 4 Wm. IV, c. 105, § 3.

[4] 3 & 4 Wm. IV, c. 106, § 2.

[5] 7 Wm. IV & 1 Vict., c. 26, § 3.

[6] 8 & 9 Vict., c. 106, § 6.

[7] For details, see Bordwell, Seisin and Disseisin, 34 Harv.L.Rev. 717, 725–740 (1921).

statute.[8] The law of disseisin has been absorbed in the law of adverse possession.   And although the word "seisin" appears in modern statutes with a fair degree of frequency it is usually treated as synonymous with "ownership".[9] A similar construction is given to the term when used by an unwary testator lured by the sound of the word "seized" but innocent of a knowledge of its meaning.[10] The modern warranty deed usually contains among the covenants for title a covenant of seisin but in the majority of states this covenant is equivalent to the covenant of right to convey an indefeasible fee simple and is not satisfied by a common law seisin in the grantor.[11]

   To sum up, we may fairly say that although a knowledge of the concept of seisin is necessary for an understanding of the historical basis of present-day law, the concept itself is no longer a vital force in that law.

   [8] The rule persisted in New York until changed by statute in 1941 (Real Prop.Law, § 260). It still obtains, for example, in Connecticut. Loewenberg v. Wallace, 166 A.2d 150 (Conn.1960).

   [9] Dial v. Dial, 378 Ill. 276, 38 N.E.2d 43 (1941) ; Mass.Gen.Laws Ann. c. 237, § 4. Sometimes "seisin" and "possession" are equated. See e. g. McKinney's N.Y.Dec.Est.Law, § 80.

   [10] Dalton v. Eash, 411 Ill. 296, 103 N.E.2d 483 (1952). Contra, Leach v. Jay, 9 Ch.D. 42 (1878).

   [11] "Possession does not satisfy a covenant of seizin. Such covenant means that the grantor, at the time of the conveyance, was lawfully seized of a good, absolute and indefeasible estate of inheritance in fee simple and had power to convey the same. Real Property Law (Cons.Laws, ch. 50) § 253." Hilliker v. Rueger, 228 N.Y. 11, 15, 126 N.E. 266, 267 (1920). Contra, Raymond v. Raymond, 10 Cush. 134 (Mass.1852) (covenant of seisin satisfied by an actual seisin in grantor).

Chapter 5

COMMON LAW TYPES OF FUTURE INTERESTS

SECTION 1. THE NATURE OF A FUTURE INTEREST

We have already seen that ownership of any parcel of land may be carved up into different successive slices or "estates" and that of these "estates" only one is presently possessory. Thus, A, owner of land in fee simple, may by a single conveyance, give it to B for life, then to C for life, then to D and his heirs. B has a present possessory life estate but C and D also have presently existing estates although they have no right to possession until some time in the future. C and D have what are called future interests. The term is somewhat misleading inasmuch as these interests have a present existence even though enjoyment of possession is postponed. The interests of both C and D are capable of transfer to third persons and D's interest is descendible or devisable. Moreover, both C and D have a right that B, the holder of the present estate, shall not commit waste. In general, a future interest in land may be defined as a present right in relation to the land by virtue of which possession will be had, or may be had, in the future.[1]

The future interests recognized at common law were: 1. the reversion; 2. the possibility of reverter; 3. the right of entry for condition broken; and 4. the remainder. To this list might be added the right of escheat, inchoate dower and curtesy initiate but these interests have different characteristics and they are not commonly classified as future interests.

---

[1] Future interests may also exist in personal property and in equitable interests in both real and personal property. In fact most of the modern law of future interests is concerned with beneficial interests in trusts the subject matter of which usually consists of stocks and bonds.

A. REVERSIONS

SECTION 2. REVERSIONS

Blackstone defined a reversion as "the residue of an estate left in the grantor, to commence in possession after the determination of some particular estate granted out by him." [1] This definition is still generally acceptable. It assumes the quantum theory of estates and that theory determines whether there is any interest "left" in the transferor. If A, owner in fee simple, transfers to B in fee simple there can be no reversion since B's fee simple represents the totality of ownership. But if A transfers to B for life or in fee tail A has a reversion in fee simple. Or if A devises land to B for life, and no further disposition of the land is contained in the will, there is a reversion in A's heirs in fee. So also, a person having a lesser estate than a fee simple will upon the transfer of an estate smaller than his own have a reversion. Thus, if B has an estate for life and transfers to C an estate for years (regardless of the number of years) B has a reversion. If C then transfers an estate for a lesser number of years to D, C also has a reversion. B and C have intermediate reversions and A has the ultimate reversion. In brief then, whenever a person has a vested estate and transfers to another a legally smaller vested estate the segment of ownership retained by the transferor is called a reversion.[2]

According to common law concepts no reversion resulted when the owner of a freehold estate created an estate for years since the termor did not have seisin. Thus, if A, owner in fee simple, conveyed to B for years, strictly speaking A had a present fee simple subject to a term for years rather than a reversion in fee

---

[1] 2 Bl.Comm. 275.

[2] Can one life estate be deemed to be legally smaller than another life estate? It would seem not, according to the quantum theory of estates. If B has an estate for his own life and conveys to C for the latter's life does B have a reversion? The Restatement affirms that B has a reversion. § 154, Comm. d. But see Simes & Smith, Future Interests § 82. If C predeceases B it is agreed that the property would revert to B.

expectant upon an estate for years. But in modern usage A is said to have a reversion in fee subject to a term of years.

Since a reversion was, by common law standards, "vested" it amounted to an estate and was transferable inter vivos and, after the Statute of Wills, was devisable. But the fact that all reversions are said to be vested does not mean that they will necessarily become possessory in the future. The reversion may be subject to defeasance. Thus, if A, owner in fee simple conveys to B for life, then to such of B's children and their heirs as survive B, the state of the title is: life estate in B, contingent remainder in fee in B's surviving children, reversion in A in fee. If B dies leaving no surviving children the land will revert to A, or if A is dead to A's heirs or his devisees. But if B dies leaving surviving children A's reversion will be divested.

B. POSSIBILITY OF REVERTER

SECTION 3. THE NATURE OF A POSSIBILITY OF REVERTER

A possibility of reverter is the interest left in a transferor who creates a fee simple determinable.[1] It will be recalled that a fee simple determinable is a fee simple on special limitation, that is, a fee simple limited to expire on the occurrence or non-occurrence of an event specified in the creating instrument.[2] Thus A, owner of Blackacre in fee simple absolute, conveys it "to B and his heirs so long as Brookline remains a town, and if Brookline becomes a city then the said premises shall revert to A and

---

[1] See c. 2, § 4, supra. An owner in fee simple who grants an estate in fee simple conditional may also be said to have a possibility of reverter. Restatement, Property, § 154, Comm. g. But since the fee simple conditional is of significance only in one state (South Carolina) this type of possibility of reverter will not be further discussed. See c. 2, § 6, supra.

[2] A fee simple determinable is sometimes called a base fee. Thus, we have three terms any one of which may be used to describe the interest of a grantee in fee simple whose estate is limited to expire automatically on the occurrence of a stated event: fee simple determinable, fee simple on special limitation, and base fee.

his heirs." B has a fee simple determinable. A's contingent reversionary interest is a possibility of reverter. If the town becomes a city, B's estate expires automatically and A becomes the owner in fee simple. A possibility of reverter, like the reversion, can exist only in the transferor or his heirs and cannot be created in a transferee. For this reason it is classified as a reversionary interest.[3] Technically, the fee simple determinable is not a legally smaller estate than a fee simple absolute; hence, the creator of a fee simple determinable cannot be said to have a reversion even though his retained interest is of a reversionary nature.

SECTION 4. THE POSSIBILITY OF REVERTER AND QUIA EMPTORES

It would seem that the English common law recognized the validity of the possibility of reverter [1] but in practice English conveyancers desiring to create a defeasible fee simple used the device of a fee simple on condition subsequent rather than a fee simple determinable hence there was no decisive case law on the point. In the nineteenth century it was questioned by some writers whether it was possible to create a determinable fee after Quia Emptores (1290). It will be recalled that that statute in prohibiting sub-infeudation destroyed tenure between the transferor and the transferee of a fee simple.[2] It was urged by Professor John Chipman Gray in his classic treatise on the Rule against Perpetuities that land conveyed in fee simple could revert to the transferor only by operation of feudal tenure and since Quia Emptores prevented tenure in such transfers a determinable fee could not be created after 1290.[3] The answer has been made that

[3] The Restatement of Property defines a possibility of reverter as "any reversionary interest which is subject to a condition precedent." § 154.

[1] Co.Litt. 18a; 2 Bl.Comm. 109.

[2] See c. 1, § 8, supra.

[3] Gray, The Rule Against Perpetuities, §§ 31–39 (4th ed. 1942). The first edition was published in 1886.

only feudal tenure was abolished by Quia Emptores and that after the statute a tenurial relation could be created by agreement of the parties.[4] In this battle of the academicians Gray's views won no judicial converts. It is not open to doubt that the fee simple determinable with its correlative possibility of reverter is a permissible estate. American courts in numerous decisions have affirmed its validity and no decision has held it inoperative. A recent English case also has recognized the existence of a fee simple determinable.[5]

SECTION 5. THE POSSIBILITY OF REVERTER DISTINGUISHED FROM RIGHT OF ENTRY FOR CONDITION BROKEN

It is necessary to distinguish carefully between a determinable fee simple and a fee simple on condition subsequent. Both of these estates are frequently created for the purpose of controlling the use of the land granted and in that respect they are functional equivalents.[1] Moreover only a slight verbal difference in the creating instrument results in the granted estate being labelled as of one type rather than the other. But the conceptual differences are important. The future interest arising in the grantor of a determinable fee simple is a possibility of reverter; the future interest arising in the grantor of a fee simple on condition subsequent is a right of entry for condition broken.[2]

---

[4] Vance, Rights of Reverter and the Statute Quia Emptores, 36 Yale L.J. 593 (1927). And see Powell, Determinable Fees, 23 Col.L.Rev. 207 (1923).

[5] Hopper v. The Corporation of Liverpool, 88 Sol.J. 213 (1944).

[1] See Goldstein, Rights of Entry and Possibilities of Reverter as Devices to Restrict the Use of Land, 54 Harv.L.Rev. 248 (1940).

[2] At times courts have added to the confusion by referring to a right of entry as a "possibility of reverter." Taylor v. Continental Southern Corp., 131 Cal.App.2d 267, 280 P.2d 514 (1955); Nicoll v. New York and Erie Railroad, 12 N.Y. 121 (1854); see also Proprietors of Church in Brattle Square v. Grant, 3 Gray 142 (Mass.1855).

These two future interests have different characteristics.[3] The principal difference between them is that the possibility of reverter automatically becomes a present estate in the grantor in fee simple, without any election on the part of the grantor, on the occurrence of the event specified in the instrument of conveyance. But a right of entry for condition broken is a power to terminate the granted estate for breach of the condition and until that power is properly exercised the grantee's estate continues despite the breach. Thus, A, owner of Blackacre in fee simple absolute, conveys it "to B and his heirs on condition that if liquor is sold on the premises conveyed A shall have the right to reenter and repossess the premises as of his former estate." B has a fee simple on condition subsequent and A has a right of entry for condition broken. If B opens a liquor store on the premises he still owns a fee simple on condition subsequent and will continue to own such estate until A enters to take possession or begins an action to regain possession. Suppose, however, that the conveyance were "to B and his heirs so long as the premises are not used for the sale of liquor and if the premises are so used they shall revert to A and his heirs." In that case B would have a fee simple determinable. If B sells liquor on the premises his fee simple automatically comes to an end and reverts to A. Let us assume that prior to any action by A to recover the property it is taken by governmental authority under the power of eminent domain. A would be entitled to the whole condemnation award.[4] But if B's interest had been a fee on condition subsequent, A's failure to exercise his power of termination within a reasonable time could result in the award being payable to B only.[5]

[3] For an argument that the differences between the two interests are insubstantial, see Dunham, Possibility of Reverter and Powers of Termination—Fraternal or Identical Twins?, 20 U.Chi.L.Rev. 215 (1953).

[4] Proprietors of Locks and Canals v. Commonwealth, 171 N.E.2d 146 (Mass. 1961).

[5] City of Santa Monica v. Jones, 104 Cal.App.2d 463, 232 P.2d 55 (1951). In the Matter of City of New York (Farragut Road), 291 N.Y. 501, 50 N.E.2d 645 (1943) ; City of New York v. Coney Island Fire Dept., 259 App.Div. 286, 18 N.Y.S.2d 923 (1940) affirmed 285 N.Y. 535, 32 N.E.2d 827 (1941) ; Simes & Smith, Future Interests, § 258 (2d ed. 1956). But cf. Restat.Prop. § 53, comm. d.

SECTION 6.   CREATION OF POSSIBILITY OF RE-VERTER—CONSTRUCTIONAL PROBLEMS

It is often difficult to ascertain whether a particular deed or will creates a fee simple determinable or a fee simple on condition subsequent. Whether it is one or the other depends on the intention of the parties. Normally, this intention is sufficiently manifested by the language of the conveyance itself but an ambiguity may be clarified by resort to the circumstances of the transaction.[1] The mode of termination of the granted estate provided for in the conveyance is the controlling test of the parties' intention. Unless an intent is manifested that the estate is to expire automatically on the happening of the stated event the transferee does not have a fee simple determinable. No particular words are necessary to create either a fee simple determinable or a fee on condition subsequent but historically certain words have come to indicate an intent to create one type of estate rather than the other. The words "while," "during," "until" or "so long as" are typical words of special limitation and are usually held to manifest an intent to create a fee simple determinable. The terms "upon condition that," "provided that," "but if," "if it happen that" are typical words of condition subsequent.[2] Normally, no express words of reverter are necessary to create a determinable fee [3] although the absence of a reverter clause may lead the court to construe the deed as not creating a determinable estate.[4] Yet the presence in the deed of a state-

---

[1] "If the four corners of the deed provide a coherent expression of the parties' intent, we need search no further, but if an ambiguity or a reasonable doubt appears from a perusal of the particular symbols of expression our horizons must be broadened to encompass the circumstances surrounding the transaction." Oldfield v. Stoeco Homes, Inc., 26 N.J. 246, 257, 139 A.2d 291, 297 (1958); Carruthers v. Spaulding, 242 App.Div. 412, 275 N.Y.S. 37 (1934).

[2] Restat.Prop., §§ 44, 45.

[3] Peters v. East Penn Township School District, 182 Pa.Super. 116, 126 A.2d 802 (1956). But cf. PCK Properties, Inc. v. City of Cuyahoga Falls, 176 N.E. 2d 441 (Ohio App.1960).

[4] In re Copps Chapel Methodist Episcopal Church, 120 Ohio St. 309, 166 N.E. 218 (1929).

ment that on the occurrence of the stated event the land shall "revert" to the grantor is not alone conclusive of the grantor's intention, especially where the instrument also contains language of condition.[5] The dislike of the courts for forfeitures is often reflected in the case of ambiguous language in a constructional preference for the fee on condition subsequent.[6] Such a construction is, of course, more favorable to the grantee.

In many of the cases in which the question of the creation of a determinable fee has arisen the grant was made to a church, hospital, school district or other public body with the proviso that the land be used for a specified purpose, such as the site of a church or school building or for park or recreational use. But the statement of the purpose or object of a conveyance does not, without more, create a determinable fee. The language may be sufficient to create a trust or a covenant but the absence of the traditional words of special limitation will normally prevent the conclusion that the intention was to create a determinable fee.[7]

[5] Dyer v. Siano, 298 Mass. 537, 11 N.E.2d 451 (1937); Trustees of Union College v. City of New York, 173 N.Y. 38, 65 N.E. 853 (1903); Oldfield v. Stoeco Homes, Inc., 26 N.J. 246, 139 A.2d 291 (1958).

[6] Oldfield v. Stoeco Homes, Inc., n. 5, supra; Storke v. Penn. Mutual Life Ins. Co., 390 Ill. 619, 61 N.E.2d 552 (1945). Cf. Charlotte Park and Recreation Commission v. Barringer, 242 N.C. 311, 88 S.E.2d 114 (1955), certiorari denied 350 U.S. 983, 76 S.Ct. 469, 100 L.Ed. 851 (1955).

One state, Kentucky, has with rare good sense abolished the fee simple determinable. Ky.Rev.St. § 381.218 provides: "The estate known at common law as the fee simple determinable and the interest known as the possibility of reverter are abolished. Words which at common law would create a fee simple determinable shall be construed to create a fee simple subject to a right of entry for condition broken. In any case where a person would have a possibility of reverter at common law, he shall have a right of entry."

[7] Hill v. Towson Realty, Inc., 221 Md. 389, 157 A.2d 796 (1960); Edward John Noble Hospital v. Board of Foreign Missions, 13 Misc.2d 918, 176 N.Y.S.2d 157 (1958); Abel v. Girard Trust Co., 365 Pa. 34, 73 A.2d 682 (1950).

SECTION 7.   CHARACTERISTICS OF POSSIBILITY
OF REVERTER

According to the English common law, contingent future interests were inalienable inter vivos except by fine or common recovery.   Such interests were thought of as possibilities of an estate or mere expectancies rather than as estates.   This view has influenced a number of American courts to hold that the possibility of reverter is not transferable inter vivos to a third person.[1]   But the modern trend is toward free transferability of all future interests and the weight of authority upholds the alienability of the possibility of reverter.[2]   In most states there are statutes providing for the transferability of future interests and these statutes are usually construed to include possibilities of reverter.[3]   Moreover, it would seem that the possibility of reverter can be transferred in equity by a specifically enforcible contract to convey, and at law by virtue of the doctrine of estoppel by deed, in the sense that if the possibility of reverter becomes a possessory estate the contract or deed will be given effect.[4]   And the courts are agreed that

[1] See e. g. Consolidated School Dist. No. 102 v. Walter, 243 Minn. 159, 66 N.W.2d 881, 53 A.L.R.2d 218 (1954) (prior to Minnesota statute expressly making such interests alienable); Magness v. Kerr, 121 Or. 373, 254 P. 1012 (1927).

[2] See e. g. Nichols v. Haehn, 8 App.Div.2d 405, 187 N.Y.S.2d 773 (1959), 45 Corn.L.Q. 373 (1960). The subject is now governed by statute in New York. The statute provides that possibilities of reverter (defined as "the residue of an estate left in the grantor or his heirs, or in the heirs of a testator, upon a conveyance or devise until the happening of a specified event") are "descendible, devisable and alienable, in the same manner as estates in possession." McKinney's N.Y.Real Property Law, §§ 59, 59–a as amended by N.Y. Laws, 1962, c. 146. The Act does not affect "any rights or interests existing prior to" September 1, 1962. The Restatement takes the view that possibilities of reverter are alienable. Restat.Prop., § 159.

[3] For a collection of these statutes, see 2 Powell, Real Property § 283, n. 4. In Illinois the possibility of reverter is by statute expressly made inalienable by inter vivos conveyance although it is releasable to the grantee or his transferee. Ill.Smith-Hurd Ann.Stat. c. 30, §§ 37b, 37g.

[4] The doctrine of estoppel by deed is a conveyancing principle of broad application. If a grantor having no title to the land purports to convey it by a

the possibility of reverter is releasable to the owner of the determinable fee. In all but a few jurisdictions this type of future interest is held to be both descendible and devisable.[5]

In recent years there has been evident a growing hostility to possibilities of reverter. They usually are of unlimited, indefinite duration [6] and any transferee of the grantee takes the determinable fee subject to the special limitation. Thus, their tendency is to clog the marketability of the title and to impede the normal economic development of the land. As a consequence, statutes have been enacted in several states restricting the duration of possibilities of reverter to a specified period of years (usually thirty) when such interests are created after the effective date of the statute,[7] and requiring periodic re-recording of pre-existing possibilities of reverter.[8] And a recently enacted New York statute makes radical changes in the enforceability of possibilities of reverter restricting the use of land where the restriction is of no actual and substantial benefit to the person seeking enforcement "either because the purpose

warranty deed he will be estopped to show that at the time of the deed he had no title to convey. If he later acquires the title, his after acquired title will pass to the grantee (without further conveyance) by way of estoppel. This doctrine was applied to the transfer of a possibility of reverter in Pure Oil Co. v. Miller-McFarland Drilling Co., Inc., 376 Ill. 486, 34 N.E.2d 854 (1941) (prior to enactment of Illinois statute).

5 See e. g. Brown v. Independent Baptist Church of Woburn, 325 Mass. 645, 91 N.E.2d 922 (1950). In Illinois, by statute, the possibility of reverter is non-devisable. Ill.Smith-Hurd Ann.Stat. c. 30, § 37b.

6 Neither the possibility of reverter nor the right of entry for condition broken is subject to the rule voiding remotely contingent interests. This rule, called the Rule against Perpetuities, is treated briefly in c. 9, § 10, infra. For an enlightening discussion, see Leach, Perpetuities Legislation, Massachusetts Style, 67 Harv.L.Rev. 1349 (1954).

7 See e. g. Ill.Smith-Hurd Ann.Stat. c. 30, § 37e (40 years); Mass.Gen.Laws Ann. c. 184A, § 3 (30 years). Statutes limiting the duration of these interests also exist in Connecticut, Florida, Maine, Minnesota, Nebraska and Rhode Island.

8 See e. g. Mass.Gen.Laws Ann. c. 260, § 31A; Minn.Stat.Ann. § 541.023; Wichelman v. Messner, 250 Minn. 88, 83 N.W.2d 800 (1957). And see McKinney's N.Y.Real Prop.Law, § 345 (1958).

of the restriction has already been accomplished, or, by reason of changed conditions or other cause, its purpose is not capable of accomplishment, or for any other reason." [9]

C. RIGHT OF ENTRY FOR CONDITION BROKEN

SECTION 8.   THE NATURE OF THE RIGHT OF ENTRY FOR CONDITION BROKEN

A right of entry for condition broken is a future interest created in a transferor who conveys an estate on condition subsequent. It can be created only in the transferor or his successors in interest, never in a third person.[1] This right of entry is not, strictly speaking, a "right" in the sense of being a present legally enforceable claim. It is rather a power to terminate the granted estate on breach of the specified condition. On breach of the condition the transferor can elect to terminate the granted estate or not as he pleases. Until he does manifest his election by making an entry on the land or bringing an action to recover it, the grantee's estate continues. Because the

---

[9] McKinney's N.Y.Real Prop.Law, §§ 346–349; McKinney's N.Y.Real Property Actions and Proceedings Law, Art. 19, §§ 1951–1955, added by N.Y.Laws, 1962, c. 142. A change of conditions is generally held, in the absence of statute, ineffective to prevent enforcement of the possibility of reverter. Simes & Smith, Future Interests, §§ 1991–1994.

[1] This rule is as old as Littleton who stated that "no entry nor re-entry (which is all one) may be reserved or given to any person, but only to the feoffer [conveyor], or to the donor, or to the lessor, or to their heirs; and such re-entry cannot be given to any other person." Littleton, Tenures, § 347. But under modern law it is possible for the grantor to create in a third person an interest comparable to a right of entry. Thus, A conveys "to B and his heirs on condition that the land be used only for residential purposes and if during B's lifetime the land is used for non-residential purposes then to C and his heirs." C has a future interest called an executory interest. This executory interest, unlike the right of entry, is subject to the rule against perpetuities and frequently the gift over will be void because violative of that rule. See e. g. Proprietors of Church in Brattle Square v. Grant, 3 Gray 142 (Mass.1855); Edward John Noble Hospital v. Board of Foreign Missions, 13 Misc.2d 918, 176 N.Y.S.2d 157 (1958). The subject of executory interests is treated in c. 9, infra.

option to terminate the granted estate for breach of the condition is the distinguishing characteristic of the right of entry it is sometimes called a "power of termination." It is so described in the Restatement of Property[2] but despite the accuracy of this term the courts continue to use the older terminology. Unhappily, they all too frequently refer to a right of entry as a "possibility of reverter." Such designation is objectionable in that it tends to confuse a right of entry with the interest left in the creator of a fee simple determinable.

It is possible to attach a condition subsequent to an estate other than a fee simple. Thus, A, owner of Blackacre in fee simple, conveys it to "B for life on the express condition that B reside on the land and in the event that he does not do so A and his heirs may re-enter and possess the premises as of his former estate." B has a life estate subject to a condition subsequent. A has a reversion in fee simple coupled with a right of entry. However, the fee simple and the estate for years are the estates most commonly created subject to a condition subsequent. In practically all standard forms of lease a right of entry is created in favor of the lessor for nonpayment of rent or breach of other covenants and conditions set forth in the lease. In such cases the right of entry for condition broken is incident to the reversion in the lessor.

SECTION 9. CREATION OF RIGHT OF ENTRY FOR CONDITION BROKEN—CONSTRUCTIONAL PROBLEMS

Although no particular words are essential to create an estate on condition subsequent the use in the conveyance of the traditional words of condition—"upon condition that," "provided that," "but if"—coupled with a provision for re-entry by the

---

[2] §§ 24, 45. The term "power of termination" is also used in a recent New York statute; it is there defined as "a power reserved to the grantor or his heirs or to the heirs of a testator to enter for breach of a condition attached to an estate granted or devised." McKinney's N.Y.Real Property Law, § 59–b as amended by N.Y.Laws, 1962, c. 146.

transferor on the occurrence of the stated event will normally be construed to manifest an intention to create an estate on condition.   According to the older cases, words of condition alone without a re-entry clause are sufficient to create the qualified estate [1] but the modern trend is to refuse to construe the conveyance as creating an estate on condition in the absence of a provision that the transferor shall have a right to re-enter or words of similar import, such as that the land shall "revert" or that the conveyance shall be "void" on the happening of the specified event.[2]   Where the language of the instrument is ambiguous the strong reluctance of the courts to enforce a forfeiture will frequently result in a construction that the parties intended to create a covenant or a trust rather than an estate on condition.[3]   A covenant is a promise under seal to do or to refrain from doing a specified thing.   If the covenant is broken the remedy of the covenantee is to sue for injunctive relief or for damages, but the breach of the covenant neither automatically terminates the estate nor gives the covenantee a power to terminate.

SECTION 10.   ENFORCEMENT OF THE RIGHT OF ENTRY

At early common law it was usually necessary for the grantor to make an actual entry on the land in order to terminate the granted estate for breach of the condition.   But the necessity of entry no longer exists in American law.   Many courts hold that the bringing of an action of ejectment or an equivalent action is a sufficient indication of the grantor's election to terminate although some courts require that notice of the elec-

---

1 Gray v. Blanchard, 8 Pick. 284 (Mass.1829).   Cf. Post v. Weil, 115 N.Y. 361, 22 N.E. 145 (1889).

2 See e. g. Taylor v. Continental Southern Corp., 131 Cal.App.2d 267, 280 P.2d 514 (1955).

3 See e. g. Post v. Weil, n. 1, supra; President and Fellows of Middlebury College v. Central Power Corp., 101 Vt. 325, 143 A. 384 (1928).

tion be given prior to the commencement of the action.   Since the grantor has an election to enforce a forfeiture for breach or not, as he pleases, he may waive the privilege either by express agreement or by his conduct.   Thus, a lessor who accepts payment of rent by the lessee after knowledge of the breach of condition waives his right to terminate for such breach although he may enforce a forfeiture for subsequent breaches.[1] Whether mere inaction without more by the grantor, short of any applicable statute of limitations, will amount to a waiver of the privilege to enforce a forfeiture is a controversial point. On principle, it would seem that failure to declare a forfeiture within a reasonable time after the grantor knows, or reasonably should have known, of the breach of condition should be held to amount to a waiver of the particular breach.[2]

Courts of equity sometimes grant relief against enforcement of a forfeiture for breach of a condition subsequent as an application of the doctrine that equity will relieve against penalties and forfeitures.   A large element of discretion is involved and normally relief will be confined to situations where the grantor can by compensation be put in the same position as if the breach had not occurred.   Thus, a lessee who pays or tenders rent past due may be granted equitable relief against enforcement of a right of entry for breach of the covenant to pay rent but not where the lessor has changed his position by leasing to a third person after making a re-entry.[3]

1 Whitehouse Restaurant, Inc. v. Hoffman, 320 Mass. 183, 68 N.E.2d 686 (1946).

2 Accord, Goodman v. Southern Pacific Co., 143 Cal.App.2d 424, 299 P.2d 321 (1956).   Cf. City of New York v. Coney Island Fire Dept., 285 N.Y. 535, 32 N.E.2d 827 (1941) (inaction by grantor for 41 years held no bar to action of ejectment where breach was continuous in nature).

3 Paeff v. Hawkins-Washington Realty Co., 320 Mass. 144, 67 N.E.2d 900 (1946); Dodsworth v. Dodsworth, 254 Ill. 49, 98 N.E. 279 (relief against forfeiture for non-payment of taxes).

SECTION 11.   ALIENABILITY OF RIGHT OF ENTRY
FOR CONDITION BROKEN

From an early date the English common law held the view that a right of entry for condition broken was not transferable by an inter vivos conveyance to a third person.   In the words of Lord Coke: "Nothing in action, entry or re-entry can be granted over" and he assigned as a reason the "avoiding of maintenance, suppression of right and stirring up of suits." [1] While the reason assigned by Coke may have been historically unsound [2] the rule itself was unquestioned and stood until changed by statute in the middle nineteenth century. [3]   American courts accepted the rule as a part of the inherited common law and even today it represents the great weight of authority where the right of entry is not accompanied by a reversion.   In a few states there are statutes expressly making the interest alienable; [4] and in some jurisdictions a general statute providing for alienability of future interests has been held to include rights of entry for condition broken but there appears to be no general movement in favor of alienability of these interests. [5]   The non-alienability rule is held to apply to assignments before and after breach of the condition.

A few American jurisdictions have held not only that a right of entry not incident to a reversion is inalienable but that an attempted alienation has the effect of destroying the right of

[1] Co.Litt. 214.

[2] Professor Thorne states that the true reason for the non-assignability rule was the lack of a remedy under medieval law to the assignee.   Since neither the assignee nor his ancestor had ever had seisin no real action to recover the seisin was available to him.   Thorne, Sir Edward Coke 14–17 (Selden Society Lecture, 1957).

[3] 7 & 8 Vict. c. 76, § 5 (1844).

[4] See e. g. West's Ann.Cal.Civ.Code § 1046; Conn.Gen.Stat.Ann., § 47–29; McKinney's N.Y.Real Property Law, § 59, as amended by N.Y.Laws, 1962, c. 146.

[5] In Illinois a statute provides that rights of entry are incapable of being alienated or devised. Ill.Smith-Hurd Ann.Stat. c. 30, § 37b.

entry—thereby adding what Professor Powell has called "a monstrous excresence on this anachronism."[6] This doctrine originated in the case of Rice v. Boston & Worcester Railroad Corporation[7] and has been followed in a handful of jurisdictions. The Restatement originally accepted the Rice case as stating American law but has since repudiated it.[8] Since most courts have not passed on the question the Restatement change may be influential in persuading them to reject a doctrine that had no English case law to support it and lacks justification both in logic and in policy. Courts which hold that a possibility of reverter is inalienable do not also hold that it is destroyed by an attempted alienation. There is no reason for applying a different rule in the case of a right of entry.

At early common law a right of entry incident to a reversion was not transferable with a grant of the reversion. But by a statute enacted in 1540[9] it was provided that a right of entry incident to a reversion resulting from a conveyance of a life estate or a term of years would pass with a transfer of the reversion. This statute, or adaptations of it, are in force in many American jurisdictions and in others the courts reach the same result as that attained by the statute. Therefore, an assignee of a lessor can enforce against the lessee a right of entry specified in the lease for breach of its conditions.[10]

All courts agree that a right of entry is releasable by the grantor (or his heirs) to the then owner of the estate on con-

---

[6] 2 Powell, Real Property, § 282.

[7] 12 Allen 141 (Mass.1866).

[8] Restat.Prop., § 160, Comm. c; Restatement of the Law (Supp., 1948) p. 415. Only six states (Colorado, Maine, Massachusetts, Michigan, New York and Oregon) have applied the destruction on transfer rule. Michigan has since abrogated it by statute and Iowa and Oklahoma have refused to apply it. A recent Ohio case rejects it. PCK Properties, Inc. v. City of Cuyahoga Falls, 176 N.E.2d 441 (Ohio App.1960). As to the present New York law, see n. 4, supra.

[9] 32 Hen. VIII, c. 34.

[10] That the subject matter of the condition must "touch and concern" the land, see Stockbridge Iron Co. v. Cone Iron Works, 102 Mass. 80, 84 (1869).

dition subsequent. And the prevailing view is that such an interest is both descendible and devisable.[11]

SECTION 12. DURATION OF RIGHT OF ENTRY ARISING FROM FEE SIMPLE ON CONDITION SUBSEQUENT

In recent years legislation has been enacted in several states limiting the duration of rights of entry arising from the creation of fees simple on condition subsequent.[1] Like the possibility of reverter, the right of entry is not, in the view of American courts, subject to the Rule against Perpetuities and is, therefore, capable of indefinite duration. Statutes restricting to a specified number of years the duration of possibilities of reverter, or requiring re-recording of claims of such interests, usually include rights of entry within their coverage.[2]

---

[11] Restat.Prop., §§ 164, 165. New York has taken the anomalous position that a right of entry for condition broken is not descendible or devisable but goes to the heirs "by representation." Upington v. Corrigan, 151 N.Y. 143, 45 N.E. 359 (1896). For a criticism of this view, see 2 Powell, Real Property, § 284. By statute in New York, a right of entry created on or after September 1, 1962 is descendible, devisable and alienable. McKinney's N.Y.Real Property Law, § 59, as amended by N.Y.Laws, 1962, c. 146. For a collection of cases, see Annotation, 16 A.L.R.2d 1246 (1951).

[1] Rights of entry incident to a reversion, such as those contained in leases, are not affected by such legislation.

[2] See e. g. Mass.Gen.Laws.Ann. c. 184A, § 3. Statutes limiting the duration of rights of entry based upon fees simple on condition subsequent also exist in Connecticut (30 years), Florida (21 years), Kentucky (30 years), Illinois (40 years), Maine (30 years), Minnesota (30 years), Nebraska (30 years), and Rhode Island (20 years). As to New York, see § 7, nn. 8, 9, supra. The Florida statute is unusual in that it permits a possibility of reverter or right of entry which exceeds the maximum period of duration to be enforced as a covenant or equitable restriction. Fla.Stat.Ann. § 689.18.

D. REMAINDERS

SECTION 13. THE CONCEPT OF A REMAINDER

A remainder is a future interest created in a transferee which can become a present possessory estate only on the expiration of a prior estate created in favor of another transferee by the same instrument. Thus, A owning Blackacre in fee simple conveys it "to B for life and then to C and his heirs." B has a possessory life estate, called the particular estate, and C has a remainder in fee simple. C's future interest was originally called a remainder because on the expiration of B's life estate the land "remained" away from A, the transferor, instead of reverting to him. At common law the number of remainders which can be created is unlimited.[1] Thus, A might convey to B for life, then to C for life, then to D for life, then to E and the heirs of his body, then to F and his heirs. All of the transferees except B have remainders since the interest of each can become a possessory estate on the expiration of the prior estates. There can be no remainder after a fee simple, whether it be a present estate in fee simple or a vested remainder in fee simple, because according to the doctrine of estates a fee simple represented the totality of ownership. And since a fee simple determinable was looked upon as having the same quality of size as the fee simple absolute, there could be no remainder after a fee simple determinable. In some circumstances a future interest limited to take effect on the expiration of a fee simple determinable is recognized as valid in modern law but such future interest is classified as an executory interest, not as a remainder.[2]

---

[1] In a few states the number of successive life estates was formerly restricted by statute to not more than two. These statutes were patterned on N.Y.Real Property Law §§ 43, 45 as those sections stood prior to their amendment in 1959. Sections 43 and 45 were repealed in 1960. See 6 American Law of Property, §§ 25.92–25.98 and Supp., 1960.

[2] Thus, if A conveys "to B and his heirs so long as the land is used during B's lifetime for residential purposes and if during B's lifetime the land is not

How does a remainder differ from a reversion? In the first place, a reversion arises by operation of law apart from the intent of the transferor, whereas a remainder is created only by express or implied limitation and by the same instrument which creates the particular estate. In the second place, a reversion arises only in favor of the transferor (or his heirs) whereas a remainder can be created only in favor of a stranger. Finally, at English common law there was tenure between the holder of the particular estate and the reversioner but there was no tenure between the holder of the particular estate and the remainderman. This last difference would, of course, be of no significance in modern law. If A, owning land in fee simple, conveys it to B for life, A has a reversion in fee simple. If A transfers this reversion to C, the latter has a reversion and not a remainder but C's interest today is practically the same as though A had originally by one instrument conveyed "to B for life, then to C and his heirs."

At common law prior to the Statute of Uses (1536) the remainder was the only future interest which could be created in favor of a person other than the transferor or his heirs. A future interest created in favor of a transferee which did not possess the characteristics of a remainder was void. A principal characteristic of a remainder is that it becomes a possessory estate only on the expiration, and not the divestment, of the preceding estates created by the same instrument. A remainder does not cut short a prior estate; it awaits its orderly termination. Thus, A, owning Blackacre in fee simple, conveys it "to B and his heirs but if B dies leaving no surviving children then to C and his heirs." C has not a remainder but a future interest that divests or displaces B's estate in fee. At common law such a future interest was void but after the Statute of Uses it was valid as an executory interest. The nature of an executory interest will be discussed in a later chapter.[3]

so used then to C and his heirs" B has a fee simple determinable and C has an executory interest. Cf. First Universalist Society v. Boland, 155 Mass. 171, 29 N.E. 524 (1891). See Restat.Prop., § 25.47.

[3] C. 9, infra.

Moreover, to qualify as a remainder the future interest must be limited to take effect in possession immediately on the expiration of the prior interest simultaneously created. A remainder cannot be so limited as to become a possessory estate following a gap after the ending of the prior estate. Thus, A conveys to B for life, and one year after B's death to C and his heirs. C does not have a remainder. Prior to the Statute of Uses C's interest was void but thereafter it could be created as an executory interest.

SECTION 14. HISTORICAL BASIS OF DISTINCTION BETWEEN REMAINDERS

The notion that a tenant of land in fee simple could convey a present possessory estate in that land and simultaneously create a future estate in favor of a third person was not readily accepted by the early common law.[1] It is probable that remainders were not recognized as valid estates until shortly after the statute De Donis (1285). But thereafter a remainder following a fee tail was given recognition and protection. Remainders following a life estate were then developed.[2] The common law, however, was not willing to recognize as a valid estate every future interest having some of the characteristics or the form of a remainder. If A conveyed "to B for life, and on B's death to C and his heirs" C was in a position to take the seisin on B's death and to discharge the feudal obligations due to the lord of the fee. C, therefore, had an estate in the land, a valid remainder. But suppose that A conveyed

---

[1] For a discussion of the historical development of remainders, see Bordwell, The Common Law Scheme of Estates and the Remainder, 34 Iowa L.Rev. 401 (1949).

[2] A freehold estate following on a term of years is classified as a remainder in modern law. Restat.Prop., § 156; McKinney's N.Y.Real Property Law, § 50. But the common law view was that such an interest was a present freehold estate rather than a remainder. Thus, A, owner in fee simple, conveys to B for ten years, then to C and his heirs. Since C had seisin the common law view was that C had a present estate in fee simple subject to a term of years in B.

"to B for life and on B's death to C (a bachelor) and his heirs if, but only if, C marries." Here there is an element of uncertainty attaching to C's interest, a condition precedent to his right to take the land on B's death. C might or might not marry and until he did he had no right to the seisin. The common law took the view that C had not an estate but the mere possibility of acquiring an estate. Not until the sixteenth century would the law extend recognition to C's interest. It was then decided that if the condition precedent of marriage was satisfied during the continuance of the preceding estate C would be permitted to take the land on the expiration of B's life estate. C's interest was labelled a "contingent" remainder to distinguish it from a "vested" remainder.

This distinction arose at a time when it was a rigid principle of the common law that on the termination of a possessory freehold estate there must be some ascertained person in existence capable of taking the seisin. There could be no gap in, or abeyance, of the seisin. A remainder was said to be "vested" when it was limited in favor of a person in existence and ascertained and was not subject to a condition precedent. If the remainder was limited to a person not ascertained or not in existence or if it was subject to a condition precedent it was said to be a "contingent" remainder. The word "vested" referred to ownership of an estate—the vested remainder was an estate, the contingent remainder was only a possibility of an estate.[3] Thus, an estate may be vested in possession as well as in interest or it may be vested only in interest. If A conveys to B for life, remainder to C and his heirs, B has an estate vested both in possession and in interest while C has an estate vested in interest.

[3] This was the primary meaning of "vested" in property law. But the word is also used in other senses, e. g. in the sense of being transmissible on death or assignable. The use of the term in the latter sense has lead a court to speak of "a vested interest in a contingent remainder!" Clarke v. Fay, 205 Mass. 228, 235, 91 N.E. 328, 330 (1910). Fortunately, such use of "vested" is not common. For a discussion of the concept of "vested," see 5 American Law of Property, §§ 21.5–21.8.

Although the concept of a remainder, as well as of other future interests, had its origin in the land law, future interests may be created at the present time in personal property, including intangibles, as well as in real property.[4] And since it is appropriate to speak of a remainder in personal property, the concept of a "vested" remainder as an estate and that of a "contingent" remainder as the possibility of an estate is now anachronistic. In modern law when we speak of a remainder as being "vested" we mean that it has certain definite characteristics, namely, that the remainderman is a presently identifiable person and that the remainder is not subject to a condition precedent.

SECTION 15. THE CLASSIFICATION OF REMAINDERS

Traditionally, remainders have been divided into two main classes: vested and contingent. At common law, substantially different legal consequences attached to these two types of interests because of the concept that a vested remainder was an estate while a contingent remainder was merely the possibility of becoming one.[1] A vested remainder was transferable; a contingent remainder was not transferable. A vested remainder was indestructible; a contingent remainder was destructible. A vested remainderman received greater protection against misuse of the land by the holder of the possessory estate than did the contingent remainderman.

In modern law the differences between these two types of remainders are less sharp. Several of the common law attributes of contingent remainders, as we shall see, have been eliminated or modified. In some situations it will be immaterial

---

[4] The topic of future interests in personalty is not specifically covered in this book. For a comprehensive treatment, see Simes & Smith, Future Interests, §§ 331–371.

[1] The modern definition of the word "estate" is sufficiently broad to include contingent remainders. See Restat.Prop., § 9.

whether the remainder is classified as vested or contingent since the end result will be the same. But there are still significant differences between the two types and the classification of a particular interest as of one type or the other may well determine the legal consequences in a given case. For example, the Rule against Perpetuities is generally applicable to contingent remainders but not to vested remainders. And even today the contingent remainder is in several respects accorded substantially less protection than the vested remainder. Therefore, it may be imperative to ascertain whether a limitation in a deed or will creates one type of remainder rather than the other.[2]

To what extent does the classification of a remainder as vested or contingent depend on the intention of the transferor? In a donative transaction the intention of the transferor as expressed in the creating instrument is given effect, when possible, in determining the disposition of the property. Thus, if the transferor manifests an intent that a particular future interest shall be subject to a specified condition precedent his intention will have controlling weight. The form of the limitation is normally important as indicative of the intention of the transferor. Where the manifestation of intention is not clear, or is absent, rules of construction are resorted to in order to ascertain the meaning of the language used.[3]

[2] The Restatement of Property discards the term "contingent remainder" because of the confusion that has arisen in its use and substitutes the term "remainder subject to a condition precedent." § 157. However, the courts continue to use the older terminology.

[3] Much of the modern law of future interests is concerned with problems of construction but no extensive treatment of these problems is herein attempted. As to theories of construction, see Simes and Smith, Future Interests, §§ 461–473; 5 American Law of Property, §§ 21.1–21.4; Restat.Prop., §§ 241–242.

SECTION 16. THE DEFINITION OF A
VESTED REMAINDER

It is difficult to formulate a simple but precise and comprehensive definition of a vested remainder. In general, it may be defined as a remainder limited to a person in existence and ascertained who is given the right to immediate possession whenever and however the preceding estate or estates come to an end. It is an estate the owner of which is entitled to immediate possession subject only to the existence of a prior right to possession in another person created by the same instrument which created the remainder. It will be noted that this definition finds its basis in the common law doctrine of the necessity of continuity of seisin.

The definition most often quoted by the courts is that given by Professor John Chipman Gray: "A remainder is vested if, at every moment during its continuance, it becomes a present estate, whenever and however the preceding freehold estates determine. A remainder is contingent if, in order for it to become a present estate, the fulfillment of some condition precedent, other than the determination of the preceding freehold estates, is necessary." [1] A present unconditional right to possession in favor of an identified person on the termination of the preceding interests may be said to be of the essence of a vested remainder. In several states there are statutes defining vested and contingent remainders.[2] These statutes are patterned on the common law concept but in a few jurisdictions they have

---

[1] Gray, Rule Against Perpetuities, §§ 9, 101 (4th ed. 1942, Little Brown & Co.)

[2] See e. g. McKinney's N.Y.Real Property Law, § 40: "A future estate is either vested or contingent. It is vested, when there is a person in being, who would have an immediate right to possession of the property, on the determination of all the intermediate or precedent estates. It is contingent while the person to whom or the event on which it is limited to take effect remains uncertain." This statute has been copied in several states. See Simes & Smith, Future Interests, §§ 154–163.

been judicially construed to reach a result different from the common law in certain situations.[3]

The following cases are illustrations of vested remainders. In each case C's remainder is vested.

1. A conveys or devises to B for life, then to C and his heirs.

2. To B and the heirs of his body, then to C and his heirs.[4]

3. To B for life, then to C for life.

4. To B for life, then to X for life if he marries, remainder to C and his heirs.

5. To B for life, then to the children of X and their heirs (X being alive and having one child, C).

6. To B for life, then to C and his heirs but if C does not marry before B dies then to X and his heirs.

7. To B for life and on his death to such of his children as he may by will appoint, and in default of appointment to C and his heirs.

SECTION 17. THE CLASSIFICATION OF VESTED REMAINDERS

It is helpful to analysis to classify vested remainders into three groupings: A. Remainders absolutely vested; B. Remainders vested subject to partial divestment; C. Remainders vested subject to complete divestment.[1] Illustrations 1, 2, 3

---

[3] See e. g. Moore v. Littel, 41 N.Y. 66 (1869). This case is discussed in § 20, infra.

[4] At common law B had a fee tail and C had a vested remainder in fee. But in a state having a statute abolishing the fee tail and substituting a different estate the future interest given to C would be a contingent remainder or an executory interest depending on the type of statute. Simes & Smith, Future Interests, § 313.

[1] The classification here adopted is similar to, but not identical with, the classification of vested remainders used in the Restatement of Property. The Restatement classifies vested remainders into: (a) remainders "indefeasibly vested;" (b) remainders "vested subject to open;" (c) remainders "vested subject to complete defeasance." § 157. The word "defeasance" is used in

and 4 given in the preceding section are examples of remainders absolutely vested; illustration 5 exemplifies a remainder vested subject to partial divestment; illustrations 6 and 7 typify remainders vested subject to complete divestment.

A. Remainders Absolutely Vested

A remainder is absolutely vested when it is limited to an ascertained or identifiable person or persons without words of condition and is not subject to divestment. Thus, A conveys to B for life, then to C and his heirs. C has a remainder absolutely vested. A remainder is none the less vested even though there is no certainty that the remainderman will ever enjoy the possession. Thus, A conveys to B and the heirs of his body, remainder to C for life. At common law, and today in a jurisdiction recognizing the estate in fee tail, C has a vested remainder even though it is possible that B will have issue who will survive C and C will never, in fact, come into possession. It is the presence or absence of a condition precedent, not the certainty or probability of enjoyment of possession, that decides whether the remainder is vested or contingent. So also, if A conveys to B for life, then to C for life, C has a vested remainder even though B's life expectancy is greater than C's.[2] Words which are conditional in form but which express nothing more than the law implies will not make the remainder contingent. Thus, if A devises to B for life and from and after B's death to C in fee it

the Restatement as including both expiration and divestment. Under the Restatement terminology a vested remainder in fee simple determinable would not be indefeasibly vested since the remainder interest could expire by the occurrence of the stated event; yet, the remainder would not be subject to divestment by reason of its being a determinable estate since it would expire but not be cut short on the happening of the stated event.

2 If A conveys to B for life, then to C for life if C survives B, is C's remainder vested or contingent? The remainder would seem to be vested on the ground that the condition of C's survivorship adds no additional element of uncertainty; since C has only a life interest he could not take in any event unless he survived B. Simes & Smith, Future Interests, § 142. But if the limitations were to B for life, then to C and his heirs if C survives B, the remainder in fee to C would be contingent because of the condition precedent of survivorship.

might be argued that B's death is a condition precedent to C's remainder. But the words "from and after" are construed to refer to the time of enjoyment of possession by C, not to the time of the vesting of C's interest. The courts universally apply a presumption in favor of construing a limitation as creating a vested rather than a contingent interest, and also a presumption in favor of early vesting rather than later vesting. Hence, when an instrument creates a life estate in B and then provides for a remainder in C "at B's death," or "when B dies," or "in the event of B's death" such language will not be construed as making the remainder contingent.

B. Remainders Vested Subject to Partial Divestment

A remainder is vested subject to being partly divested when the remainderman is in existence and ascertained but the amount of his estate is subject to diminution in favor of other members of a class. This type of remainder, frequently called a remainder vested subject to open, is illustrated by a common kind of class gift. Thus, A devises land to B for life, then to the children of B in fee. At the time of A's death B has one child, C. C's remainder is vested because he is in existence, ascertained and he (or his heirs) is certain to acquire a possessory interest on the expiration of B's life estate. According to common law standards the seisin can pass to him immediately on B's death. But C's remainder is subject to open up and let in after born children of B because they also come within the terms of the gift. If after A's death two more children are born to B they take equally with C as remaindermen and C's interest is reduced to a one third share.[3]

In Minnig v. Batdorff,[4] the court summarized the rule thus: "When there is an immediate gift to children, those only living at the testator's death will take; but it is now settled, that where a particular estate or interest is carved out, with a gift

---

[3] If the devise were to B for life, then to the children of C, the class of remaindermen would close at B's death and only those children of C born during B's lifetime would take.

[4] 5 Pa. 503 (1847).

over to the children of the person taking that interest, or of any other person, the limitation will embrace not only the objects living at the death of the testator, but all who shall subsequently come into existence before the period of distribution. Such a remainder vests in the objects to whom the description applies at the death of the testator, subject to open and let in others answering the description as they are born successively." The interest of the unborn children is usually classed as a contingent remainder, not an executory interest.[5]

C. Remainders Vested Subject to Complete Divestment

A remainder is vested subject to complete divestment when the remainderman is in existence and ascertained and his interest is not subject to a condition precedent but his right to possession or enjoyment on the expiration of the prior interests is subject to termination by reason of an executory interest, or a power of appointment, or a right of entry. Thus, A conveys to B for life, then to C and his heirs but if C die leaving no surviving children then to D and his heirs. C has a remainder vested subject to complete divestment on the death of C without surviving children. D's interest is not a remainder but an executory interest. So also, if A conveys to B for life, remainder as B shall appoint, and in default of appointment to C and his heirs, C has a remainder vested subject to complete divestment.[6] Due to the strong preference for construing an interest as vested, C's remainder is viewed as being subject to divestment by the exercise of the power of appointment rather than as being contingent on the non-exercise of the power. A third example of this type of remainder would be: A conveys to B for life, remainder to C and his heirs on the express condition that if the

---

[5] See 1 American Law of Property, § 4.34.

[6] A power of appointment may be generally defined as a power or authorization given by the owner of a property interest (the donor) to another person (the donee) to designate a transferee or transferees of that interest (the appointees) or the shares which the appointees are to take. Instruments creating powers of appointment usually make a gift over in default of appointment to take care of the situation where the donee of the power fails to exercise it.

premises are used for the sale of intoxicating liquor A shall have the power to re-enter and repossess himself as of his former estate.[7]

Difficult problems of construction frequently arise in determining whether words of condition in a limitation amount to a condition precedent of the interest or a condition subsequent. If the conditional words amount to a condition precedent the remainder is contingent; if such words amount to a condition subsequent the remainder is vested subject to divestment. Thus, where A devises to B for life, then, if C (a bachelor) marries before B dies, to C and his heirs, C's remainder is contingent. But if A devises to B for life, then to C (a bachelor) and his heirs but if C does not marry before B dies then to D and his heirs, C has a remainder vested subject to divestment. It is true that the difference is principally one of form since C will not take in either case unless he marries during B's lifetime yet the distinction is usually adhered to by the courts. So also, if A devises to B for life, then to such of B's children and their heirs as survive B, the remainder is contingent because of the condition precedent of survivorship even though B has a child at the time A's will became effective.

The test suggested by Professor Gray is often quoted and adopted by the courts: "Whether a remainder is vested or contingent depends upon the language employed. If the conditional element is incorporated into the description of, or into the gift to, the remainder-man, then the remainder is contingent; but if, after words giving a vested interest, a clause is added divesting it, the remainder is vested."[8] Gray's test is

---

[7] A further illustration of a remainder vested subject to complete divestment is where property is given in trust for the benefit of a person for life with power in the trustee to invade the principal for the benefit of the life tenant, followed by a remainder over. Thus, A transfers to T in trust to pay the income to B for life together with such portion of the principal as T may deem necessary for B's comfortable maintenance, remainder to C in fee.

[8] Gray, Rule Against Perpetuities, § 108 (4th ed. 1942, Little Brown & Co.). In Howard v. Batchelder, 143 Conn. 328, 122 A.2d 307 (1956) the court quoted

helpful in many cases but it may be difficult to determine in some cases whether the conditional element is "incorporated into the gift to the remainderman." It may first be necessary to resort to rules of construction to determine the meaning of the language. Thus, if A devises to B for life, then to C and his heirs when C attains the age of twenty-one, C has a contingent remainder. The requirement of survival to the stated age is viewed as a condition precedent of C's interest. But suppose the limitations were as follows: to B for life, then to C and his heirs when C attains the age of twenty-one, but if C dies under twenty-one to D and his heirs. Here the addition of the supplanting limitation (but if C dies under twenty-one to D in fee) will cause C's interest to be viewed as a vested remainder subject to divestment because of the strong constructional preference in favor of vested interests.[9] But if A devises to B for life, then to such of B's children as shall attain the age of 21, and for want of any such issue to X and his heirs, the remainder to B's children is contingent prior to the attainment of the specified age by a child.[10] The condition of age attainment is viewed as being incorporated into the description of the remaindermen. Yet if the limitations read: to B for life, then to B's children, if they attain 21; and for want of such issue to X in fee, it is probable that the remainder to the children (assuming all are under 21) would be viewed as vested subject to divestment. The requirement of age attainment could

Gray and also stated: "The form of the limitation is of primary importance in solving the difficulty. If the form indicates that the condition is to happen before the remainderman is to take, the remainder is ordinarily held to be contingent. If the form is that of an unconditional gift followed by language to the effect that the remainder is to be taken away from the remainderman if a condition happens, then the remainder is generally construed as vested subject to complete defeasance." Cf. 1 American Law of Property, § 4.36.

[9] This is basically the often cited old English case of Edwards v. Hammond, 3 Lev. 132 (C.P.1683). See 5 American Law of Property, § 21.32; Simes & Smith, Future Interests, §§ 148–149; Restat.Prop., § 253, Comm. e.

[10] The case given is basically that of Festing v. Allen, 12 M. & W. 279 (Ex 1843). See 5 American Law of Property, § 21.32; Simes & Smith, Future Interests, § 148.

be treated as not being a condition inhering in the designation
of the remaindermen.

SECTION 18.   THE NATURE OF A CONTINGENT REMAINDER

A contingent remainder is any remainder which is created in
favor of an ascertained person but is subject to a condition
precedent; is created in favor of an unborn person; or is created in favor of an existing but unascertained person. It was
not, according to the older common law definition, an estate
but merely the possibility of an estate. In the medieval period,
the law refused to recognize the validity of contingent remainders on the ground that the contingent remainderman had at
the time of the conveyance no present capacity to take the
seisin on the expiration of the preceding freehold estate and
the conveyance could not be effective to give him the seisin after
a gap following the freehold estate. But in the fifteenth century, if not earlier, a contingent remainder in favor of the heirs
of a living person was recognized; and other types of contingent
remainders were gradually given recognition and the rules governing them were developed. These rules bore a deep impress
of the doctrine of seisin.

A contingent remainder becomes a vested remainder if any
condition precedent is fulfilled and if the remainderman is ascertained before the termination of the preceding estate. Thus,
A conveys to B for life, then to C and his heirs if C marries.
At the time of the conveyance C is unmarried. The state of
the title at that time is: life estate in B, contingent remainder
in fee simple in C, reversion in fee simple in A. C marries
while B is yet living. C's remainder becomes vested immediately
on his marriage and all of the characteristics of a vested remainder attach thereto. The vesting of C's remainder operates
to divest the reversion in A. Since the condition precedent has
been satisfied the seisin or possession will pass to C as soon as
B's estate ends. If C dies before B his now vested remainder

goes to his heirs or devisees in the absence of a prior transfer by him of the remainder.

SECTION 19. REMAINDERS SUBJECT TO A CONDITION PRECEDENT

A remainder subject to a condition precedent is a contingent remainder even though the remainderman is an ascertained person. This is so for the reason that the remainderman, so long as the condition remains unsatisfied, has no right to immediate possession if the preceding estate should come to an end. From the common law viewpoint, his inability to take the seisin, should the freehold become vacant, makes his interest contingent.

The most common type of condition precedent is one requiring the remainderman to survive the life tenant or to survive to a specified age. Thus, A devises to B for life, then, if C survives B, to C and his heirs. Or, A devises to B for life, then to such of B's children as shall survive B and their heirs. So also, if A devises to B for life, then to C and his heirs, if but only if, C attains the age of twenty-one (C being under 21 at A's death). Frequently, a will contains alternative limitations each being subject to a condition precedent. Thus, A devises to B for life, then to such of B's children and their heirs as survive him and if no child of B survives him then to C and his heirs. Here the state of the title would be: Life estate in B, alternative contingent remainders in fee in B's children and in C, reversion in A's heirs in fee (assuming that there is no residuary clause in A's will).[1]

---

[1] Although the alternative contingencies are mutually exclusive and will exhaust all possibilities, A's heirs (A is, by hypothesis, dead) will be deemed to have a reversion because at common law contingent remainders were destructible. Hence, the reversion might take effect in possession. The doctrine of destructibility of contingent remainders is explained in §§ 21, 22, infra.

It will be recalled that in certain situations the strong preference for construing a remainder as vested may cause a court to construe the first limitation as creating a vested remainder subject to divestment by an executory

The creation of alternative limitations sometimes raises the question whether there can be a vested remainder after a contingent remainder in fee. Thus, A conveys to B for life, and on B's death to his surviving children and their heirs, then to C and his heirs. In form, C's remainder is vested. But the limitation to the surviving children is clearly a contingent remainder in form. Yet if it takes effect in possession it will do so by divesting C's apparent vested remainder—something which a contingent remainder cannot do. It can be argued, therefore, that C's interest should be construed as being subject to the condition precedent of B dying without surviving children. Moreover, a dictum in the English case of Loddington v. Kime,[2] stated that "no remainder limited after a limitation in fee, can be vested." This dictum, although not universally accepted, has represented the traditional view. Hence, the preferred construction is to treat the limitations as creating alternative contingent remainders. This is the view taken by the Restatement.[3]

SECTION 20.　REMAINDERS TO UNASCERTAINED PERSONS

A remainder limited in favor of an unascertained person is necessarily a contingent remainder. This is so because until the remainderman is ascertained there is no one ready to take the seisin or possession should the preceding freehold estate come to an end. The remaindermen may be unascertained because they are unborn or because some event, such as survival

interest. See § 17, supra. Thus, A devises to B for life, then to the children of B in fee and if any child predeceases B his share to go to X in fee. B has one child, C. C's remainder is vested subject to divestment. The limitation to X is viewed not as an alternative limitation imposing a requirement of survival as a condition precedent to C's remainder but as a supplanting or divesting limitation if C does not survive the life tenant. See 2 Powell, Real Property, §§ 329, 330.

[2] 1 Salk. 224 (1695).

[3] § 278. See Simes & Smith, Future Interests, § 145.

to a specified time, must occur before it can be determined who are to take the remainder. Thus, A devises to B for life, then to the children of C, a bachelor. The remainder to C's children is contingent. If a child is born to C during B's lifetime, that child has a remainder vested subject to open in favor of other children of C born before B dies. The concept of a remainder in favor of persons not yet in existence may seem strange. It is true, of course, that legal relations with respect to property can exist only between persons in being. When we speak of a contingent remainder in unborn persons we mean that the law recognizes the possibility of a legal relationship arising in the future and that the recognition of this potential interest has present legal consequences, e. g. the inability of the life tenant to deal with the property as though no such potential interest had been created.

Frequently, the remaindermen are in existence but their identity is uncertain until the happening of a future event. Thus, A grants to B for life, then to such of B's children in fee as survive him. Since the identity of the remaindermen cannot be known until B dies the remainder to B's children is contingent. Or, suppose that A devises to B for life, then to C or his children (or to C or his heirs, or to C or his issue). If we construe the word "or" as meaning the disjunctive, there are alternative dispositions here and it is uncertain until B's death who will take. C's interest is deemed to be subject to the condition precedent of survival until B's death. Therefore, the remainders to C and to the children are usually held to be contingent.[1] So also, if A devises "to my son B for life, then to his widow for her life, then to my daughter C and her heirs." Unless we construe "widow" as meaning B's present wife, the first remainderman is unascertained until B's death since "widow" literally means such spouse of B as survives him. But if we construe "widow" as meaning B's present wife, that is, his wife at the time A's will was drafted, the remainder is vested.

[1] 2 Powell, Real Property, § 329; Simes & Smith, § 153.

A very common instance of a remainder contingent by reason of uncertainty of the remaindermen is found in a limitation
of a remainder to the heirs of a living person. Heirs are those
persons entitled to take real property under the statutes of
descent upon the death of the owner thereof intestate. It is
obvious that a man's heirs cannot be determined until his death
because until then it cannot be known who those persons will
be who will inherit his property. The common law expressed
this thought in the maxim *"Nemo est haeres viventis"* (No one
is the heir of the living.) A living person may have heirs apparent or heirs presumptive but not heirs. It follows, then,
that if A devises to B for life, remainder to the heirs of C (a
living person), the remainder is contingent. So, also, if A devises to B for life, then to the heir of C during such heir's life,
the remainder is contingent. And if A devises to B for life,
then to the next heir male of B in fee tail, there is, at common
law, a contingent remainder in fee tail.[2] At times the context of the instrument may indicate that the testator used the
word "heirs" not in its technical sense but as meaning "children" or "issue." Where such construction is adopted the
children already in existence would have vested remainders subject to partial divestment in favor of after-born children.

In a jurisdiction where the rule in Shelley's Case[3] has been
abolished a conveyance to B for life, then to the heirs of B
creates a contingent remainder in the heirs according to orthodox concepts of vested and contingent remainders. Yet in the
New York case of Moore v. Littel[4] the court took the anomalous
view that such a remainder was vested, subject to divestment,
in those persons who would be entitled to take should the life
estate now come to an end. This conclusion was based in part
on the New York statute[5] defining vested and contingent re-

2 These were the limitations in Archer's Case, 1 Co.Rep. 66b (1597).

3 This rule is explained in c. 6, infra.

4 41 N.Y. 66 (1869). See 6 American Law of Property, § 25.34.

5 The language of the statute (now McKinney's N.Y.Real Property Law, §
40) is set out in § 16, n. 2, supra.

mainders although the statute did not necessitate the holding. The case has been subjected to much criticism but it is apparently still law in New York although it has not been extended beyond similar fact situations.[6] It has had some influence in other jurisdictions having statutes on vested and contingent remainders similar to the New York statute.

SECTION 21. DESTRUCTIBILITY OF CONTINGENT REMAINDERS AT COMMON LAW

At common law the usual method of creating a freehold estate was by a transaction called a feoffment with livery of seisin. This involved a transfer or delivery of seisin and possession of the land. It became a fundamental rule of common law conveyancing that there can be no livery of seisin to take effect in futuro. Livery of seisin is a present act and A cannot convey a freehold estate to B today to take effect next month. From the nature of livery of seisin the rule was derived that there could be no conveyance, by feoffment or otherwise, of a freehold estate to commence in futuro.[1] The limitation of a remainder did not violate this rule since a remainder follows after the present, particular estate created by the same conveyance. When A enfeoffed B to have and to hold to B for life, remainder to C and his heirs, B was invested with the seisin on his own behalf and on behalf of C, and upon his death, or upon the termination of the life estate from any cause, the seisin would continue in C in his own behalf. In this example C has a vested remainder and there is, therefore, no possibility of a lapse in the seisin. But suppose A conveyed to B for life, remainder to the eldest son of C, a bachelor. The remainder is contingent. If B dies before C has any children, what be-

---

[6] For an extensive treatment, see Simes & Smith, §§ 154–163. The unkind statement has been made that the old Court of Appeals which decided Moore v. Littel was abolished because it did not know the difference between a vested and a contingent remainder. Wheeler, Moore v. Littel and the Jackson Title, 1 Col.L.Rev. 347 (1901).

[1] Roe d. Wilkinson v. Tranmer, 2 Wils. 75, 95 Eng.Rep. 694 (1757).

comes of the contingent remainder? The seisin cannot be suspended or put in abeyance. It must vest in some one. The remainderman is not yet in existence, hence the seisin must be in A or if A is dead then in A's heirs. If C later marries and has a son will the seisin then pass to the son? No, because it will take a new conveyance to get the seisin out of A. The result is that the contingent remainder is destroyed.

From the feudal doctrines of seisin there arose the well settled common law rule that a freehold contingent remainder which does not vest at or before the termination of the preceding freehold estate is destroyed. Such termination of the preceding estate might result from the natural expiration of that estate, or from forfeiture, or from merger.

a. *Destructibility by Normal Expiration of Supporting Freehold Estate*

A contingent remainder of its very nature is subject to the possibility of not becoming vested prior to the normal termination of the supporting freehold estate. If the supporting estate, usually a life estate, should come to an end while the remainder is yet contingent the remainder must fail. Thus, A conveys to B for life, then to the heirs of C (a living person). B dies while C is still living. Since the remaindermen are not ascertained the seisin must revert to A and the contingent remainder is destroyed. If, however, the remainder vests at the same time as the expiration of the supporting estate the remainder will be given effect. Thus, A conveys to B for life, then to B's surviving children. Here the same event which marks the termination of the supporting freehold (B's death) also causes the contingent remainder in B's "surviving children" to become vested in possession in those of his children who in fact survived him. If the conveyance had been to B for life, then to C for life, then to the surviving children of C, the death of B during C's life would not cause the remainder in the surviving children to fail because it would be supported by C's estate. The English courts admitted one exception to the strict logic of the common law rule prohibiting a gap in the seisin and the creation of a freehold estate to commence in the future—a posthumous child may be considered as being in existence prior to his birth. Thus, in Reeve v. Long [2] A devised to B for life, remainder to B's first son in fee tail, with remainders over. B died before any son was born to him but he left his wife "great with child." Six months later a son was born. The House of Lords, reversing the King's Bench, held that the son was entitled to take.[3]

b. *Destructibility Arising from Forfeiture of Supporting Freehold Estate*

The rule of destructibility was applied also in cases where the supporting freehold estate terminated prior to the time of its natural expiration. Such premature termination would result from a forfeiture of the supporting life estate. At common law it was possible for a person having a life estate to transfer a greater estate than his own. This resulted from the doctrines of seisin and disseisin. If B had a life estate in Blackacre he could make a feoffment (livery of seisin) to X and his heirs and thereupon X acquired a tortious fee simple. This would also follow if the conveyance were made by fine or common recovery. As a consequence of his act B's life estate was forfeited and the reversioner or vested remainderman had a right of entry against X.[4] It followed that any contingent remainder dependent on the life estate for support was destroyed.

---

[2] 3 Lev. 408, 83 Eng.Rep. 754 (1695).

[3] The reporter tells us that "all the judges were much dissatisfied with this judgment of the Lords" because it created an exception "where the law was so clear and certain." It should be noted that at the time lay members of the House of Lords voted on cases coming up on appeal. It may be presumed that they were not overly impressed by the nice technicalities of property law.

[4] The reason usually given to explain the forfeiture of the life tenant's estate was that his conveyance was a breach of the feudal obligation of loyalty which he owed to his lord. The validity of this explanation is open to question. The law of reversions and remainders was not developed until the late thirteenth century and at that time feudalism was in its decline. It took a statute enacted in 1278 to give an heir an immediate right of action (equivalent to forfeiture) against a tenant in dower who wrongfully alienated her

Archer's Case [5] affords a good illustration of the operation of this rule. A, being seised of land in socage tenure, devised it to B for life, then to the next heir male of B in fee tail. A son was born to B. Then B enfeoffed X in fee simple. B died and his son entered on the land. In an action brought to try the title the court held for X, saying: ".   .   . by the feoffment of the tenant for life, the remainder was destroyed; for every contingent remainder ought to vest, either during the particular estate, or at least *eo instanti* that it determines; for if the particular estate be ended, or determined in fact or in law, before the contingency falls, the remainder is void. And in this case, inasmuch as by the feoffment of (B), his estate for life was determined by a condition in law annexed to it, and cannot be revived afterwards by any possibility; for this reason the contingent remainder is destroyed.   .   .   ."

c. *Destructibility by Merger*

A third situation in which a contingent remainder would fail by reason of the termination of the supporting life estate arose from the doctrine of merger of estates. By this doctrine, whenever successive vested estates are owned by the same person the smaller of the two estates will be absorbed by the larger. Thus, if A conveys to B for life, then to B and his heirs, B has only one estate, a fee simple. By the doctrine of merger, the life estate merges in, or is swallowed by, the larger estate. So also if A, owning in fee simple, conveys to B for life and A later transfers his reversion to B the latter will have one estate—a fee simple, not a life estate plus the reversion in fee. In order for a merger to take place the two estates must be successive and vested. Therefore, a merger will not be effected where a vested estate in-

dower lands. A similar remedy was later extended to reversioners and remaindermen. But not until 1310 was a writ of entry available to the holder of a vested remainder against the alienee of an ordinary life tenant. Thus, the doctrine of forfeiture of a life estate for a tortious feoffment first emerges as an offshoot of a statutory remedy. See Plucknett, Concise History of the Common Law 362, 569–570 (5th ed. 1956); Bordwell, Common Law Scheme of Estates And the Remainder, 34 Iowa L.Rev. 400, 405–406 (1949).

5 1 Co.Rep. 66b, 76 Eng.Rep. 146 (1597).

tervenes between the two estates. Thus, A conveys to B for life, then to C for life, then to B and his heirs. B has both a life estate and a vested remainder in fee. C's vested remainder will prevent a merger of B's two estates. But a contingent remainder, not being an estate according to common law standards, would not prevent two estates owned by the same person from being treated as successive estates. Thus, A conveys to B for life, then to C for life if C marries. Before C marries A assigns his reversion to B. B's life estate merges in his reversion in fee and C's remainder is destroyed.

Since the merger of a life estate with another vested estate causes a premature termination of the life estate, any contingent remainder dependent on the life estate for support will be destroyed. Thus, A conveys to B for life, then to C and his heirs if C arrives at the age of twenty-one. If at a time when C is ten years old A conveys his reversion in fee to B, or B conveys his life estate to A, or both A and B convey their estates to a third person, C's contingent remainder will be destroyed. Since C's contingent remainder failed to vest at or prior to the termination of the supporting life estate it is extinguished.

The general rules of merger and destructibility of contingent remainders are subject to two qualifications: 1. a fee tail will not merge into a fee simple; 2. a contingent remainder will not be destroyed by a merger of a life estate and the next vested estate when the two estates are created simultaneously with the contingent remainder. As to the first exception, the statute De Donis was thought to prevent the destruction of a fee tail by merger. It is true that once a tenant in tail acquired the power to convey a fee simple (at common law by suffering a common recovery) a contingent remainder following the fee tail would be destroyed by such a conveyance but this had nothing to do with the doctrine of merger. So also would a vested remainder expectant on the fee tail be eliminated by such conveyance. As to the second exception if it were held that merger of the two estates destroyed the contingent remainder created simultaneously with them, the intention of the transferor would be completely defeated. Therefore, if A conveys to B for life, then to C for life if C marries, then to B and his heirs, C's contingent remainder is initially valid. So also, if A devises to B for life, then to C for life if C marries, and the reversion simultaneously descends to B as heir of A the contingent remainder in C is not destroyed by merger of the life estate and the reversion.[6] But if there is a later transfer by B to a third person of his two estates there will be a merger in the transferee and C's contingent remainder will be destroyed.[7]

d. *Trustees to Preserve Contingent Remainders*

The destructibility of contingent remainders posed a threat to the stability of English family settlements of land and the conveyancing bar set to work to circumvent the destructibility rule. In the seventeenth century the conveyancers began to resort to the device of inserting in the settlement after the particular life estate an additional remainder to trustees "to preserve contingent remainders." Thus, A would convey to B for life, then to X and Y and their heirs for the life of B in trust for B and to preserve contingent remainders, then to B's first born son in fee tail male, remainders successively to B's other sons in fee tail male, with remainders over (B having no son at the time). It was held, partly for policy reasons, that the remainder to the trustees was vested.[8] Therefore, if B made a tortious conveyance in fee and thereby forfeited his legal life estate the right of entry in the trustees would support the contingent remainders

---

[6] Would it be correct to say that there is no merger here or to say that there is a merger but that it will not have the effect of destroying the contingent remainder? There are theoretical difficulties in either answer but there is no doubt about the rule itself. Perhaps we can say there is a merger subject to a split-up if the contingent remainder vests.

[7] In Purefoy v. Rogers, 2 Wm.Saund. 380, 85 Eng.Rep. 1181 (1670) A devised to B for life, then if B should have a son and name him after A to such son in fee. The reversion passed to X. Before B had a son X conveyed the reversion to B. Later a son was born to B. It was held that B's life estate merged in the reversion and the son's contingent remainder was destroyed.

[8] Dormer v. Packhurst, 6 Bro.P.C. 351 (1740); see Duncomb v. Duncomb, 3 Lev. 437 (1697).

in the unborn sons. Moreover, the vested estate in the trustees would prevent any merger of B's life estate in the fee simple. Thus, the estate of the trustees continued until B's death and protected the contingent remainders from being destroyed by a premature termination of B's life estate.

SECTION 22.   THE DESTRUCTIBILITY RULE TODAY

In the nineteenth century American courts generally accepted the English doctrine of destructibility as a part of the common law. Since conveyance by feoffment was rare, only a few cases dealt with destructibility resulting from forfeiture of the supporting life estate; but, in several states destruction by merger and by failure to vest at or before the normal expiration of the preceding life estate was held to be in effect. Yet there was a growing dissatisfaction with the rule. The original reasons for the rule bore little relation to contemporary property concepts. The feudal doctrine of the necessity of continuity of seisin and the prohibition of the creation of a freehold estate to commence in the future were devoid of practical significance in the nineteenth and twentieth centuries. More importantly, the rule operated to defeat the intention of the grantor or testator. In England a series of statutes commencing in 1845 abolished the destructibility rule. In the United States approximately one half of the states have enacted statutes abrogating the rule in whole or in part.[1] In a few jurisdictions there are decisions rejecting the rule without the aid of legislation.[2] Only in Florida, Oregon, Pennsylvania, and Tennessee do the cases recognize that the rule continues to exist. Since it is no longer the law that a life tenant who purports to convey a fee simple forfeits his life estate,[3]

---

[1] The statutes are collected in 1 American Law of Property, § 4.63, n. 1; Powell, Real Property, § 314; Simes & Smith, Future Interests, § 207. Some of these statutes do not in terms cover the situation of failure of the remainder to vest prior to the normal termination of the prior freehold estate.

[2] See e. g. Rouse v. Paidrick, 221 Ind. 517, 49 N.E.2d 528 (1943); Hayward v. Spaulding, 75 N.H. 92, 71 A. 219 (1908).

[3] In a few states forfeiture for tortious alienation is expressly abolished by statute. See e. g. Mass.Gen.Laws Ann. c. 184, § 9: "A conveyance by a

destructibility in these latter states will usually arise only from merger or on a failure of the contingent remainder to vest at or before the natural determination of the supporting life estate.[4] In about twelve states there are no decisions on the point and no legislation. The position taken by the Restatement of Property that contingent remainders are indestructible[5] may influence these uncommitted jurisdictions to reject the doctrine of destructibility.

SECTION 23. ALIENABILITY OF REMAINDERS

A vested remainder has always been considered an estate and, therefore, is as transferable by deed or by will as any similar possessory estate. If it is a remainder in fee simple it will descend on the death of the remainderman intestate to his heirs. A remainder vested subject to partial or complete divestment is as freely alienable as a remainder absolutely vested but remains subject after alienation to the divesting condition.

It was the accepted view at English common law that a contingent remainder was inalienable inter vivos except by fine or common recovery. The argument of champerty, which for so long made choses in action nonassignable, was advanced as a reason for the non-transferability inter vivos of this interest which was looked upon as a mere possibility or expectancy. Yet it was held that a contingent remainder was releasable to the

tenant for life or years which purports to grant a greater estate than he possesses or can lawfully convey shall not work a forfeiture of his estate but shall pass to the grantee all the estate which such tenant can lawfully convey."

[4] In some states there are statutes providing for forfeiture of the life estate where the life tenant commits waste. See e. g. Mass.Gen.Laws Ann. c. 242, §§ 1, 2. In a state retaining the destructibility rule contingent remainders dependent on the forfeited life estate would seem to be destroyed.

[5] § 240. The comments on this section of the Restatement set out the English and American historical background. It should be mentioned that the destructibility rule does not apply to equitable contingent remainders or to legal contingent remainders in terms for years or in personal property. These interests do not involve the concept of seisin.

holder of the possessory estate or to the person whose interest would be divested by the happening of the contingency. In 1845 contingent remainders were made alienable in England by statute.

The earlier American cases followed the English rule of the non-alienability of contingent remainders. But at the present time contingent remainders are freely alienable in the great majority of the states.[1] In more than half of the American jurisdictions this result is reached by statute. These statutes are not uniform in scope. Some of them provide that "expectant estates" are as alienable as estates in possession;[2] others declare that "future interests" are alienable;[3] and others specify that certain types of contingent remainders are alienable.[4] Even in the absence of statute in all but a handful of jurisdictions the courts have held such interests freely transferable inter vivos.[5] And it is probable that in all states contingent remainders are transferable by way of estoppel and specifically enforceable contract. Thus, if the owner of the contingent remainder conveys his interest by warranty deed, or other deed containing representations of title, and the contingency later happens, the after-acquired title of the grantor will inure to the grantee by estoppel.[6] So also, if the contingent remainderman for consideration contracts to convey his interest courts of equity will grant specific performance of the contract when the remainder vests.

[1] The Restatement of Property declares that all remainders and executory interests are transferable by ordinary conveyance. § 162.

[2] E. g. McKinney's N.Y.Real Property Law, § 59: "An expectant estate is descendible, devisable and alienable, in the same manner as an estate in possession."

[3] E. g. West's Ann.Cal.Civ.Code § 699.

[4] E. g. Mass.Gen.Laws Ann. c. 184, § 2 (descendible contingent remainders made assignable).

[5] For a full treatment of the topic of alienability, see 1 American Law of Property, §§ 4.64–4.67; 2 Powell, Real Property, §§ 283–292; Simes & Smith, Future Interests, §§ 1852–1859.

[6] See e. g. Smith v. Town of Groton, 147 Conn. 272, 160 A.2d 262 (1960) (estoppel based on quitclaim deed).

The courts agree that contingent remainders are releasable, and they are devisable and descendible subject to the contingency inhering in the interest.[7]

---

[7] For a discussion of other characteristics of remainders, such as protection against conduct of the life tenant and third persons, creditors' rights, partition, and representation in proceeding affecting the title, see 1 American Law of Property, §§ 4.78–4.117.

Chapter 6

THE RULE IN SHELLEY'S CASE AND THE DOCTRINE OF WORTHIER TITLE

There are two special rules relative to the creation of remainders that are of sufficient importance to call for separate treatment. The first is the Rule in Shelley's Case; the second is the Doctrine of Worthier Title.

A. THE RULE IN SHELLEY'S CASE

SECTION 1. STATEMENT OF THE RULE

The Rule in Shelley's Case may be stated in its simplest form as follows: If in a conveyance or a will a freehold estate is given to a person and in the same conveyance or will a remainder is limited to the heirs or to the heirs of the body of that person, that person takes both the freehold estate and the remainder.[1] The Rule takes its name from Shelley's Case,[2] the report of which contains the argument of counsel wherein the Rule was stated as follows: " . . . it is a rule in law, when the ancestor by any gift or conveyance takes an estate of freehold, and in the same gift or conveyance an estate is limited either mediately or immediately to his heirs in fee or in tail; that always in such cases, 'the heirs' are words of limitation of the estate, and not words of purchase."

The effect of the Rule is to convert what would otherwise be a remainder in the heirs or heirs of the body into a remainder

---

[1] For other statements of the Rule and a thorough discussion of its operation, see 1 American Law of Property, §§ 4.40–4.52; 3 Powell, Real Property, §§ 378–380; Simes & Smith, Future Interests, §§ 1541–1572; Restat.Prop., §§ 312, 313.

[2] 1 Co.Rep. 93b (1581).

in the ancestor. Thus, A conveys or devises land to B for life, and after B's death to the heirs of B. Apart from the Rule in Shelley's Case the state of the title would be: life estate in B, contingent remainder in fee simple in B's heirs, reversion in A in fee. But by virtue of the Rule the state of the title is: life estate in B, vested remainder in B in fee simple. The doctrine of merger will then cause B's life estate to coalesce with his remainder so that the ultimate result is that B gets a present estate in fee simple. So also, if A grants or devises to B for life, remainder to the heirs of B's body, by virtue of the Rule plus the operation of merger B, at common law, gets a present estate in fee tail. Under the Rule the limitations are treated as though they read: to B for life, remainder to B and the heirs of his body.

SECTION 2. ORIGIN AND DEVELOPMENT OF THE RULE

It may seem strange that the origin of, and the reasons for, one of the most famous rules in the entire field of real property law are not definitely known, yet the beginnings of the Rule are hidden in the obscurity of legal history. It is certain that the Rule did not originate in Shelley's Case. It was applied as early as 1366 in the Provost of Beverley's Case [1] and there are indications of its earlier existence. When the law of remainders was in its early stage of development a conveyance to B for life, then to the heirs of B would not seem greatly dissimilar from a conveyance to B and his heirs. Perhaps for that reason both kinds of conveyance were held effective to give B a fee simple. However that may be, the Rule had from the beginning a close connection with feudal tenure. It will be recalled that when an owner of land in fee simple died the lord of the fee was entitled to profitable incidents of tenure deriving from the descent to the heir. Depending on the type of tenure, the lord was entitled to primer seisin, relief or wardship and marriage. But these incidents would not attach if the heir took by purchase—as remainderman, for example. The Rule in Shelley's Case served

1 Y.B. 40 Ed.III, f9, 18.

to protect the feudal rights of the lord by taking the remainder away from the heir and giving it to the ancestor, thereby forcing the heir to take by descent if he was to take at all.[2]

This is well illustrated by the Provost of Beverley's Case.[3] In that case A gave lands to B for life, remainder to his son John and the latter's wife and the heirs of their bodies, and in default of such issue to the right heirs of B. B died, then John and his wife died leaving no issue. B's heir entered and thereupon the chief lord of the fee levied a distress to compel the heir to pay a relief. It was argued on behalf of the heir that he took by purchase under the conveyance and not by descent, hence was not liable to pay a relief. But the court held that the lord was entitled to a relief, one of the justices saying: "If the lease was made to your father for life with remainder to his right heirs then the father had the fee . . . and if you were under age the lord would have wardship and consequently relief."

The Rule had such hardy vitality that it survived in full force for many centuries after the conditions which gave it birth were only dimly discernible in history. It became "part and parcel of the law of England." When feudal conditions could no longer justify its existence, its continuance was assured by the inertia of precedent and the fact that it tended to increase the alienability of land. It was extended in scope so as to include equitable interests in land. But the Rule did not have a peaceful existence. A mass of literature grew up on the subject and a legion of cases, containing many fine distinctions, filled the reports. Lord Macnaghten eloquently described the situation as it existed about the beginning of the nineteenth century: "Things were not going well with the rule. Its feudal origin was a disgrace. Its antiquity was a reproach. Some judges thought that on those grounds it ought to be discountenanced. Then it was constantly made a matter of complaint that the rule disappointed the inten-

---

[2] The strong policy of the law in favor of protection of the lord's feudal dues is evidenced by a statute of 1267 making ineffective a feoffment to his eldest son by an owner in fee simple. 52 Hen.III, c. b.

[3] n. 1, supra.

tion, as if that were not its very end and purpose—as if it had not been at the outset 'levelled against the views of the parties.' It was always being disparaged, and what was perhaps worse, it was always being explained. It led to profound discussions and some very pretty quarrels." [4] Yet the Rule persisted in England until abolished by the Law of Property Act, 1925.[5]

In the United States the Rule was almost universally accepted by the courts as an integral part of the common law. Here, as in England, it had its critics and its defenders but only in Hawaii, Kentucky and Vermont did the courts refuse to recognize the Rule. The great majority of the courts held, in accordance with the English view, that it was a positive rule of law, not a rule of construction, that is, that its operation did not depend on the intention of the conveyor or testator but would apply, if its requirements were satisfied, regardless of the transferor's intention. Indeed, an express declaration in the instrument that no more than a life estate is intended to be given to the ancestor, or that the heirs shall take as purchasers, will not prevent the ancestor from also taking the remainder under the Rule.[6] In one respect a few of the American courts extended the scope of the Rule beyond its English boundaries—they applied it to interests in personal property. And occasionally, the Rule was said

[4] Van Gruten v. Foxwell, (1897) App.Cas. 658. One of these "pretty" quarrels arose between Lord Mansfield, Chief Justice of the King's Bench, and the conveyancing bar over Mansfield's decision (1770) in the famous case of Perrin v. Blake, 1 Coll.Jur. 318 (1791). Mansfield held that the Rule would not apply where the testator made it clear that he intended the devisee to take only a life estate even though there was a further limitation of a remainder to the heirs of his body. His decision was reversed in the Exchequer Chamber. 1 W.Bl. 672, 96 Eng.Rep. 392 (1772). It thus became settled that the intention of the grantor or testator that the ancestor should take no more than a life estate would not prevent the application of the Rule. Charles Fearne, a conveyancer, published the first edition of his work on Contingent Remainders for the purpose of exposing the "heresies" in the opinion of Lord Mansfield.

[5] 15 & 16 Geo.V, c. 20, § 131.

[6] Bishop v. Williams, 221 Ark. 617, 225 S.W.2d 171 (1953); Wilson v. Harrold, 288 Ill. 388, 123 N.E. 563 (1919); Sybert v. Sybert, 152 Tex. 106, 254 S.W. 2d 999 (1953).

to apply to chattels by analogy as a rule of construction. But most American courts have confined its application to interests in land.[7] The nineteenth century witnessed the Rule's period of ascendancy. As we shall see, legislation in the great majority of states has made the Rule a doctrine of declining importance in American law.

SECTION 3. OPERATION OF THE RULE

The Rule in Shelley's Case operates only on the remainder given to the heirs of the ancestor. It in no way affects or disturbs the freehold estate given to the ancestor. Thus, in the simple case of A conveying to B for life, then to the heirs of B, the Rule leaves undisturbed the life estate given to B but converts what would be a contingent remainder in B's heirs into a vested remainder in B himself. A freehold estate in the ancestor is an indispensable pre-requisite for the application of the Rule but in the application of the Rule the remainder alone is affected.

The application of the Rule may or may not result in a merger of the freehold and the remainder. The effect of the Rule may be to create a situation to which the doctrine of merger will apply (as in the case of a devise to B for life, remainder to B's heirs) but the Rule itself is entirely independent of that doctrine. It will apply even though a vested estate be interposed between the freehold and the remainder. Thus, in the Provost of Beverley's Case the Rule was applied where the limitations were to B for life, remainder to B's son and his wife in fee tail, remainder to the heirs of B. The interposition of the vested estate would prevent a merger of the freehold and the remainder but the Rule will nevertheless operate on the remainder. So also, if a contingent remainder be interposed between the ancestor's freehold and the remainder to the heirs there will be no merger but the Rule applies. Thus, A devises to B for life, remainder to C

[7] The Restatement asserts that the Rule applies only to transfers of interests in land. § 312(3), Comm. b. For a collection of cases, see Simes & Smith, Future Interests, § 367.

for life if C marries, remainder to the heirs of B. The state of the title would be: life estate in B, contingent remainder for life in C, vested remainder in B in fee simple. If C predeceases B there will then be a merger. So also, if B conveys his entire interest to a third person C's contingent remainder would be destroyed (apart from statutes abolishing destructibility of contingent remainders) and a merger would result so as to give the third person a fee simple.

In order for the Rule to apply the following requirements must be satisfied: 1. there must be a freehold estate given to the ancestor; 2. by the same instrument a remainder must be limited to the heirs or to the heirs of the body of the ancestor; 3. the freehold and the remainder must be of the same quality, that is, both legal or both equitable. As to the first requirement, in the American cases the freehold is invariably a life estate although under the classic English view the freehold estate could be a fee tail. The life estate may be one pur autre vie as well as for the ancestor's own life. And it may be a defeasible life estate. Thus, A conveys to B for life or until she remarries, then to the heirs of B. By the operation of the Rule plus the effect of merger B gets a present estate in fee simple. The life estate need not be one in possession.[1] Thus, A devises to B for life, then to C for life, remainder to the heirs of C. The Rule operates to convert the remainder in the heirs of C into a vested remainder in C. There will be a merger and the end result will be: life estate in B, vested remainder in C in fee.

The requirement of a life estate in the ancestor is satisfied where the life estate is one held in co-tenancy with another. Thus, A conveys to B and C for their lives as tenants in common,

[1] If the life estate limited to the ancestor expires before the instrument takes effect does the Rule apply? Thus, A devises to B for life then to the heirs of B. B predeceases A and the life estate lapses. Illinois has held that the Rule applies, hence the heirs of B do not take under the will. Lydick v. Tate, 380 Ill. 616, 44 N.E.2d 583, 145 A.L.R. 1216 (1942); Belleville Savings Bank v. Aneshaensel, 298 Ill. 292, 131 N.E. 682 (1921). The Restatement takes the position that since there is no life estate in the ancestor the Rule does not apply. § 312, Comm. c. For arguments pro and con, see Simes & Smith, Future Interests, § 1561.

remainder to the heirs of B. The Rule operates on the remainder so as to give B a remainder in fee simple. The cases seem to hold that B takes the whole remainder in fee simple.[2] The Restatement takes the position that where B has only a one half interest in the estate for life he should be held to take only a one half interest in the remainder, the other half interest in the remainder going to B's heirs as purchasers.[3] Under this view, the Rule operates on the remainder only to the same extent as the fractional interest of the ancestor in the life estate.

The second requirement for the operation of the Rule, that the same instrument which creates the life estate must also limit a remainder to the heirs or heirs of the body of the life tenant, prevents the Rule from applying when the future interest given to the heirs is an executory interest. Thus, A conveys to B for life, and one year after B's death to the heirs of B. Because of the gap following B's life estate the interest limited to the heirs of B is an executory interest, not a remainder, and the Rule is not applicable.

Most of the difficulties arising in the application of the Rule involve the question whether the remainder which has been limited in the instrument is a remainder to the heirs or heirs of the body of the ancestor. Where the conveyance or devise gives a life estate to B and then a remainder "to the heirs of B" or "to the heirs of B's body" and the quoted words are used without qualification it is clear enough that the Rule applies. But frequently the conveyor or testator, instead of using the standard formula, will use language which may or may not be substantially

---

[2] The leading case is Bails v. Davis, 241 Ill. 536, 89 N.E. 706 (1909). The conveyance was to B and C "during their natural lives and after their death to the heirs of said" B. The court said that B and C took an estate as tenants in common during their joint lives with a remainder in fee in B. Thus, C had a life estate in an undivided half interest and B had a present fee simple in an undivided half interest plus a remainder in fee in the other half interest. Cf. Powell, Real Property, § 379.

[3] § 312, Comm. r. The Restatement agrees that the Rule operates on the entire remainder where the life estate is limited to B and C as joint tenants or tenants by the entirety since each tenant is seised of the whole life estate.

equivalent. The court, therefore, is confronted with a preliminary problem of construction. Before it can determine the applicability of the Rule, it must first construe the language of the particular limitation to ascertain its meaning. The English courts took the view that in order to satisfy the requirements of the Rule the remainder must be limited to heirs or heirs of the body of the ancestor as a class taking in succession from generation to generation. It was not sufficient that the remainder be limited to that person or persons who at the moment of B's death would be his heir. This view was undoubtedly a product of the English system of descent under which there could be only one heir in each generation. Primogeniture cast the descent on the eldest male; where the descent was to females they took together as one heir. It was natural, therefore, to view the requirement of a remainder to "heirs" as meaning something more than a remainder to the individual or individuals who would inherit in the first generation. Thus, in Archer's Case [4] the Rule was held not to apply where land was devised to B for life, with remainder to the next heir male of B and the heirs male of the body of such next heir male. Here the remainder was neither to heirs generally nor to heirs who were lineal descendants.

Some of the American courts have adopted the English view that the remainder must be limited to heirs or heirs of the body of the ancestor from generation to generation in an indefinite line of succession. Under this view the Rule does not apply if the remainder is limited to those persons who on the death of the ancestor intestate will inherit his real property.[5] But the weight of American authority rejects this technical meaning given to the words "heirs" or "heirs of the body" by the English courts and

---

[4] 1 Coke 66b, 76 E.R. 146 (1597).

[5] See e. g. Taylor v. Cleary, 29 Gratt. 448 (Va.1877). The conveyance was to B for life and after his death to such person or persons as shall at that time answer the description of heir or heirs at law of said B "and such person or persons shall take the said land under that description as purchasers under and by virtue of this deed, and not by inheritance as heirs of the said" B.

holds that the Rule operates where the remainder is limited to those persons who would be the heirs of the life tenant at the time of his death.[6] Thus, A conveys land in State X to B for life, and after B's decease to such person or persons as may be entitled to inherit real estate from him by virtue of the statutes of State X. B takes a fee simple.[7]

Whichever view is adopted as to the meaning of the requirement that the remainder must be one to the heirs or heirs of the body of the life tenant, difficult problems of construction may arise when the draftsman of the instrument substitutes other words for the standard formula or adds words to it. The following illustrations are suggestive of some of the problems: 1. A devises to B for life, then to his heir during its life;[8] 2. to B for life, then to his children and their heirs;[9] 3. to B for life, remainder to his heir;[10] 4. to B for life, then to his heirs in fee simple;[11] 5. to B for life, then to his heirs of blood;[12] 6. to B for life, then to the heirs of his body, their heirs and assigns;[13]

---

[6] Accord, Restat.Prop., § 312, Comm. f, g. The Restatement calls this the "American rule". For an extensive discussion, see Simes & Smith, Future Interests, § 1548.

[7] See e. g. People v. Emery, 314 Ill. 220, 145 N.E. 349 (1924). But compare the language of the same court in Bails v. Davis, 241 Ill. 536, 89 N.E. 706 (1909).

[8] The Rule does not apply. Bennett v. Morris, 5 Rawle 9 (Pa.1834).

[9] The Rule does not apply unless from the context it appears that the word "children" was used in the sense of heirs. Hough v. Farmers Bank & Trust Co., 359 Pa. 555, 60 A.2d 11 (1948) (to B for life, then to her children, share and share alike or heirs at law; Rule applies).

[10] The Rule applies, apparently on the theory that the singular word includes the plural.

[11] Most courts hold that the Rule applies. For a collection of cases, see Simes & Smith, Future Interests, § 1549, n. 77.

[12] The Rule has been held not applicable. Cahill v. Cahill, 402 Ill. 416, 84 N.E.2d 380 (1949). The court based its decision on the ground that the remainder was not to heirs generally of the life tenant but to a restricted class of heirs which would not include all persons who would inherit as heirs under the statute of descent, for example, a widow or adopted child of the life tenant.

[13] There are decisions both ways in this situation. See e. g. Sybert v. Sybert, 152 Tex. 106, 254 S.W.2d 999 (1953) (to B for life only and after his death

7.   to B for life then to his issue.[14]

At times the question has arisen whether the Rule applies when the remainder to the heirs or heirs of the body is subject to a condition precedent in addition to the contingency arising from the fact that the remaindermen are unascertained. Thus, A conveys to B for life, and after B's decease to his wife, C, and her heirs if C survives B, and if she does not survive B then to the heirs of B. The Rule is generally held to apply. The state of the title is: life estate in B, contingent remainder in C in fee, alternative contingent remainder in B in fee, reversion in A in fee. There will be no merger of B's life estate and his contingent remainder. But if C predeceases B the remainder in B will vest and there will then be a merger of B's two estates.

The third requisite for the operation of the Rule, that the life estate in the ancestor and the remainder to the heirs or heirs of the body must both be legal or both equitable, may create a problem when the conveyance is in trust. If A transfers to T for the life of B in trust for B for life, and on B's death the property to belong absolutely to the heirs of B, the Rule will not apply. Here there is an equitable life estate in B and a legal remainder in B's heirs since the duration of the trust is limited to B's life. But suppose that the conveyance is to T in trust for B for life, and on B's death the trustee to convey to the heirs of B. Is the remainder legal or equitable? The majority of courts have held that the direction to the trustee to convey to the heirs imposes an active duty on him so that the trust continues until the conveyance. Therefore, the remainder as well as the life estate is equitable and the Rule applies.[15]

to vest in fee simple in the heirs of his body; Rule applies); Aetna Life Insurance Co. v. Hoppin, 214 F. 928 (C.C.A.7th, 1914) (to B for life, then to the heirs of the body of B, their heirs and assigns; Rule does not apply).

14 It is usually held that the Rule applies, the word "issue" being construed as meaning "heirs of the body." Restat.Prop., § 312, Comm. g. Cf. Baker v. Forsuman, 15 Ill.2d 353, 155 N.E.2d 24 (1958). As to the effect on the Rule of statutes abolishing the fee tail and substituting some other estate, see Simes & Smith, Future Interests, § 1569.

15 Restat.Prop., § 312, Comm. h. See Burnham v. Baltimore Gas & Electric Co., 217 Md. 507, 144 A.2d 80 (1958).

SECTION 4. THE RULE IN MODERN LAW

Mr. Justice Holmes once said: "It is revolting to have no better reason for a rule of law than that so it was laid down in the time of Henry IV. It is still more revolting if the grounds upon which it was laid down have vanished long since, and the rule simply persists from blind imitation of the past." [1] This criticism is strikingly applicable to the Rule in Shelley's Case. The Rule is a troublesome anachronism that has no substantial justification for its continued existence. The only argument that can be advanced in favor of its retention is that it makes land more freely alienable but it does this by defeating the intention of the conveyor or testator. Moreover, the argument of freer alienability in this context would seem to be inconsistent with the present trend of the law towards making contingent remainders indestructible. The Rule has produced a mass of litigation. It operates as a trap for the unwary testator or attorney. A skilled draftsman can easily circumvent the Rule by creating a non-freehold estate in the ancestor or by giving to the heirs an executory interest instead of a remainder. Thus, A devises to B for 100 years if B so long live, then to the heirs of B; or, A devises to B for life, and one day after B's death to the heirs of B.

Such considerations as these have led the legislatures in almost two-thirds of the states to abrogate the Rule. In thirty-six states and the District of Columbia statutes have abolished the Rule either wholly or in part.[2] In some states the wording of the statute is such as not to cover explicitly all situations to which the Rule might be applicable and a question may arise as to the scope of the statute.[3] Normally, the effect of a statute abolishing the

---

[1] Holmes, The Path of the Law, 10 Harv.L.Rev. 457, 469 (1897).

[2] For a collection of these statutes, see 1 American Law of Property, § 4.51; 3 Powell, Real Property, § 380; Simes & Smith, Future Interests, § 1563.

[3] See e. g. Fla.Stat.Ann. § 689.17. The Illinois statute is a model of effective simplicity. It provides: "The rule of property known as the rule in Shelley's Case is abolished." Ill.Smith-Hurd Ann.Stat. c. 30, § 186. It is said that Mr. Justice Holmes **as a young man** sought the advice of Ralph

Rule is to give a life estate to the ancestor and a contingent remainder to the heirs but this is not universally true.[4] A few of the abrogating statutes are of relatively recent enactment and since they do not apply to instruments taking effect prior to the operative dates of the statutes it will be many years before the Rule will become, in those states, purely a matter of legal history.   In Illinois, for example, the Rule was not abolished until 1953.[5] In states where the legislature has not afforded relief the courts and the profession must continue to struggle with the intricacies of the Rule.   At the present time the Rule still exists in Arkansas, Colorado, Delaware, Indiana, North Carolina and Texas.

B. THE DOCTRINE OF THE WORTHIER TITLE

SECTION 5.   STATEMENT OF THE DOCTRINE

At English common law a man could not either by conveyance or by devise limit a fee simple to his own heirs.   The heirs of the transferor were not permitted to take as purchasers under the conveyance or will and the attempted limitation was void.   Let us consider this statement first with respect to wills, and then with respect to inter vivos conveyances.   Where a will devised to the heirs of the testator an estate of the same kind and quality as the heirs would have taken by descent if the devisor had died intestate the heirs were required to take by descent instead of by purchase.   Thus, A, owner of land in fee simple, devises it to B for life, then to the heirs of A.   The remainder to the heirs of A

Waldo Emerson in connection with a paper he was writing on a difficult subject.   Emerson cautioned him: "When you shoot at a king you cannot afford to miss."   Illinois took no chance of missing.   The Rule was indeed a king in the realm of property law.

4 See Moore v. Littel, 41 N.Y. 66 (1869).   This case is discussed in c. 5, § 20, supra.

5 It should be mentioned that in Illinois, throughout the years, draftsmen of wills and deeds have shown a remarkable propensity to play tag with the Rule in Shelley's Case.

is void as such and they take the reversion by descent. So also, if land was devised to a designated person who turned out to be the testator's heir that person took by descent, not by devise. Thus, A devises land "to my son John and his heirs." At A's death John is his heir. John takes the land by descent, not as purchaser under the will. It will be noted that the rule in its application to wills determined the character or manner in which the heir took the land.

The rule in its application to inter vivos transfers came to this: a conveyor cannot create a remainder in his own heirs. Lord Coke expressed it as follows: "If a man makes a gift in taile or a lease for life, the remainder to his own right heires, this remainder is void, and he hath the reversion in him   .   .   ." [1] In the case of a conveyance the effect of the rule is to convert what would otherwise be a contingent remainder in the heirs of the conveyor into a reversion in the conveyor himself. Thus, A conveys to B for life, and after B's death to the heirs of A. By virtue of the rule the state of the title is: life estate in B, reversion in fee simple in A. In its application to conveyances the rule prevents the heir from taking under the conveyance. In fact, the heir may never take because of the ancestor's power to transfer the reversion to a third person by conveyance or by devise.

This rule, or combination of rules, became known in American law as the worthier title doctrine. The rule in its testamentary aspect required the heir to take by descent rather than by devise and title by descent was said to be "worthier" or better than a title derived by purchase for the reason that a descent of lands from a disseisor to his heir barred the right of entry of the person disseised (but not the right of action), whereas if the title were acquired by purchase the disseisee's entry was not barred.[2]

---

[1] Co.Litt. 22b. Coke went on to give a specious explanation for the rule: "for the ancestor during his life beareth in his body (in judgment of law) all his heirs, and therefore it is truly said that *haeres est pars antecessoris.*" Professor Thorne has pointed out that Coke was adept at inventing a maxim to fit the occasion. Thorne, Sir Edward Coke 7 (Selden Society Lecture, 1957).

[2] In the leading case of Ellis v. Page, 7 Cush. 161 (Mass.1851) the court said: "It is a well settled rule of real property, that a limitation to an heir in a

At times it has been objected that it is inappropriate to label as the worthier title doctrine the rule prohibiting a conveyor from creating a remainder in his own heirs on the ground that in this situation the rule does not force the heir to take by descent but prevents him from taking at all unless, perchance, the conveyor later dies intestate still owning the land.[3] But both aspects of the rule, or the two rules if you prefer, had a common origin and a common purpose in feudal society, and modern courts and writers usually apply the same term to both types of transactions. The two aspects of the rule are often differentiated by referring to one as the testamentary branch of the worthier title doctrine and to the other as the inter vivos branch of the doctrine.

SECTION 6.   ORIGIN OF THE DOCTRINE

It is highly probable that the same considerations which led to the development of the Rule in Shelley's case also shaped the doctrine of the worthier title in both its testamentary and inter vivos aspects. Feudal policy dictated that the incidents of tenure accruing to the lord on the death of the tenant should not be evaded. At the time, feudal policy was public policy and the feudal estate tax must be paid. The incidents of relief, wardship and marriage accrued to the lord on the descent of the fee but not where the fee was acquired by purchase; hence, the necessity of rules requiring the heir to take by descent and not by purchase. A thirteenth century statute made void, as against the

devise is void, and that the heir cannot be a purchaser; Co.Litt. 22b; or, to state the rule more fully, if a man devises by his will his land to his heir at law and his heirs, in such case the devise, as such is void and the heir will take by descent and not by purchase, for the reason that the title by descent is the worthier and better title, by taking away the entry of those who might have a right in the land."

3 See Warren, Remainder to the Grantor's Heirs, 22 Tex.L.Rev. 22 (1943). In the fifteenth and earlier centuries inter vivos transfers of land were much less frequent than in later centuries; and land was devisable only in a few areas by special custom. Therefore, under those conditions the rule forbidding a remainder to the heirs of the conveyor would normally result in the heir taking by descent on the later death of his ancestor.

lord of the fee, a feoffment (conveyance) by the tenant to his eldest son, who was his heir apparent.[1] In the next century when the law of remainders was being developed a rule prohibiting the limitation of a remainder to the heirs of the conveyor would seem a natural corollary. And a devise by a tenant to his own heir would be too obvious an evasion of the lord's seignorial rights to be tolerated.

But the doctrine survived and flourished long after wardship and marriage had been abolished and the incidents of tenure had become inconsequential. The wills branch of the doctrine, in particular, had important results since it affected the course of descent of land and the rights of creditors of the testator. Descent was traced from the last purchaser and if the heir took by descent he would not be a stock or root of descent for subsequent inheritance by collaterals. Certain creditors of the testator could reach the land in the hands of the heir taking by descent but not in the hands of a devisee. The cases applied the doctrine in both of its branches as a positive rule of law but restricted its application to real property only.[2] But by the nineteenth century it was felt that the doctrine had outlived whatever utility it formerly had and it was totally abrogated by Parliament in 1833.[3]

---

[1] This was the Statute of Fraudulent Feoffments. 52 Hen. III, c. 6 (1267). For the text of the statute, see Pickering, Statutes at Large 59–60. With the abolition of wardship and marriage by the Statute of Tenures (12 Car. II, c. 24) in 1660 the statute became a dead letter although it was not formally repealed until 1863. 26 & 27 Vict. c. 125. For Tudor legislation designed to prevent evasion of the tenurial incidents, see 34 & 35 Hen. VIII, c. V, § 15 (1542–3).

[2] The earliest cases thus far uncovered are from the second half of the sixteenth century but it is highly unlikely that the doctrine originated at that relatively late time. The English cases are collected in Morris, The Inter Vivos Branch of the Worthier Title Doctrine, 2 Okl.L.Rev. 133 (1949); Morris, The Wills Branch of the Worthier Title Doctrine, 54 Mich.L.Rev. 451 (1956).

[3] 3 & 4 Will.IV, c. 106, § 3.

SECTION 7. THE DOCTRINE IN AMERICAN LAW

In a substantial number of states the worthier title doctrine in both of its branches has been recognized and accepted as a part of the common law. But the two branches of the rule have had a different course of development in American law and, therefore, must be considered separately.

SECTION 8. THE TESTAMENTARY BRANCH OF THE DOCTRINE

Most of the cases applying the testamentary or wills branch of the doctrine arose in the nineteenth century and in the early part of the present century. As usually formulated by the courts the rule was stated to be that where a devise to the heirs purports to give them an estate of the same quantity and quality as they would have taken by descent in the absence of a will then the heirs must take by descent and not under the will. The rule applied whether the estate given to the heir was a present or a future interest and whether given to the heir by name or under the form of a limitation to the heirs of the testator. The English concept of quantity referred to the type of estate devised to the heir but some American courts refused to apply the rule where the heir would have taken by descent a different share or proportion of the testator's estate.[1] But rule was held to be applicable where the devise gave the heir an equitable interest under a trust. In a very few jurisdictions the doctrine was expanded to include bequests of personal property to the next of kin.[2]

At the present time it will usually make no difference whether the person who takes an interest in the estate of the testator takes in the capacity of heir or of devisee. Therefore, the in-

[1] For an excellent discussion of the "same quantity and quality" concept in American law, see Morris, The Wills Branch of the Worthier Title Doctrine, 54 Mich.L.Rev. 451, 488–491 (1956).

[2] See e. g. In re Warren's Estate, 211 Iowa 940, 234 N.W. 835 (1931); Parsons v. Winslow, 6 Mass. 169 (1810).

stances in which the question of the applicability of the wills branch of the doctrine can arise are relatively rare.[3] And on principle, there should be no difference in legal consequences in any case. The Restatement of Property takes the advanced position that the wills branch of the doctrine is no longer a part of American law.[4] Whether this is an accurate statement of existing law or only "a consummation devoutly to be wished" is open to some question.[5] The doctrine would seem to have a slumbering or potential existence in many jurisdictions. In a few states (California, Illinois, Kansas, Minnesota, and Nebraska) it has been abolished by statute.

SECTION 9.   THE INTER VIVOS BRANCH OF THE DOCTRINE

If the wills branch of the doctrine is a moribund rule (with the Restatement administering the *coup de grace*), the inter vivos branch, by contrast, plays a vigorous and important role in mod-

[3] In some states there are still a few situations where under the local statutes the course of descent of property depends upon whether it was acquired by the decedent by inheritance or by purchase. See Morris, *op. cit.* n. 1 at 470. A second area of possible significance of the wills branch of the doctrine exists in connection with the marshalling of assets of the estate of a decedent. If the assets are not sufficient for the payment of debts, legacies and expenses, intestate realty and personalty must be sacrificed before resorting to the property passing under the will. Hence, if a devise to the heir is void and he takes by intestacy his interests may be adversely affected. **Ellis v. Page,** 7 Cush. 161 (Mass.1851); cf. Biederman v. Seymour, 3 Beav. 368, 49 Eng.Rep. 144 (1840). See Restat.Prop., § 314(2) Comm. j.

[4] § 314(2).

[5] Recent cases recognizing the wills branch of the doctrine are: McNeilly v. Wylie, 389 Ill. 391, 59 N.E.2d 811 (1945); National Shawmut Bank v. Joy, 315 Mass. 457, 53 N.E.2d 113 (1944) (dictum); Cordon v. Gregg, 164 Or. 306, 101 P.2d 414 (1940); Braswell v. Braswell, 195 Va. 971, 81 S.E.2d 560 (1954) (dictum). In his article on the subject Morris lists cases from twenty-one jurisdictions recognizing the doctrine and cases from only two jurisdictions (Kentucky and Georgia) repudiating the doctrine. 54 Mich.L.Rev. 451, 486–487. Connecticut may also reject it. See Phoenix State Bank & Trust Co. v. Buckalew, 15 Conn.Super. 149 (1947).

ern law.[1] The earlier American cases, following the English precedents, applied the doctrine as a positive rule of law applicable normally only to conveyances of realty. From the relatively simple rule that a grantor cannot limit a remainder to his own heirs the doctrine has evolved into a rule of construction applicable to the limitation by inter vivos transfer of an interest in real property to the heirs of the transferor or of an interest in personal property to his next of kin. The point of departure came in the landmark case of Doctor v. Hughes.[2] In that case A conveyed real property to T in trust to pay the income therefrom to the settlor (A) for life, and upon his death "to convey the said premises (if not sold) to the heirs at law of" A. The settlor, who was still living, had two daughters one of whom conveyed to her husband all of her interest in the trust property. A judgment creditor of this daughter and her husband brought an action to reach the interest alleged to have been given the daughter under the trust. The court held that the limitation to the heirs of the settlor operated as a retention of a reversion in the settlor, not as a remainder to the heirs, and, therefore, the daughter took no interest under the trust. Although the court, speaking through Cardozo, J., applied the doctrine of worthier title it did so on the basis that the settlor actually intended to retain a reversion and thereby control the disposition of the principal of the trust property rather than to create a remainder and confer an interest on his heirs apparent. In the course of his opinion Judge Cardozo stated: "We do not say that the ancient rule survives as an absolute prohibition limiting the power of the grantor. At the outset, probably, like the rule in Shelley's Case, it was a rule, not of construction, but of property . . . But at least the ancient rule survives to this extent: That, to transform into a remainder what would ordinarily be a reversion, the intention

---

[1] Professor Edward H. Warren, a master of the vivid phrase, in objecting to the inter vivos branch being bracketed with the wills branch under the name "doctrine of the worthier title" asked: "Why tie a bull-pup to the tail of a dead cat?" 22 Tex.L.Rev. 22, 28 (1943).

[2] 225 N.Y. 305, 122 N.E. 221 (1919).

to work the transformation must be clearly expressed. Here there is no clear expression of such purpose."

The decision in Doctor v. Hughes gave new strength and a new direction to the doctrine in American law. The importance of the court and the eminence of the judge who wrote the opinion gave the rule a prominence it had hitherto lacked; [3] and changing the rule from a positive rule of law to one of construction appeared to have the merit of effectuating the intention of the grantor. As a consequence, most courts have since followed the lead of New York and have accepted the doctrine as a rule of construction.[4] In substance, then, the rule has the effect of creating a rebuttable presumption that when a conveyor limits a remainder to his own heirs, in the case of realty, or to his next of kin in the case of personalty, he intends to retain an indefeasible reversion and not to create a remainder in the heirs or next of kin. This presumption will yield to the manifestation of a contrary intent.[5]

[3] Prior to Cardozo's opinion in Doctor v. Hughes there are not a few instances where courts dealt with limitations to the heirs of the grantor without referring to the worthier title doctrine. For instance, the lower New York court's opinion in Doctor v. Hughes gives no indication that the court was aware of the applicability of the doctrine. 174 App.Div. 767, 161 N.Y.S. 634. Another example is Sands v. Old Colony Trust Co., 195 Mass. 575, 81 N.E. 300 (1907).

[4] The influence of Doctor v. Hughes is evident in such cases as National Shawmut Bank v. Joy, 315 Mass. 457, 53 N.E.2d 113 (1944) and McKenna v. Seattle-First Nat. Bank, 35 Wash.2d 662, 214 P.2d 664 (1950).

[5] The Restatement of Property states the modern rule as follows: "When a person makes an otherwise effective inter vivos conveyance of an interest in land to his heirs, or of an interest in things other than land, to his next of kin, then, unless a contrary intent is found from additional language or circumstances, such conveyance to his heirs or next of kin is a nullity in the sense that it designates neither a conveyee nor the type of interest of a conveyee." § 314(1). The justification for the rule is stated to be that "it represents the probable intention of the average conveyor" who in making a gift in remainder to his own heirs "seldom intends to create an indestructible interest in those persons who take his property by intestacy, but intends the same thing as if he had given the remainder 'to my estate'." Comm. a. (Copyright 1940. Reprinted with permission of The American Law Institute.)

But the rule in its modern form has not had a happy existence in the state of its origin. As a rule of construction it has proved difficult of application and the numerous New York cases involving the doctrine have been marked by inconsistency and confusion.[6] The problem most frequently has arisen in connection with transfers in trust. Thus, A transfers stocks and bonds to a bank or trust company in trust to pay the income to A for life, and at A's death to distribute the principal to A's next of kin as though A had died intestate. The question whether A has retained an indefeasible reversion or has created a remainder can become important in several situations.[7] For example, A may later change his mind and desire to revoke the trust even though no power to revoke was reserved in the trust instrument. It is well established that the settlor (creator) may revoke the trust with the consent of all persons beneficially interested therein. If the limitation to the next of kin amounts to the retention of a reversion in A there is no one beneficially interested except A and he can revoke. But if it is found that A intended to create a remainder in his next of kin their consent to the revocation will be necessary; and if the living next of kin are minor children they have no power to consent to the termination of the trust.[8]

Although in Doctor v. Hughes [9] Cardozo, J. spoke of the necessity of a "clear expression" of an intention by the grantor "to transform into a remainder what would ordinarily be a reversion" later New York cases have indicated a readiness to find an intent to create a remainder in circumstances where the grantor's intention is at best doubtful. The strong presumption in favor of a reversion formulated by Judge Cardozo was gradu-

---

[6] 3 Powell, Real Property, § 381.

[7] If it is found that A has a reversion his creditors can reach this interest; and A can transfer his reversion by deed or will.

[8] Many of the New York cases have arisen from an attempt by the settlor of a trust to terminate it. In that state the termination of a trust "upon the written consent of all the persons beneficially interested in" the trust property is provided for by statute. McKinney's N.Y.Personal Property Law, § 23; McKinney's N.Y.Real Property Law, § 118.

[9] n. 2 supra.

ally diluted into a rather weak constructional preference for a reversion.[10] In Whittemore v. Equitable Trust Co.[11] it was held that the trust could not be terminated by the settlor because of a found intent to create a remainder. In that case three settlors transferred certain bonds in trust, the income to be paid to B and C during their lives and at the death of the surviving life beneficiary the property to be returned to the settlors in equal shares if living; but if any be dead his share to be paid to such persons as such deceased settlor should by his will appoint, and in default of appointment to such persons as would be entitled thereto if the settlor had been the owner thereof at his death and had died intestate. In finding an intention of the settlors to create a remainder in the next of kin the court seems to have relied on the fact that the settlors made a "rather full and formal disposition of the principal of the trust estate" in case they died before the life beneficiaries, and also on the fact that they reserved a power of disposition "only by will." [12] In later cases the New York Court of Appeals has attempted, with qualified success, to state the factors deemed to be significant in determining the intention of the settlor.[13] Not the least of the factors

[10] "It is clear from the cases in this state since Doctor v. Hughes, supra, . . . that, despite the language in that opinion that a reversion exists unless there is clear evidence to the contrary, the rule has been less limited in application . . . While we have not yet adopted a rule, either by statute or judicial construction, under which language limiting an interest to heirs is unequivocally given its full effect, the presumption which exists from the use of the common law doctrine as a rule of construction has lost much of its force since Doctor v. Hughes, supra." Matter of Burchell, 299 N.Y. 351, 359, 87 N.E.2d 293, 297 (1949).

[11] 250 N.Y. 298, 165 N.E. 454 (1929).

[12] But compare City Bank Farmers Trust Co. v. Miller, 278 N.Y. 134, 15 N.E.2d 553 (1938). In this case the trust agreement provided for weekly payments to the settlor of specified amounts from income and principal until the principal was reduced to $5000 and in that event the principal was to be returned to the settlor. On the settlor's death the trust property was to be paid as the settlor should by her will appoint, and in default of appointment to the persons entitled to take as her intestate successors. The court held the trust agreement gave rise to a reversion, not a remainder.

[13] In Richardson v. Richardson, 298 N.Y. 135, 81 N.E.2d 54 (1948) the court stated: "To summarize, therefore, we believe that the settlor evidenced her

indicating an intention to create a remainder, according to the court, is the reservation by the settlor of a testamentary power of appointment of the principal without the retention of any other power of disposition of the corpus of the trust estate.[14] Perhaps the clearest conclusion to be drawn from these cases is that there is no reliable standard of predictability of the court's action in the reversion-remainder situation. However, the New York legislature has afforded partial relief. In 1951 it amended the statutes regulating the power of the settlor to revoke an inter vivos trust by providing that, for the purpose of determining revocability, a limitation contained in a trust in favor of heirs or next of kin of the settlor does not create a beneficial interest in such persons.[15] Although the amendatory statute has been of substantial assistance in the trust termination situation it leaves the modern rule operative in all other areas.

Litigation in other states involving the doctrine has been much less extensive than in New York but, as previously stated, the doctrine, in the form of a rule of construction based on the presumed intent of the transferor, has won general acceptance. In order to invoke the doctrine the conveyance must limit a future interest to the intestate successors of the transferor, that is, to his heirs in the case of land, and to his next of kin in the case of personal property. Therefore, the rule is not applicable where

intention to give a remainder to her next of kin because she (1) made a full and formal disposition of the principal of the trust property, (2) made no reservation of a power to grant or assign an interest in the property during her lifetime, (3) surrendered all control over the trust property except the power to make testamentary disposition thereof and the right to appoint a substitute trustee, and (4) made no provision for the return of any part of the principal to herself during her lifetime."

14 Matter of Burchell, 299 N.Y. 351, 360, 87 N.E.2d 293, 297 (1949). For an excellent summary and discussion of the New York cases, see Verrall, The Doctrine of Worthier Title: A Questionable Rule of Construction, 6 U.C.L.A. L.Rev. 201 (1959).

15 N.Y.Laws, 1951, c. 180 amending McKinney's N.Y.Personal Property Law, § 23 and McKinney's N.Y.Real Property Law, § 118. The statute applies only to trusts executed on and after September 1, 1951. It should be noted that the statute represents a retreat to the common law rule in the area of its application.

the gift is to "children" or "issue" of the transferor or where the persons to take are to be determined as of a time other than the transferor's death.[16] Nor does the rule apply where the gift is limited to named persons who later turn out to be the heirs or next of kin of the transferor. Although the limitation must be to the heirs or next of kin, the use of the words "heirs" or "next of kin" in the instrument is not necessary and any equivalent words are sufficient to satisfy this requirement of the rule.[17] Almost invariably the interest given to the heirs or next of kin is a remainder, but on principle the doctrine, as a rule of construction, should also be applicable where the limitation to them is an executory interest instead of a remainder.[18] In both situations it may be presumed, in the absence of a manifested contrary intention, that the transferor intended to retain a reversion or reversionary interest in himself rather than to create an interest in his intestate successors.

At times the doctrine is confused with the Rule in Shelley's Case.[19] Both rules involve a problem of remainders but they are separate and distinct rules despite their probable common origin. The worthier title doctrine, in its inter vivos aspect, is concerned only with remainders to the heirs of the conveyor whereas the Rule in Shelley's Case is concerned with remainders to the heirs of any person to whom a life estate has been given by the same conveyance. Thus, if A conveys to B for life, then to the heirs of B, the Rule in Shelley's Case will apply but not the worthier title doctrine. And if A conveys to B for life, then to the heirs of A, the worthier title doctrine will apply but not the Rule in Shelley's Case. In one situation the possible application of both

---

[16] Restat.Prop., § 314, Comm. c. But see Bottimore v. First & Merchants Nat. Bank, 170 Va. 221, 196 S.E. 593 (1938).

[17] See e. g. Richardson v. Richardson, 298 N.Y. 135, 81 N.E.2d 54 (1948) ("to such persons as would be entitled to the same under the intestacy laws of the State of New York.")

[18] The Restatement takes this view. § 314, Comm. f. And see 1 American Law of Property, §§ 4.20, 4.57.

[19] See e. g. Sutliff v. Aydelott, 373 Ill. 633, 27 N.E.2d 529 (1940); Loring v. Eliot, 16 Gray 568 (Mass.1860).

rules must be taken into consideration.   Assume that A conveys land to T in trust for A for life, and on A's death in trust for the heirs of A.   It is sometimes said that in this situation both rules are applicable.[20]   But before the Rule in Shelley's Case can apply it must first be determined that the conveyance limits a remainder to the heirs of the life tenant.   If the worthier title doctrine is accepted as a positive rule of law its effect, when applied to this conveyance, is to eliminate the remainder in the heirs of A and there is nothing on which the Rule in Shelley's Case can operate. If, taking the modern view, the worthier title doctrine is accepted as a rule of construction expressing the intention of the conveyor, we reach the same result.   There is no remainder in the heirs of A because, presumably, A did not intend to give them a remainder.   Again, there is nothing on which the Rule in Shelley's Case can operate.   Only if, as a matter of construction of the conveyance, it is first determined that the worthier title doctrine does not apply because of a manifested intention of the conveyor to create a remainder, does the Rule in Shelley's Case come into operation.   On the bare facts of the case given above, the conveyor has not manifested an intention to create a remainder in his heirs and, therefore, the limitation to the heirs will operate as a reversion in A and the Rule in Shelley's Case will not be applicable.

SECTION 10.   STATUTORY MODIFICATION OF THE DOCTRINE

In recent years there has been a trend in the direction of statutory abrogation of the worthier title doctrine in both of its branches.   As a rule of construction the inter vivos aspect of the doctrine has been productive of litigation and confusion; and it has been questioned whether the modern rule does in fact express the intention of the normal settlor of a trust.[1]   As a consequence,

---

[20] Simes & Smith, Future Interests, § 1607.   Cf. Restatement Property, § 314, Comm. g.

[1] Verrall, The Doctrine of Worthier Title: A Questionable Rule of Construction, 6 U.C.L.A.L.Rev. 371 (1959).

statutes abolishing the doctrine have been enacted in California, Illinois, Kansas (wills only), Minnesota and Nebraska.[2] The New York statute modifying the doctrine has been previously discussed.[3]

[2] The Nebraska statute (Neb.Rev.Stat. §§ 76–114, 76–115) is an adoption of Sections 14 and 15 of the Uniform Property Act. The latter Act was drafted by the American Law Institute and approved by the Commissioners on Uniform State Laws. See 9B U.L.A. 405.

[3] § 9, supra.

Chapter 7

COMMON LAW METHODS OF CONVEYANCING

SECTION 1.   CREATION AND TRANSFER OF PRESENT FREEHOLD ESTATES

Prior to the seventeenth century the typical form of conveyance of a present freehold estate in land was the feoffment with livery of seisin.   A feoffment was the grant of a fief or feudal tenement and livery of seisin was the means by which the grant was effected.   At a time when seisin was tantamount to ownership it was logical enough that the law should take the position that a transfer of seisin was essential to the creation of a freehold estate.   If A was seised of Blackacre in fee simple and wished to convey his estate to B, it was necessary that he invest B with the seisin.   This was done by means of a feoffment with livery of seisin, or more shortly, a feoffment.   A and B, or their agents, would go upon the land and A would formally "give" or "deliver" the seisin to B in the presence of witnesses from the neighborhood.   A would usually hand over to B a branch, twig or piece of turf as a symbol of the land itself although this ceremonial act was not essential.   What was essential was the investiture of B with the seisin—the feoffor, A, must declare that he gives the seisin to the feoffee, B; and having installed B in occupancy of the land, A must completely relinquish the possession.   The feoffor would declare at the time of the livery what estate he gives to the feoffee.   Livery of seisin could also be made in view of the land without the parties actually going on it but in that case it was necessary for the feoffee to make an entry on the land during the lifetime of the feoffor, otherwise the feoffment was void.

Until the enactment of the Statute of Frauds in 1677 [1] no writing was necessary to make the feoffment valid. The estate conveyed passed to the feoffee solely by virtue of the transfer of the seisin. From the thirteenth century onward it was, in fact, customary for the feoffor to deliver to the feoffee a deed or charter of feoffment but the function of the charter was to furnish evidence of the livery of seisin and of the nature of the estate given, as well as to set forth the covenant of warranty. The language of the charter, written in the past tense, indicated its purpose: it recited that the feoffor had "given and granted" the land and had delivered the seisin to the feoffee. The operative act in the transaction was the delivery of seisin, not the giving of the charter or deed. In the course of time, the reverse of this was to become true, the deed becoming essential and livery of seisin obsolete. As we shall see, the enactment in the sixteenth century of the Statute of Uses [2] gave rise to new modes of conveying freehold estates which took effect through the execution and delivery of deeds, and the medieval conveyance by feoffment with livery of seisin fell into disuse. The Real Property Act of 1845 [3] provided that a present freehold estate could be transferred by a simple deed of grant. Yet conveyance by feoffment, evidenced by a deed, continued to be theoretically possible in England until the present century when the Law of Property Act, 1925,[4] finally made it invalid as a mode of conveyance.[5]

---

[1] 29 Car. II, c. 3, § 1. The statute provided that an estate "made and created by livery and seisin only, or by parol, and not put in writing, and signed by the parties so making or creating the same, or their agents . . ." should have the effect of an estate at will only.

[2] 27 Hen. VIII, c. 10 (1536).

[3] 8 & 9 Vict. c. 106.

[4] 15 & 16 Geo. V, c. 20, § 51.

[5] Feoffments were occasionally used to convey land in colonial times in America. In Massachusetts a provincial act of 1697 provided that a deed of lands, signed, sealed and acknowledged by the grantor and recorded "shall be valid to pass the same, without any other act or ceremony in the law whatsoever." At the present day valuable land in Ipswich, Massachusetts is owned by a charitable corporation bearing the ancient name "The Feoffees of the

Livery of seisin was in its very nature a present act which operated to take the seisin out of the feoffor and put it in the feoffee. Therefore, a feoffment with livery of seisin could not be made to take effect at a future date. A could not enfeoff B of Blackacre, the feoffment to take effect on B's subsequent marriage, or on A's death. The transaction was deemed void and the seisin continued in A. Herein lies the probable reason for the common law rule that a freehold estate could not be created to commence *in futuro*.[6] Since seisin passed to the feoffee at the time of the feoffment, or not at all, there could be no springing freehold estate to arise in the conveyee out of the estate of the conveyor at a future time. Nor could seisin be suspended or in abeyance for any period of time since under the medieval law there must always be a tenant to answer to the lord of the fee's demand for the feudal dues and to the plaintiff's writ in a real action.

Although conveyance by feoffment was the usual method of creating and transferring a present freehold estate, it was not the only method available. Conveyance by fine was also rather widely used in the medieval period. A fine was the compromise of a feigned action, usually an action begun by writ of covenant, between the parties to the conveyance.[7] The compromise set forth the terms of the conveyance and a copy of this compromise became an official record of the court and was preserved as such. Thus, conveyance by fine had the great advantage of giving the conveyee an official record of his title—one which, unlike the charter of feoffment, was subject neither to theft nor forgery. Yet, the fine was incomplete until seisin had been delivered to the conveyee. Another mode of conveying land

Grammar School in the Town of Ipswich." The land was conveyed to the Feoffees at some time between 1650 and 1660 "for the use of school-learning in the said town forever."

6 The effect of this rule on the destructibility of contingent remainders has been discussed in c. 5, § 21, supra.

7 The word "fine" is derived from the Latin term *"finalis concordia"*, meaning final concord or agreement of the parties. The whole process was called "levying a fine."

through the use of the judicial machinery was the common recovery. Unlike the fine, the common recovery was a real action prosecuted to a final judgment ordering the "recovery" of the lands by the plaintiff. In its classical form, as developed in the late fifteenth and in the sixteenth centuries, the collusive common recovery became an effective means whereby a tenant in tail could alienate in fee simple and destroy reversions and remainders expectant on the estate tail, as well as the rights of his issue.[8] The Fines and Recoveries Act (1833) [9] abolished both of these methods of conveyancing. There are a few instances of the use of fines and recoveries in early American law but they were never an important factor in this country and were supplanted by conveyance by deed.

SECTION 2.   CREATION OF NON-FREEHOLD ESTATES

Since the tenant for years and the tenant at will did not have seisin such estates were not created by a feoffment. An agreement between the parties that the transferee should have a specified estate for years or a tenancy at will followed by an entry into possession by the tenant was sufficient to create the estate. Prior to the Statute of Frauds (1677) a lease for years need not in any case be in writing but as a practical matter a leasehold estate for any substantial period would be evidenced by a writing under seal in order that the parties might maintain an action of covenant for breach of the promises set forth in the lease. Until the lessee entered into possession he had no estate in the land but the peculiar interest called an *interesse termini*. This interest was assignable even before the doctrine of assignability of contract rights in general had evolved. The insistence of the common law on the taking of possession by the lessee before his position as tenant would be recognized is analogous to the neces-

---

[8] For an excellent discussion of fines and recoveries, see Plucknett, Concise History of the Common Law 619–622 (5th ed. 1956); Simpson, An Introduction to the History of the Land Law 115–129 (1961).

[9] 3 & 4 Will. IV, c. 74.

sity of the conveyee of a freehold estate obtaining seisin in order to acquire the status of a freehold tenant. This curious concept of *interesse termini* is now obsolete.[1]

SECTION 3.   CREATION OF FUTURE INTERESTS

Since a reversion arises by operation of law and not by agreement of the parties, no manifestation of an intention by the conveyor to create a reversion was necessary to produce that result. A conveyance by the conveyor of a legally smaller estate than his own automatically resulted in the retention of a reversion.[*] But if the conveyor wished to reserve a right of entry for condition broken (power of termination) it was necessary to manifest such intention by appropriate language in the charter of feoffment or other conveyance. So also, a possibility of reverter arose from the words of express limitation creating a determinable fee in the conveyee.

At common law, that is, prior to the Statute of Uses (1536), the only two types of future interests that could be created in a conveyee were the vested remainder and the contingent remainder. Both of these interests were created by appropriate language in the feoffment, or in the conveyance by way of fine. Thus, if A, seised of land in fee, wished to give B a present life estate therein and a remainder to C in fee tail followed by a remainder to D in fee simple, he would enfeoff B by delivering the seisin to him and as part of the transaction would declare, orally or in writing, that B should hold the land for life and that on B's death it should go to C and the heirs of his body and on failure of such issue to D and his heirs. B received the seisin in his own right and also on behalf of the remaindermen. Therefore,

---

[1] As to *interesse termini* under modern law, see c. 3, § 2, supra.

[*] It will be recalled that, strictly speaking, an owner of a freehold estate who created an estate for years did not by common law standards have a reversion; he retained a present freehold estate subject to the term of years. But under the modern law the transferor has a reversion expectant upon the estate for years. See c. 5, § 2, supra.

on B's death the seisin would automatically pass to C. The necessity of seisin passing to the remainderman delayed the recognition of the validity of a contingent remainder. If A enfeoffed B for life, remainder to the heirs of C, a living person, who was the remainderman and where did the seisin of the inheritance go at the time of the feoffment? If seisin of the fee remained in A it would take another conveyance to get it out of him. Not until the middle of the fifteenth century were these theoretical difficulties overcome, or ignored, by acceptance of the view that if the remainder vested at or prior to the termination of B's estate seisin could pass to the remainderman on B's death.

It was permissible for A, seised in fee simple, to give a term of years to B and by the same transaction to give to C a fee simple subject to B's term. In other words, it was possible for the conveyor to create what we would now call an estate for years followed by a remainder in fee simple. This was done by having A deliver the seisin to B on behalf of C; at the same time A would declare the grant of the term of years to B and of the fee simple to C. In receiving the seisin B was acting as though he were C's agent and the seisin vested immediately in C. As Littleton puts it: "But if he (the feoffor) maketh livery of seisin to the lessee, then is the freehold, together with the fee to them in the remainder, according to the form of the grant and the will of the lessor." [2] Since, under the medieval law, the term of years was not an estate, C's interest was regarded as a present fee simple, not a remainder in fee simple. The present freehold was in C subject to B's term for years. But it has become customary to describe these limitations as creating an estate for years in B, with a remainder in fee simple in C.

[2] Littleton, Tenures, sec. 60 (c. 1481).

SECTION 4.   COMMON LAW RULES RESTRICTING THE CREATION OF FUTURE INTERESTS

It may be helpful at this point to summarize and recapitulate the principal restrictive rules at common law governing the creation of future interests in transferees:

A.   No freehold estate could be created to commence *in futuro*.   This was a consequence of the concept of livery of seisin as a presently operative act.

B.   A freehold contingent remainder could not be supported by a term of years.   Thus, A conveys to B for ten years, then to the heirs of C, a living person.   The attempted remainder to C is void and A has an estate in fee simple subject to B's term of years.   B receives possession but not seisin and since C's heir will not be ascertained until C's death there is no one capable of taking the seisin.   Inasmuch as the seisin cannot be in abeyance it must remain in A.   It cannot pass to C's heir when the latter is ascertained since this would violate the rule forbidding the creation of a freehold to commence in the future.

C.   A limitation operating to shift the seisin from one transferee to another transferee by cutting short or divesting a precedent estate was void.   A grantor could reserve a right of entry in favor of himself but there could be no cut-off in favor of a stranger.   Thus, A enfeoffs B and his heirs but if B dies without having married then to C and his heirs.   The limitation to C is void.   So also, if A enfeoffs B for life but upon C paying B a sum of money then to C and his heirs, again the limitation to C is void.   C's interest is not a remainder because a remainder, by its very nature, awaits the termination of the preceding estate before becoming a possessory estate.[1]   It does not displace or cut off a prior estate.   And since the common law did not permit the creation of a springing or a shifting interest in a conveyee, it follows that the only future interest which could be limited in favor of a conveyee was a remainder.

[1] See c. 5, § 13, supra.

D.   A future interest limited to take effect after an interval of time following the termination of the preceding estate was void.   There could be no gap between the preceding estate and the remainder.   Thus, A enfeoffs B for life, and one year after B's death to C and his heirs.   The limitation to C is void.   The seisin cannot be suspended during the year following B's death hence it will, on B's death, revert to A.   Once the seisin has come back to A it will take a new conveyance to transfer it to C.   The original conveyance is not effective to give the seisin to C because of the rule forbidding the creation of a freehold estate to take effect *in futuro*.   A gap for even a short interval of time was not permitted.   Thus, A enfeoffs B "for ten years, then to C for life and if D gives C a good funeral then to D and his heirs." D takes nothing by the conveyance.

As we shall see in a later chapter,[2] after the enactment of the Statute of Uses (1536) it became possible for a conveyor to give an estate to one person and to provide that upon the occurrence of a specified event that estate should be cut short and an estate should arise in a third person.   It also became possible at that later period of time to create a freehold estate to commence *in futuro;* that is, a freehold estate could be created to become effective at a future date without any precedent estate being limited, or after a gap following the termination of the precedent estate.   But in none of these cases would the future interest take effect by way of remainder.

SECTION 5.   TRANSFER OF FUTURE ESTATES

A reversion or remainder expectant upon a freehold estate could not be transferred by livery of seisin for the simple reason that the seisin was in the holder of the particular estate.   Thus, A, seised of Blackacre in fee simple, enfeoffs B for life.   Since B and not A has the seisin, if A wishes to transfer the reversion to C he cannot do so by livery of seisin.   He could do so by the type of conveyance called a grant.   A grant was effectuated by the

---

[2] c. 9, § 7, infra.

execution and delivery of a deed from the transferor to the transferee.[1] Although the term "grant" is, in its modern usage, practically synonymous with "conveyance" and is used generically without reference to a particular type of conveyance, in its technical common law meaning it referred to a special type of conveyance. It was the appropriate method of transferring reversions, remainders and other incorporeal interests. The notion that certain interests in land were transferable by livery of seisin and other interests by grant was summed up in the maxim that "all lands lie in livery or in grant." [2]

The owner of a freehold estate subject to a term of years could transfer his estate by grant. Thus, A, seised of Blackacre in fee simple, leases to B for ten years. The present freehold and seisin are in A but because of B's possessory estate A could not transfer his reversion by livery of seisin to C unless B temporarily surrendered the possession to A.[3]

A grant of a reversion or of a remainder was not effective until the holder of the present particular estate assented to the transfer. This assent was known as attornment. The requirement of attornment by the tenant probably finds its origin in the personal relation existing between lord and tenant in feudal times. The necessity of attornment was abolished in England in 1705 by the statute 4 & 5 Anne, c. 16, sec. 9, and is an obsolete doctrine in all American jurisdictions at the present time.

If the holder of a possessory estate for life or years desired to transfer it to the person having the immediate reversion or next vested remainder he could do so by surrender. Lord Coke described a surrender as "a yielding up an estate for life, or years,

---

1 The term "grant" derives from the language of the deed which recited that the conveyor "gives and grants" to the conveyee.

2 Doe v. Cole, 7 B. & C. 243, 108 Eng.Rep. 714 (1827). This distinction between conveyance by livery and conveyance by grant continued to exist as a matter of legal theory until 1845 when, by statute, present freehold estates became transferable by deed of grant. 8 & 9 Vict. c. 106, § 2.

3 Doe v. Cole, n. 2, supra. The practice was, prior to the Statute of Uses, for the lessee to give up possession for a moment to the lessor to enable the lessor to make livery of the seisin subject to the lease.

to him that hath an immediate estate in reversion or remainder, wherein the estate for life, or years, may drown by mutual agreement between them." [4]   The estate surrendered would merge in the estate of the surrenderee.   Prior to the Statute of Frauds no writing was necessary but under the provisions of that Statute the surrender had to be by deed or note or "by act and operation of law." [5]

A release was the converse of a surrender.   As in the case of the surrender, the release could be used only when both parties to the transaction already had estates or interests in the land. It could, as between holders of successive estates in the same parcel of land, be given only by a person out of possession to a person in possession.   Thus, if B has a life estate in land, followed by a remainder in C in fee simple, C could convey his remainder to B by means of a release.   A release, being an instrument in writing under seal, was a species of grant.   It was also the appropriate type of conveyance where the joint tenant of a freehold estate desired to transfer his estate to the other joint tenant or where a disseisee wished to convey his right of entry to the disseisor.

It was possible for an owner of land in fee simple to convey his estate without livery of seisin by means of a lease and release. Thus, A, seised of Blackacre in fee simple, wishes to convey it to B in fee simple.   A could, by agreement and entry, create in B an estate for one year and upon B's entry into possession give B a deed of release of the reversion "to have and to hold to B and his heirs," thereby putting the whole fee in B.   This method seems not to have been in common use prior to the Statute of Uses (1536) but thereafter it became the established practice to convey land by means of a bargain and sale of a term of years followed by a common law release of the reversion.

[4] Co.Litt. 337b.

[5] As to surrender in the modern law of landlord and tenant, see c. 3, § 6, supra.

Chapter 8

USES AND THE STATUTE OF USES

SECTION 1. THE NATURE OF A USE

Thus far we have been discussing estates and interests in land from the viewpoint of the common law. We have now to consider English land law from the viewpoint not only of a court of law but also of a court of equity. There existed in England until 1875 a separate court, called the Court of Chancery, which dispensed justice in a way that was designed to afford a remedy where none was available under the rigid, formulary common law procedure. The Chancellor, as keeper of the king's conscience, sought to give relief where justice and equity required it even though, or rather because, the suppliant or petitioner could obtain no redress for his grievance in the king's common law courts. In course of time, the principles which the Chancellor applied in the adjudication of cases coming before him became integrated into a system of jurisprudence called by the distinctive name "Equity". The law of real property of today is a result of the application of both common law and equitable doctrines; and it was by means of the institution of "uses" that equity came into contact with the land law.

In the fourteenth century there became prevalent a practice whereby land owners conveyed their lands to friends to hold for the use and benefit of the feoffors or of third persons.[1] The per-

---

[1] The "use" as a device for putting the beneficial enjoyment of land in a person other than the owner was resorted to as early as Domesday Book but the practice was not widespread until the thirteenth and fourteenth centuries. For an account of the origin and development of the use, see Plucknett, Concise History of the Common Law 575–587 (5th ed. 1956); 2 Powell, Real Property §§ 265–267; 1 American Law of Property, §§ 1.17–1.25; 4 Holdsworth, History of English Law 409–443 (1924).

son for whose use or benefit the land was thus held was called the *cestui que use*.[2] The purpose of such conveyances frequently was to enable the landowners to deal with their lands in a manner not countenanced by the common law or to evade the liabilities incident to legal ownership. Thus A, seised of Blackacre in fee simple and wishing to dispose of it by will, would enfeoff B in fee simple to hold to A's use during A's lifetime and after his death to transfer the land according to his will. (The student will recall that land generally was not devisable prior to 1540.) A landowner could by a feoffment to uses place his lands beyond the reach of his creditors seeking to levy an execution thereon. Again, a dying land owner could by a conveyance to several feoffees to uses (who would take as joint tenants) deprive the lord of the fee of the important incidents of wardship, marriage or relief. For these and other reasons men sought to rid themselves of the legal title to land and yet retain the beneficial ownership. A feoffment to uses or in trust was generally adequate to accomplish this purpose.

It is obvious that the success of a feoffor's attempt to put the legal ownership of his land in someone else and retain the beneficial ownership in himself depended on the feoffee keeping his promise to deal with the land according to the agreement made at the time of the feoffment. Unless some way could be found to enforce the feoffee's promise the feoffor's position was indeed precarious. In law the feoffee was the true owner; the cestui que use in possession was only a tenant at will. Seisin had vested in him by virtue of the feoffment and the law was not at all concerned with the feoffee's promise to deal with the land for the benefit of the feoffor or his nominees. That promise in no way affected the legal estate in the land and beyond the legal title the common law would not inquire.[3] The situation was one naturally calling for the exercise of the extraordinary jurisdic-

[2] The term "cestui que use" is a corruption of the law French phrase "*cestui a que use le feoffment fuit fait*" (he to whose use the feoffment was made).

[3] When the remedy of assumpsit had developed it would have enabled the feoffor to recover damages against the feoffee to uses for breach of his undertaking but by then far more effective relief was obtainable in Chancery.

tion of the Court of Chancery, and the Chancellor accepted jurisdiction in the early fifteenth century.

The principle upon which the Chancellor decided to give protection to the cestui que use against faithless feoffees to uses was a simple one: a man ought to keep his promises, and should not be allowed profit by his own breach of faith. The Court of Chancery, therefore, began to apply its peculiarly powerful sanctions of fine and imprisonment to force feoffees to uses to perform their undertakings. The Chancellor did not interfere with the legal title of the feoffee to uses. He recognized the legal title as being in the feoffee but compelled the latter to refrain from making use of that legal title in a manner inconsistent with the promise under which he had received it. Did the Chancellor recognize an *in rem* right on the part of the cestui que use, a right in the land itself, or only an *in personam* right against the feoffee? That is a theoretically debatable point, but the rights of the cestui que use were so similar to in rem rights that for practical purposes we may treat those rights as being rights in the land itself—a species of ownership.[4] We arrive, then, at this result: as a consequence of Chancery's protection of cestui que use there is now a dual ownership of land, the legal title of the feoffee to uses, or trustee, and the equitable title of cestui que use—an equitable title that is transferable, inheritable and devisable.

Having decided to enforce the use against the feoffee to uses, would the Chancellor also enforce it against others who were transferees from that feoffee? The answer ultimately formulated was that those who took legal title with notice of the use and those who took without notice but paid no value for the transfer were bound by the use. Thus, heirs of the feoffee to uses, donees, and purchasers with notice took subject to the use but bona fide purchasers for value, without notice, from the feoffee to uses took the legal title unencumbered by the equitable title of the

---

4 No doubt, in its origin and later development the use did not bind the land; it bound only the conscience of the person acquiring the legal ownership.

cestui que use. A person taking the legal estate under a title independent of that of the feoffee to uses, such as a disseisor, was not bound by the use. The only remedy of the cestui que use in such a case would be to petition the Chancellor to compel the trustee to institute an action to recover possession of the land.

As to the duties imposed on the feoffee to uses, these depended for their details on the terms of the particular feoffment. In general, however, those duties were as follows:

1. The feoffee to uses must permit the cestui que use to occupy the land or to take the rents and profits thereof;

2. He must convey the legal estate according to the instructions of the cestui que use;

3. He must take all necessary proceedings to defend the legal title against the claims of third persons.

In turn, the feoffee could compel the cestui que use to indemnify him for the costs and expenses incurred in discharging these duties. And in some instances, at least, the feoffee to uses demanded and got compensation for his services.[5]

SECTION 2. USE ESTATES AND INTERESTS INCLUDING SPRINGING AND SHIFTING USES

We have thus far spoken chiefly of feoffments to the use of the feoffor or to the uses to be declared by the will of the feoffor, but a use estate could be and frequently was created in favor of third persons. Thus, A, seised of Blackacre in fee simple, en-

But the extensive, although not complete, protection given by Chancery to the cestui que use amounted to a type of equitable "ownership." See 1 Scott, Trusts, § 1 (2d ed. 1956).

[5] Particularly when one of the feoffees to uses was a lawyer, as was often the case. Holdsworth points out that it was most unusual to have only one feoffee to uses. If only a single feoffee was availed of, his death would entitle the lord of the fee to the feudal incidents. Hence, the feoffment was normally made to as many as six or more feoffees to uses. When their number became dangerously low there would be a re-enfeoffment to a larger group. 4 Holdsworth, History of English Law 421–422 (1924).

feoffs B and his heirs to the use of C for ten years, then to the use of D for life, then to the use of E and his heirs. B has the legal estate in fee simple but C, D and E have equitable or use estates. In according recognition to uses the Chancellors in a general way followed the common law pattern of estates as their model. There could be equitable possessory estates, and equitable remainders, for years, for life, in fee tail and in fee simple corresponding to legal estates and remainders. But as the Chancellors were not in any way dealing directly with the legal title they were not bound by the categories of interests in land emanating from the common law doctrine of seisin. Hence, a degree of flexibility was permissible in the limitation of equitable interests which did not obtain in the creation of common law estates. These differences require examination.

We have in our discussion of conveyancing at common law pointed out four restrictions on the creation of future estates:[1]

1. No freehold estate could be created to commence in futuro. Thus, A enfeoffs B and his heirs, the feoffment being declared to go into effect the following Christmas. B takes nothing.

2. A freehold contingent remainder preceded only by a term of years is void in its inception as an attempt to create a freehold to commence in futuro. Thus, A conveys to B for ten years, then to the heirs of C, a living person. The heirs of C take nothing.

3. A limitation providing that a freehold estate should on the happening of a specified event be cut short and an estate commence in a third person was void. Thus, A enfeoffs B and his heirs but if B dies childless then to C and his heirs. C takes nothing.

4. There could be no gap between the particular freehold estate and a freehold future interest or between two freehold "remainders." Thus, A enfeoffs B for life

---

[1] See c. 7, § 3, supra.

and one year after B's death to C and his heirs. C takes nothing.

None of these restrictions applied to the creation of equitable interests. To illustrate:

1. On July 1, A enfeoffs B and his heirs to the use of C and his heirs beginning on August 1. The legal estate is in B before and after August 1. There is a resulting use [2] in A in fee for the period of a month and on August 1 the use springs up in favor of C. Thus, a use could be created to commence in futuro. Such a use was called a springing use.

2. A enfeoffs B and his heirs to the use of C for ten years then to the use of the heirs of D, a living person. The heirs of D have a valid equitable contingent interest.[3]

3. A enfeoffs B and his heirs to the use of C and his heirs but if C dies unmarried then to the use of D and his heirs. B has the legal estate in fee simple. C has an equitable estate in fee simple but on C's death unmarried that use estate is cut short and the use shifts to D in fee. The use limited in favor of D was called a shifting use. A shifting use is one which cuts short a prior use estate in a person other than the conveyor; a springing use is one which cuts short a use estate in the conveyor.

4. A enfeoffs B and his heirs to the use of C for life and one year after C's death to the use of D and his heirs. B has the legal estate in fee simple. C has an equitable life estate followed by a resulting use to A in fee simple subject to a use in D in fee simple commencing one year after C's death. This use in D cutting short the resulting use in A was also a springing use. Thus,

---

[2] The concept of a resulting use is explained in § 4, infra.

[3] If D is still living at the end of C's term, the interest given to the heirs of D would not fail but would take effect as a springing use which would divest the resulting use in A on D's death.

there could be a gap between the use estates limited in favor of strangers.

In brief, by virtue of the doctrine of uses it was possible to create equitable interests, in the nature of springing and shifting uses, that had no counterpart in the common law scheme of estates.

SECTION 3. METHODS OF CREATING OR RAISING A USE

It is evident from what we have already said that a use could be created or raised by a feoffment to uses. That was indeed the common method of creating a use but it is not to be assumed that it was the only method. A use could also be created in connection with any other common law type of conveyance such as a fine, common recovery, lease, release or grant. Broadly speaking, a use could be created with or without a transfer of possession. A use was raised with a transfer of the possession where it was created upon an actual transfer of the seisin as in the case of a feoffment to uses. No technical words were necessary to create a use, and the declaration of the use could be oral or written. The word "use" was frequently employed but it was not essential.[1] Any words expressing the feoffor's intention that the legal estate should be held for the benefit of another person were sufficient. A declaration that the feoffee should hold the land upon trust or confidence for C and his heirs, or that he should permit C and his heirs to take the profits, was sufficient to raise a use.

At the beginning of the sixteenth century it was settled that a use could be raised without a transfer of the seisin by means of a bargain and sale. A bargain and sale was an agreement whereby the owner of land for a pecuniary consideration promised to sell the land to, or to hold it for the benefit of, the promisee. Thus, in 1530 (before the Statute of Uses) A, seised of

---

[1] When the use was declared by written instrument the medieval Latin phrase "*ad opus*" (to the use of) was commonly inserted in the earlier documents.

Blackacre in fee simple, orally or in writing promises B, in consideration of the payment of the purchase price by B, to sell Blackacre to B in fee simple, or promises to hold the land for the benefit of B and his heirs. Since no legal conveyance has been made A is still the legal owner of the land, but in equity B will be given protection and will be treated as the beneficial owner. The Chancellor will compel A to allow B to have the use of the land, the rents and profits thereof, and to convey the legal title at B's request. A bargain and sale, therefore, raised a use in the bargainee.[2]

SECTION 4.   RESULTING USES

So common had become the practice of conveying lands to uses that the Chancellor would sometimes imply a use where none had been expressed.   Where A enfeoffed B in fee simple and no use was expressly declared and B gave no value for the conveyance, the Court of Chancery presumed that it was A's intention not to make a gift to B but to retain the beneficial ownership in himself. This was a wholly reasonable construction to put upon the transaction at a time when feoffments to uses were so numerous. The use was said, therefore, to result or come back to A. An express declaration of the use in the feoffee or in a third person, or the giving of consideration for the feoffment, negatived any resulting use.   There would be no resulting use in the case of a conveyance of a smaller estate than the conveyor had since the tenure existing between conveyor and conveyee was held to be sufficient, by reason of the obligations consequent thereon (such as fealty), to rebut the presumption of a resulting

---

[2] Here again the underlying reason for recognizing a use in the bargainee was that it would have been unconscionable for the seller, after receiving the purchase price, to violate the trust imposed in him by the buyer. Although the doctrine of a use arising from a "bargain and sale" of lands seems to have originated in the situation where the bargainee had paid the agreed purchase price, it was later extended to cases where the bargainee had paid any valuable consideration for the bargainor's promise to convey. Ultimately, a mere recital of consideration in a deed of bargain and sale was sufficient to raise a use. Jackson ex dem. Hudson v. Alexander, 3 Johns. 484 (N.Y.1808).

use. Thus, A holding land in fee simple enfeoffs B for life. B has a legal life estate unencumbered by any use in favor of A, and A has a legal reversion in fee.* It should be noted that there would be no question of a resulting use on a bargain and sale since that transaction was, prior to the Statute of Uses, essentially a transfer of the use estate only.

SECTION 5.   THE STATUTE OF USES

The system of divided ownership of land that resulted from the practice of conveying lands to uses undoubtedly resulted in much inconvenience, litigation and fraud. As abuses crept in, Parliament felt it necessary from time to time to enact remedial legislation. In 1377 a statute was passed to prevent frauds on creditors, and in 1392 one to prevent evasion of the statutes of mortmain (which forbade conveyances of land to religious houses and corporations). The culmination of legislative attempts to control conveyances to uses came in 1535 in the famous Statute of Uses.[1]

This statute is probably the most important piece of legislation dealing with the English land law, and its far-reaching consequences are still felt in our own times. The causes which led to its enactment are to be found in an English King's need of money. The Statute was primarily designed to restore to the Crown the feudal revenues which were being lost by means of the conveyance of lands to uses. In the sixteenth century the incidents of tenure, such as wardship, marriage, relief, primer seisin and es-

---

* In fact, prior to the Statute of Uses it was not possible to create even an express use on a feoffment for life or in tail because of the tenure between feoffor and feoffee. Only a feoffee in fee simple could hold to the use of another. 4 Holdsworth, History of English Law 429 (1924).

[1] 27 Hen. VIII, c. 10. The Statute became effective in 1536. Statutory developments prior to the Statute of Uses are traced in 4 Holdsworth, History of English Law 443–449. That Parliament was gradually tightening control over uses is evidenced by a statute of 1489 making the heir of the cestui que use of lands held by knight service liable to wardship or relief where the cestui que use died intestate

cheat, were burdensome exactions on the tenant and, correspondingly, a profitable source of revenue for the lord of the fee. Since the king "alone was always lord and never tenant" he lost heavily when landowners by conveyances to joint feoffees to uses rid themselves of the incidents of tenure by retaining only the beneficial ownership. Henry VIII by means of the Statute of Uses sought to put an end to this drainage of the royal revenues.

The long preamble to the Statute sets forth in detail the real and fancied grievances flowing from uses but the true purpose of the Statute is to be found in that clause which recites as one of the reasons for its enactment "to the intent that the king's highness * * * shall not in any wise hereafter by any means of inventions be deceived, damaged or hurt, by reason of such trusts, uses or confidences". The abolition of uses was not looked upon with favor by the land owning class who feared the loss of the power to devise their lands, but Henry was able to enlist the support of the common law lawyers in Parliament in putting through the Statute because of their deep-rooted jealousy of the Court of Chancery. As Maitland well puts it, the Statute "was forced upon an extremely unwilling Parliament by an extremely strong-willed king." [2]

Strictly speaking, the Statute of Uses was aimed at the control of the creation of uses rather than at their abolition. It did not declare presently existing uses to be void nor did it forbid the creation of uses in the future. It sought to accomplish its purpose by uniting the legal and equitable title in the cestui que use. Its operating principle was to convert the equitable title of the cestui que use into a legal estate by drawing the seisin and legal title from the holder thereof and vesting it in the cestui que use. The essence of the Statute is to be found in these words: " * * * where any person or persons stand or be seised, or at any time hereafter shall happen to be seised, of and in any * * * lands * * * to the use, confidence or trust of any

---

[2] Maitland, Equity 35 (1909). The classic exposition of the causes leading to the enactment of the Statute is set forth in 4 Holdsworth, *op. cit.* supra, n. 1 at 450–461.

other person or persons　＊　＊　＊,　by reason of any bargain, sale, feoffment,　＊　＊　＊　that in every such case, all and every such person and persons　＊　＊　＊　that have or hereafter shall have any such use, confidence or trust　＊　＊　＊　shall from henceforth stand and be seised,　＊　＊　＊　of and in the same ＊　＊　＊　lands　＊　＊　＊　of and in such like estates as they had or shall have in use, confidence or trust of or in the same; and that the estate, title, right and possession that was in such person or persons that were, or hereafter shall be seised of any lands,　＊　＊　＊　to the use, confidence or trust of any such persons　＊　＊　＊　be from henceforth clearly deemed and adjudged to be in him or them that have, or hereafter shall have, such use, confidence or trust　＊　＊　＊."

In substance, the Statute provides that where one person stands seised of land to the use of another person that other person shall be seised of a like estate as he had in the use. Hence, in cases to which the Statute is applicable, its effect is to convert an equitable or use estate into a corresponding legal estate. Use estates or interests thus converted or changed into legal estates or interests are said to be "executed". For example, A, tenant of Blackacre in fee simple in 1540, enfeoffs B to have and to hold to B and his heirs to the use of C and his heirs. By virtue of the Statute, C has a legal estate in fee simple. The use declared in favor of C is executed into a legal estate by drawing to it the legal title and seisin which momentarily vested in B by virtue of the feoffment. B in reality serves merely as a conduit for the passing of the seisin to C. So also, if A in 1540 for value received, bargains and sells land to B and his heirs by a deed duly enrolled, B gets a legal estate in fee simple. The use raised by the bargain and sale in favor of B is executed into a legal estate. To spell this out more fully: A, by virtue of the bargain and sale, stands seised to the use of B; since the Statute of Uses provides that where one person is seised to the use of another, the seisin shall be deemed to be in the one having the use to the extent of the use estate, A's legal estate is vested in B and united with B's use estate thereby giving B a legal estate in fee simple. Similarly, where A enfeoffs

B and his heirs to the use of C and his heirs, since B stands seised to the use of C the Statute takes B's fee simple estate from B and vests it in C.

It should be noted that the legal estate vested in the cestui que use would usually be of the same size as the use estate declared in him, but in any event the person to whom the use estate was given would get no larger legal estate than that given to the feoffee to uses since it was the estate of the feoffee which was taken from him and vested in the person to whom the use estate was given. Thus, A enfeoffs B for life to the use of C and his heirs. C gets only a legal life estate since B's life estate was all that could be vested in C. The state of the title would be: estate pur autre vie in C, reversion in A in fee simple.[3]

---

[3] The old rule that a use could not be raised on a feoffment for life disappeared after the Statute of Uses.

Chapter 9

THE EFFECT OF THE STATUTE OF USES

The effect of the Statute of Uses upon the law of real property was threefold: 1, it introduced new methods of creating and transferring estates; 2, it made possible the creation of new types of legal future interests; 3, it gave rise to the modern trust in the form of an unexecuted use.

SECTION 1.   THE EFFECT OF THE STATUTE ON CONVEYANCING

The older common law methods of conveyancing were not abrogated by the Statute of Uses. A freehold estate could still be conveyed by livery of seisin; a term of years could be created by agreement and entry; a reversion or vested remainder could be transferred by grant. Unless a use were in some way declared or raised on such a conveyance the Statute had no application and the validity and efficacy of the transaction depended exclusively on common law principles. The rigid rules of the common law, such as the prohibition of an attempt to create a freehold to commence in futuro, continued to be applicable to common law conveyances. Thus, in Roe ex dem. Wilkinson v. Tranmer,[1] it was held that a release of a reversion purporting to take effect after the releasor's death was void *as a release.*

The Statute, however, gave rise to new methods of conveyancing in addition to the still existing common law methods and also made possible a combination of the new and old methods.

[1] 2 Wils. 75, 95 Eng.Rep. 694 (1757).

SECTION 2. FEOFFMENT TO USES

As before the Statute of Uses so afterwards, an owner of land could convey it to a feoffee to hold to such uses as were declared at the time of the feoffment. The Statute would, of course, convert the use estates thus raised into legal estates by uniting the seisin of the feoffee with the use in the cestui que use. Thus, A enfeoffs B and his heirs to the use of A for life, then to the use of the eldest unborn son of A and the heirs of the body of that son, then to the use of C and his heirs. The state of the legal title would be: life estate in A, contingent remainder in fee tail in A's unborn son, vested remainder in fee simple in C. At common law a man could not convey to himself or his wife but after the Statute this could be done by raising a use estate in favor of himself or his wife which would be executed into a legal estate. After the rise of the newer methods of conveyancing in the seventeenth century feoffments to uses were rarely used in practice.

SECTION 3. RESULTING USES AFTER THE STATUTE

We have already seen that if, prior to the Statute of Uses, A seised of land in fee simple, enfeoffed B and his heirs and no uses were declared and no consideration was paid, there would be a resulting use in fee simple so that B would hold the legal title to the use of A. What would be the result of such a transaction after the Statute of Uses? A literal application of the Statute would execute the resulting use in the feoffor so as to vest in him the entire estate, thereby rendering the transaction nugatory. Although such a conveyance was undoubtedly due to ineptness on the part of the conveyancer, the courts applied the Statute rigorously and held that the resulting use was executed.[1] The danger of a common law conveyance being made ineffective by reason of an executed resulting use led to the practise of inserting

---

1 Armstrong dem. Neve v. Wolsey, 2 Wils. 19, 95 Eng.Rep. 662 (1755).

in such conveyances an express declaration of a use in the conveyee in order to rebut a resulting use.[2]

A resulting use would also arise in the case of a partial declaration of a use as well as in the case of a common law conveyance of an estate in fee simple with no declaration of a use. Thus, A enfeoffs B and his heirs to the use of C for life, or in tail, or for years. The undeclared residue of the use results to A thereby giving A a legal reversion in fee simple, expectant upon the particular legal estate given to C. B, it will be noted, takes nothing, since the Statute of Uses divests him of the seisin momentarily vested in him by the feoffment. A use will not result to the feoffor, however, where by the terms of the conveyance a use is expressly limited to him for life or for years. Thus, A enfeoffs B and his heirs to the use of A for life. There is no resulting use and the state of the title (legal and equitable) is life estate in A, remainder in B in fee simple. The reason for such construction is this: if a resulting use were implied in favor of A, the life estate expressly limited to A would merge in the reversion in fee simple thereby vesting the entire estate in A, contrary to his declared intention to give himself a life estate.[3]

---

2 Older types of deeds in use in the United States guarded against a resulting use by declaring that the land was conveyed to the conveyee "and his heirs to have and to hold to his and their own use and behoof forever." An occasional statute deals explicitly with the problem. Mass.Gen.Laws c. 183, § 14 provides: "If no use is declared in a conveyance or devise of real estate, the same shall take effect as if it were expressed to be for the use of the grantee or devisee." Since modern deeds almost invariably contain a recital of consideration the question of a resulting use is not a matter of practical importance at the present time. It will be recalled that in a conveyance by bargain and sale there could be no resulting use because the transaction raised a use in the bargainee.

3 But there could be a resulting use where a use estate in tail was declared in the feoffor. Thus, A enfeoffs B and his heirs to the use of A and the heirs of his body. The state of the title would be: estate in fee tail in A, reversion in fee simple in A. The statute De Donis would prevent a merger of the fee tail in A's reversion in fee simple.

SECTION 4.   CONVEYANCE BY BARGAIN AND SALE

Since before the Statute of Uses a use could be raised by a bargain and sale, after the Statute a legal freehold estate could be created or transferred by means of a bargain and sale.   The use raised by the bargain and sale would be executed by the Statute into a legal estate.   Thus an entirely new method of conveying freehold estates was made possible by the Statute, dispensing with the necessity of livery of seisin.   The Statute itself operated to vest the seisin of the bargainor in the bargainee. Prior to the Statute no writing was required for a valid bargain and sale.   The framers of the Statute of Uses foresaw that, unless supplementary legislation were enacted, it would be possible to convey a freehold estate in land by an oral bargain and sale without the presence of witnesses.   Such a secret conveyance, if permitted, would contravene the long established policy of the law.   To avoid this situation the same Parliament which passed the Statute of Uses also enacted the Statute of Enrolments.[1]

The Statute of Enrolments provided in substance that no conveyance of an estate of *inheritance* or *freehold* by means of a bargain and sale should be effective unless the bargain and sale should be in writing, under seal, and enrolled in certain public offices mentioned therein.   These requirements for the public recording of a deed of bargain and sale made impossible secret oral transfers of estates of freehold.

SECTION 5.   CONVEYANCE BY LEASE AND RELEASE

The requirement of registration resulting from the Statute of Enrolments was displeasing to large landowners who desired to make family settlements without rendering the transaction a matter of public record but still wished to make use of the newer methods of conveyancing introduced by the Statute of Uses.   The

---

[1] 27 Hen. VIII, c. 16 (1536).

ingenuity of conveyancers eventually found a loophole whereby the Statute of Enrolments could be evaded and yet advantage taken of the Statute of Uses. The Statute of Enrolments was by its express terms applicable only to a bargain and sale of a freehold estate. A non-freehold estate, such as a term for years, might still be created by an oral or written bargain and sale which need not be recorded. The conveyancers hit upon the device of creating a term for years by means of a bargain and sale and then transferring the reversion by means of a common law release to the bargainee, thereby vesting the complete estate in the bargainee. Thus, A, seised of land in fee simple, wishes to convey it to B. A would by a written instrument of bargain and sale, reciting a consideration of five shillings paid to him in hand by B, create an estate for one year in B. Then A would, by a common law release, convey the reversion to B and his heirs. The estate for a year would merge in the fee simple and B would then have a present estate in fee simple. The bargain and sale would, by force of the Statute of Uses, vest the term of years in B without the necessity of B's entering into possession and he was, therefore, in a position to accept a release of the reversion.[1] Had the estate for years been created by the common law method of agreement and entry, B could not have validly accepted a release until after making an actual entry.

From approximately 1620 until 1845 the conveyance by lease and release was the most commonly used method of conveying land in England. It had the advantage (from the viewpoint of the parties) of transferring the title by means of a secret conveyance that involved none of the inconveniences of the common law methods. It was not necessary for the parties to go upon the land as in the case of a transfer by feoffment, nor was it necessary for the conveyee to make an actual entry as in the case of a transfer of an estate for years by agreement and entry. Moreover, the requirement of recording and payment of a fee therefor under the terms of the Statute of Enrolments was circumvented. In actual practice the bargain and sale, in the

[1] Lutwich v. Mitton, Cro.Jac. 604, 79 Eng.Rep. 516 (1621).

form of a deed, and the release would be drawn up on the same paper, the bargain and sale being dated the day before the release. It was customary to insert a consideration of five shillings in the deed of bargain and sale, although in fact it was rarely ever paid. The mere recital of consideration, without actual payment, was considered sufficient to raise a use.[2] Another advantage of conveyance by lease and release was that it could be used to effectuate family settlements of land by declaring uses on the release. Thus, A, seised in fee simple, would bargain and sell a term of one year to B. Then A would release the reversion to B and his heirs to the use of A for life, then to the use of A's eldest son in fee tail, with further remainders by way of use. All of the uses would be executed by the Statute of Uses into legal estates or interests.

SECTION 6. THE COVENANT TO STAND SEISED

In addition to the bargain and sale, another entirely new method of conveying a legal estate which originated in the Statute of Uses was the covenant to stand seised to uses. Normally, the Chancellor would not enforce a use unless there was "good" consideration—that is, a sound or worthy reason for doing so. The equitable doctrine of consideration was not confined to the notion of recompense or value. It was clear enough that where there had been a feoffment to uses the Chancellor's intervention was warranted. So also, in a bargain and sale the payment of the purchase price or, in the sixteenth century, a recital of consideration, was sufficient to raise a use. But a gratuitous agreement to hold land to the use of another was not sufficient to persuade the Chancellor to enforce the use. Nevertheless, in the middle of the sixteenth century it was held that if a land-

---

[2] As later stated by Chancellor Kent: "The rule requiring a consideration to raise a use, has become merely nominal, and a matter of form; for if a sum of money be mentioned, it is never an inquiry whether it was actually paid, and the smallest sum possible is sufficient; nay, it has been solemnly adjudged, that a pepper corn was sufficient to raise a use." Jackson ex dem. Hudson v. Alexander, 3 John. 484 (N.Y.1808).

owner by written instrument under seal promised to hold the land to the use of a relative in consideration of natural love and affection, or to the use of another in consideration of marriage, the covenant was effective to raise a use.[1] And the use thus raised would be executed by the Statute of Uses, thereby transferring the legal estate to the covenantee.

The covenant to stand seised, therefore, became valid as a method of conveyance where the parties thereto were related by blood or marriage. Since it could not be used for the purpose of conveying to a stranger, its principal use was in effectuating family settlements of land. Unlike the bargain and sale of a freehold estate, it was not required to be recorded under the Statute of Enrolments and, therefore, had the advantage of a private family arrangement. But its usefulness was somewhat impaired after the device of a limitation to trustees to preserve contingent remainders had been invented in the seventeenth century, because of the necessity that such trustees be relatives.

No technical words were required to have the conveyance operate as a covenant to stand seised, nor was a formal recital of a covenant or promise necessary. Indeed, the word "grant" was held to be a sufficient expression of intention to stand seised to the use of the conveyee.[2] Although the required degree of relationship between covenantor and covenantee was probably a close one in the early development of the doctrine, it was later somewhat relaxed. A covenant in favor of a wife, brother, nephew or spouse of a blood relation was valid.

---

[1] Sharrington v. Strotton, Plowden 298 (1566).

[2] Roe dem. Wilkinson v. Tramer, 2 Wils, 75, 95 Eng.Rep. 694 (1757). In Jackson ex dem. Wood v. Swart, 20 Johns. 85 (N.Y.1822) it was said: "It is scarcely necessary to observe that in such a conveyance no technical words are required; such as that the grantor covenants to stand seised, to the use of A etc.; but any other words will create a covenant to stand seised, if it appears to have been the intention of the party to use them for that purpose." Accord, Gale v. Coburn, 18 Pick. 397 (Mass.1836).

SECTION 7.   THE EFFECT OF THE STATUTE ON FUTURE
INTERESTS—EXECUTORY INTERESTS

The principal effect of the Statute of Uses on the law of future
interests was that it made possible the creation of new types of
legal future interests.   The rigid rules of the common law forbade the limitation of a freehold estate to begin in the future
and forbade the cutting short of the estate of one grantee in
favor of another grantee.   As a consequence, the one type of future interest that could be created in a conveyee was a remainder.
As we have seen, however, it was permissible in equity to create
future interests in the form of springing and shifting uses that
were not subject to these common law restrictions.[1]   By virtue
of the Statute of Uses, such equitable future interests became
converted into legal future interests and acquired the name "executory interests."   An executory interest, therefore, may be defined, in the primary sense of the term, as a legal future interest
created by means of an executed springing or shifting use.

These new types of legal future interests made possible a variety of limitations that were unknown to the common law and imparted to the land law a much needed flexibility.
To illustrate:

1.   By means of a springing use, a freehold estate could now be
     limited to commence in futuro.   Thus, A bargains and sells
     land to B and his heirs to have and to hold from and after
     the marriage of B to C.   The state of the title is: estate in
     fee simple in A subject to an executory interest in B in
     fee simple taking effect in possession on B's marriage.   Or,
     A enfeoffs X and his heirs to the use of B and his heirs

[1] The extent to which, in fact, the Chancellor, prior to the Statute of Uses,
recognized springing and shifting uses is far from clear but it is commonly
assumed that such uses were then enforced.   Shifting and springing uses
were recognized at law in the middle of the sixteenth century and it is hardly
likely that they were given legal recognition so soon after the Statute of
Uses without prior chancery precedent.   Cf. Simpson, Introduction to the
History of the Land Law 171, 184–185 (1961).

from and after the marriage of B. The state of the title is: estate in fee simple in A (by means of an executed resulting use) subject to an executory interest in B in fee simple. In each case B acquires his estate by means of an executed springing use.

2. There could now be a gap between the limitations of freehold estates to successive grantees. Thus, A bargains and sells land to B for life, and one year after B's death to C and his heirs. The state of the title is: life estate in B, reversion in fee simple in A subject to an executory interest in C in fee simple to take effect in possession one year after B's death. The interest of C which is now executory will become a possessory estate by means of the execution of a springing use which will cut short A's resulting use.

3. There could now be a valid limitation of a future interest taking effect by cutting short a prior estate in another grantee. Thus, A bargains and sells land to B for life but if B becomes a bankrupt then to C and his heirs. The state of the title is: life estate in B subject to an executory interest in fee simple in C, reversion in A. The interest of C which is now executory may become a possessory estate by means of the execution of a shifting use cutting short B's life estate.

4. An owner of land could now validly create a contingent future interest preceded by a term of years. Thus, A bargains and sells land to B for ten years, then to the heirs of C, a living person. The state of the title is: estate for years in B, executory interest in the heirs of C in fee simple, reversion in A in fee simple. The interest of C's heirs takes effect by means of an executed springing use. It was, at first, doubtful whether a contingent use preceded by an estate for years was good but later decisions seem to have settled the point.

In each of the situations above, the executory interest could be created by a conveyance in the form of a bargain and sale, a covenant to stand seised (assuming that the parties were related by blood or marriage), or, except in the fourth illustration, a feoffment to uses.

The case of Roe ex dem. Wilkinson v. Tranmer,[2] is a good illustration of the creation of an executory interest by means of a covenant to stand seised. There A, being seised of certain lands in fee simple, bargained and sold the lands to his brother B, in consideration of five shillings paid by B, for a term of one year. Then A, by an instrument in the form of a deed of release reciting a consideration of £100 paid by B, released the lands to B to have and to hold, *from and after the death of A,* to B and the heirs of his body, then to his cousin, C, and his heirs. B having died without issue, C brought an action of ejectment after the death of A. It was held that C could recover. The decision rests upon three main propositions: 1, since the estate in fee tail in B was not to become possessory until the death of A, it was an attempt to limit a freehold estate to commence in futuro and, therefore, the conveyance was void as a release; 2, although the deed was void as a release, it had all of the essential attributes of a covenant to stand seised and would be treated as such, on the principle that although a conveyance cannot be given effect as a conveyance of the particular type intended, if it fulfills the requirements of another type of conveyance it will be given effect as such rather than have it fail entirely; 3, a freehold estate which is limited to commence in the future may be created by a covenant to stand seised to uses.[3] Apparently, the deed of release was not enrolled and, therefore, would be void as a deed of bargain and sale because of failure to comply with the Statute of Enrolments.

---

2 Wils. 75, 95 Eng.Rep. 694 (1757).

3 The state of the title immediately after the conveyance was: estate for years in B, reversion in A in fee subject to executory interests in B in fee tail and C in fee simple. On A's death during B's lifetime, the state of the title would be: present estate in fee tail in B, vested remainder in C in fee. An interest which at the time of its creation was an executory interest can become a remainder by reason of subsequent events. See Simes & Smith, Future Interests, § 225; Restat., Prop. § 156, Comm. c.

SECTION 8.   THE STATUTE OF WILLS AND EXECUTORY DEVISES

One immediate consequence of the Statute of Uses was the loss of the power to transmit a use estate by will. The common law, apart from special custom in certain localities, did not permit a devise of a freehold estate but, as we have seen, landowners were able to circumvent this restriction by means of a feoffment to the uses declared in the feoffor's will. After the Statute of Uses this device was no longer effective because the Statute united the legal title and the use in the same person. The loss of the power to devise caused such deep resentment and discontent on the part of the land owning class that Henry felt compelled to restore that power and did so in 1540 by the Statute of Wills (32 Hen. VIII, c. 1).[1]

The Statute of Wills gave a limited power to tenants in fee simple to devise their lands by a will in writing.[2]   Since livery of seisin was not required, the courts construed this statute as permitting the creation of future interests which were not subject to the restrictions pertaining to the common law forms of conveyance. There could be a devise of a freehold estate to begin in the future, and an estate could be devised to take effect in defeasance of a prior devised estate. No declaration of a use was necessary, although devises could be limited by way of a use. These new types of legal future interests, originating in the Statute of Wills and analogous to springing and shifting uses,

[1] One of the grievances of the rebels in the rising known as the Pilgrimage of Grace (1536) was that the Statute of Uses had deprived men of the power to devise their lands.   Primogeniture had little appeal for Tudor England. "The Englishman would like to leave his land by will.   He would like to provide for the weal of his sinful soul, and he would like to provide for his daughters and younger sons.   That is the root of the matter."   Maitland, 3 Collected Papers 335 (Fisher, ed. 1911, Cambridge Univ. Press).

[2] The landowner was empowered by the Statute of Wills to devise all of his lands held in socage tenure and two-thirds of his lands held by knight service.   Moreover, those taking by devise were liable for the feudal dues as though they took by descent.   The Statute of Tenures (1660) removed the restriction on the power to devise.

were called executory devises. In common usage, the term "executory interest" includes executory devises as well as springing and shifting uses. The term "conditional limitation" is sometimes used as synonymous with "executory interest." [3]

SECTION 9. CHARACTERISTICS OF EXECUTORY INTERESTS

The addition of executory interests to the category of permissible future interests imparted a desirable elasticity to the land law but at the same time it made that law much more complex. Inasmuch as executory interests had some legal attributes different from those possessed by the common law future interests (reversions, possibilities of reverter, rights of entry for condition broken, and remainders) it frequently became necessary to decide whether a limitation in a conveyance or a will created an executory interest or a common law type of future interest.

The type of conveyance used to create a future interest would not in all cases determine the nature of that interest. An executory interest, by its very nature, could not be created by a common law conveyance on which no uses were raised. Thus, if A, after the Statute of Uses, enfeoffed B for life and one year after B's death to C and his heirs, C's interest would be void. The rule prohibiting the creation of a freehold estate to take effect in futuro still applied to common law conveyances. But it does not follow that every future interest created by a conveyance operating under the Statute of Uses, or by a will, is an executory interest. Common law types of future interests could be, and usually were, created by such conveyances. A remainder, for example, could be limited by the newer methods of conveyancing as well as by a common law conveyance. Thus, A bar-

[3] See e. g. Proprietors of the Church in Brattle Square v. Grant, 3 Gray 142 (Mass.1855). To make matters slightly more confusing the Massachusetts court has, at times, used the term "conditional limitation" in the sense of special limitation, that is, language in an instrument creating a determinable estate. See e. g. Markey v. Smith, 301 Mass. 64, 16 N.E.2d 20 (1938).

gains and sells to B for life, then to C and his heirs.   C has a legal remainder in fee simple expectant upon B's legal life estate.   C's interest is none the less a remainder although created by means of an executed use.

An executory interest, like a remainder, can be created only in a transferee, never in the transferor.   There is, therefore, usually no difficulty in determining whether a limitation creates an executory interest or gives rise to a reversion, a possibility of reverter, or a right of entry for condition broken.[1]   In some respects, an executory interest that divests an estate in a prior grantee resembles a common law right of entry but a right of entry could be created only in favor of the transferor.   Thus, A devises to B and his heirs but if B dies leaving no surviving children then to C and his heirs.   C has an executory interest, not a right of entry.   C's interest vests automatically on the happening of the specified event and no entry or election by him is necessary to cause the fee to shift to him.

The principal difficulty comes in determining whether a future interest in a transferee created under a will or by a conveyance operating under the Statute of Uses is a remainder or an executory interest.   This difficulty can only be resolved by examining the characteristics of the particular limitation.   A remainder can take effect in possession only at the expiration of the preceding estate in another grantee, not by divesting it.   By contrast, an executory interest can take effect only by di-

---

[1] This is not invariably true. Suppose that A devises land to a church to have and to hold so long as the land is used for church services, and if the land ceases to be used for such church services then to C and his heirs. A also devises the residue of his estate to C. The devise to the church with the gift over to C creates a determinable fee in the church and an executory devise in C. The gift over to C violates the Rule against Perpetuities and is, therefore, void. This would normally leave a possibility of reverter in the transferor.   Does the gift of the residue to C give C a possibility of reverter or a void executory interest? Under American law a possibility of reverter is not subject to the Rule Against Perpetuities. This, in substance, was the problem in Brown v. Independent Baptist Church of Woburn, 325 Mass. 645, 91 N.E.2d 922 (1950). The court held that under the residuary clause C received a possibility of reverter.

vesting a preceding estate in another grantee (except where the preceding estate is a fee simple determinable), or by divesting a freehold estate in the transferor or his successors in interest.[2] Put another way, a remainder is a successive interest; an executory interest is, normally, a divesting interest. Thus, A devises land to B for life, then to C and his heirs; but if C dies before B leaving no issue surviving him then to D and his heirs. D's interest is an executory interest because it takes effect by divesting or cutting short C's vested remainder. But suppose that the limitations were as follows: to B for life, and on B's death to C and his heirs, if C survives B; and if C dies before B, to D and his heirs. The limitations to C and D in this illustration are alternative contingent remainders.[3] Or, to take an actual case,[4] suppose A devises to "my son for life, and from and after his decease to his children who shall attain the age of twenty-one and their heirs; and in case my son shall become bankrupt or insolvent, the estate to my son shall become void and shall vest in his children as above limited." In discussing the nature of the interest given to the children, Lopes, L. J. said: "If the first part of the disposition had stood alone, the limitations to the children of the son would have been contingent remainders. But the forfeiture defeats the life estate before its natural determination, and the limitations to take effect on that premature determination are not contingent remainders, but executory devises."

2 If A conveys to B (a bachelor) to have and to hold to B and his heirs from and after B's marriage to C, the future interest given to B is an executory interest which takes effect in possession by divesting a fee simple in A. The estate in A is not a reversion because it is not a future interest. The state of the title is: fee simple in A subject to an executory interest in B in fee simple. A contingent remainder can divest a reversion by becoming vested. Thus, if A conveys to B for life, then to the heirs of C (a living person), the death of C during B's lifetime will cause the remainder to C's heirs to become vested in fee simple thereby extinguishing A's reversion.

3 Limitations such as these are a recurrent problem. See e. g. Cotter v. Cotter, 176 A.2d 316 (N.H.1961); Doe d. Planner v. Scudamore, 2 B. & P. 289 (Common Bench, 1800).

4 Blackman v. Fysh, 3 Ch.Div. 209 (1892). The language of the limitations has been changed slightly in the text.

Although it is a characteristic of an executory interest that it normally takes effect in possession by divesting a prior freehold estate in another grantee (shifting executory interest) or a vested freehold estate in the grantor (springing executory interest), there is an exception in the case of an executory interest limited after a fee simple determinable. There can be no remainder after a determinable fee; therefore, any interest limited to succeed such an estate is called an executory interest even though it will take effect on the expiration of, not the divestment of, the determinable fee. Thus, A bargains and sells land to B and his heirs so long as the land is used only for residential purposes, and if, during C's lifetime, the land is not so used, then to C and his heirs. B has a determinable fee followed by an executory interest in C in fee.

SECTION 10. CONTINGENT REMAINDERS AND EXECUTORY INTERESTS [1]

We have seen that at common law contingent remainders could be destroyed by a tortious alienation by the owner of the supporting freehold estate.[2] When executory interests were first recognized in the middle of the sixteenth century it was generally thought that they were as destructible as contingent remainders. This view was repudiated in Pells v. Brown [3] and by

[1] At this point the student may be interested in knowing that England's great legal historian, Frederic W. Maitland, once asked: "For who shall interest us in contingent remainders or the Statute of Uses, while Chinese metaphysics remain unexplored?" 1 Collected Papers 190 (Fisher, ed. 1911, Cambridge Univ. Press). But this rhetorical question was put to laymen, not to law students.

[2] C. 5, § 21, supra. The doctrine of forfeiture of a life estate on a tortious alienation was confined to common law conveyances, that is, conveyance by feoffment, fine or common recovery. It was not extended to conveyances operating under the Statute of Uses. Thus, if B having a life estate bargained and sold the land to X and his heirs, X would get only an estate for the life of B, not a tortious fee simple. Any contingent remainders dependent on B's life estate would not be destroyed.

[3] Cro.Jac. 590 (1620). The limitations in Pells v. Brown were these: A devised land to Thomas and his heirs; and if Thomas died without issue "living

virtue of that case it became settled that an executory interest was indestructible by an act of the owner of the preceding estate. The quality of indestructibility attaching to executory interests then became the principal characteristic of such interests and set them apart from contingent remainders. The courts continued to hold that contingent remainders were destructible by forfeiture, merger or other termination of the supporting freehold estate and they refused to draw a distinction between contingent remainders created by way of use or by will and those created by means of a common law conveyance. This refusal to treat contingent remainders created by way of use or by will differently from common law contingent remainders was due to a fear on the part of the judges that a consequence of holding such remainders indestructible would be to permit the creation of "perpetuities" and thereby impede the free alienability of land. At the time, the basis for the modern Rule against Perpetuities had not yet been formulated and it is a matter of some surprise not that early seventeenth century judges held all contingent remainders destructible but that they ruled executory interests to be indestructible.[4]

The rule that a contingent remainder created by way of use or by will was as destructible as a common law contingent remainder was given additional importance by the refusal of the courts to allow a contingent remainder to take effect as an ex-

William, his brother," then to William and his heirs. After entering into possession Thomas suffered a common recovery to the use of himself and his heirs. Thomas later died without issue and William claimed the land. The court held: 1. the phrase "if he (Thomas) died without issue" meant definite failure of issue because the failure of issue on which the gift over was to take effect was failure in the lifetime of William; therefore, Thomas had a fee simple, not a fee tail; 2. the gift over to William was valid as an executory devise which would divest the fee in Thomas; 3. the executory devise in William was not destroyed by the common recovery.

[4] The holding in Pells v. Brown, n. 3, supra, that an executory interest could not be destroyed by a common recovery did not meet with general acceptance at the time. Indeed, it was later remarked that it "went down with the Judges like chopped hay." Scattergood v. Edge, 12 Mod. 278, 281, 88 Eng.Rep. 1320, 1322 (1697). As to the law prior to Pells v. Brown, see Plucknett, Concise History of the Common Law 594 (5th ed. 1956).

ecutory interest in order to save it from failing as a contingent remainder. It became firmly settled that a future interest which, at the time of its creation, could take effect as a contingent remainder must take effect as such or fail. This rule, frequently called the rule of Purefoy v. Rogers [5] because of its application in that case, was stated by Hale, C. J. as follows: "where a contingency is limited to depend on an estate of freehold which is capable of supporting a remainder, it shall never be construed to be an executory devise, but a contingent remainder only, and not otherwise." In applying the rule to future interests created by way of use Lord St. Leonards said: "Now, if there be one rule of law more sacred than another, it is this, that no limitation shall be construed to be an executory or shifting use, which can by possibility take effect by way of remainder." [6] To illustrate: A devises land to B for life, and after B's death to such of his children as shall attain the age of twenty-one. It is possible that the children of B will reach twenty-one before B dies. The limitation to the children could, therefore, at the time of its creation, take effect as a contingent remainder. Since that is so, the limitation must, regardless of subsequent events, take effect as a remainder or not at all. If, at the time of B's death, all of his children are under twenty-one their interest fails and will not be preserved by treating it as an executory interest.[7]

[5] 2 Wm. Saunders 380, 85 Eng.Rep. 1181 (1670).

[6] Cole v. Sewell 4 Dr. & War. 1, 27, 4 Ir.Eq.Rep. 66, 68–69 (1843).

[7] Festing v. Allen, 12 Mees. & W. 279, 152 Eng.Rep. 1204 (1843). Contra, Bass River Savings Bank v. Nickerson, 303 Mass. 332, 21 N.E.2d 717 (1939). But suppose that at B's death he left surviving a son over twenty-one and a daughter under twenty-one. Would the daughter take on attaining twenty-one after B's death? Under the English view the daughter's interest would be classed as a contingent remainder and it would fail. But it is arguable that when the son reached twenty-one during B's lifetime he then had a vested remainder subject to open in favor of younger children who might later attain twenty-one and, therefore, the interest of such younger should be classed as an indestructible executory interest. There is some slight American support for this second view. See Simonds v. Simonds, 199 Mass. 552, 85 N.E. 860 (1908). The problem is discussed in 1 American Law of Property, § 4.62; Simes & Smith, Future Interests, §§ 204, 205.

The rule of Purefoy v. Rogers was a rule of law, not a rule of construction.[8] It undoubtedly operated to defeat the intention of the conveyor or testator in most of the cases in which it was applied. In the illustration given above, for example, (to B for life, then to such of B's children as shall attain twenty-one) it is almost certain that the testator intended that all of B's children who attained the age of twenty-one should take, whether they attained the specified age before or after B's death. But the rule implemented a concept of public policy. Since contingent remainders were destructible and executory interests were indestructible, it was thought desirable to classify future interests, where possible, as contingent remainders and thereby avoid the danger of permitting the creation of remotely contingent interests. In truth, the rule was an aspect of the doctrine of destructibility.

Until contingent remainders were made indestructible by statute in the latter half of the nineteenth century it was necessary for the conveyancer to guard against their destruction.[9] The device commonly used in the English family settlement of lands was the limitation of a remainder (after the life estate) to trustees to preserve contingent remainders. Another device available to the draftsman was to create limitations of future interests which could never take effect as contingent remainders,

---

8 White v. Summers, (1908) 2 Ch. 256. Two American cases have taken the opposite view and held that a limitation will not be treated as a contingent remainder if to do so would defeat the intention of the transferor. Simonds v. Simonds, 199 Mass. 552, 85 N.E. 860 (1908); Hayward v. Spaulding, 75 N.H. 92, 71 A. 219 (1908). Cromwell, it is said, described the law of real property in the seventeenth century as an "ungodly jumble." With considerable truth, the same might be said of the opinion in Simonds v. Simonds.

9 Contingent remainders were made indestructible in England by forfeiture or merger of a preceding freehold estate in 1845 but they continued to be destructible by failure to vest before the natural termination of the supporting freehold estate until 1877. 8 & 9 Vict. c. 106, § 8 (1845); 40 & 41 Vict. c. 33 (1877). The latter statute applied only to instruments executed after the enactment of the statute. It should be remembered that the destructibility doctrine was not applicable to equitable contingent remainders in land or to interests in personal property analagous to contingent remainders. The concept of seisin was inapplicable to equitable interests in land, and to personalty.

thereby avoiding the rule of Purefoy v. Rogers.   Thus, A by
lease and release conveys to X and his heirs to the use of B for
one hundred years if he so long live, then to the use of B's first
son who shall attain the age of twenty-one and the heirs of his
body.   Since B has a determinable estate for years, not a life
estate, the interest limited to B's first son is necessarily an executory interest.   Or, A could similarly convey to B for life, and
one day after B's death to B's first son who shall attain the age
of twenty-one in fee tail.   Again, the interest given to B's first
son is an executory interest since it follows a gap after the life
estate and can take effect only as a springing use.

   Moreover, it became possible to avoid the rule of Purefoy v.
Rogers by couching the gift of the future interest in the form of
alternative limitations one of which could take effect only as an
executory interest.   An example of such alternative limitations in
a gift to a class is found in the case of In re Lechmere & Lloyd.[10]
There, A, in substance, devised land to B for life, and after B's
death to such of her children living at her death as either before
or after her death shall attain the age of twenty-one years.
B died leaving seven children, of whom five had attained twenty-
one and two had not.   The question arose whether the two minor
children would take if they lived to the age of twenty-one.   The
court held that they would take with the other five children
on meeting the age requirement.   The court treated the "before
or after" death clause as creating "two distinct classes as the
objects of the devise," one class being children who attained
twenty-one before B's death, and the second class being children
who reached majority after B's death.   The court then stated:
"But to enable the second class to participate it is necessary to
read the gift to them as an executory devise.   The rule is that you
construe every limitation, if you possibly can, as a remainder,
rather than as an executory devise.   It is a harsh rule: why
should I extend it?   Why should a gift which cannot possibly
take effect as a remainder not take effect as an executory devise?   I see no good reason why it should not." [11]

[10] 18 Ch.Div. 524 (1881).

[11] Accord, **Dean** v. **Dean** [1891] 3 Ch. 150.

Although the alternative limitations in In re Lechmere & Lloyd were contained in a gift to a class, it is also possible to phrase a gift to an individual in the form of alternative limitations, one of which is a contingent remainder and the other an executory interest. In a dictum in White v. Summers [12] it was said by Parker, J.: "Thus, in case of a devise to A. for life, and after his death to B. if he shall have then attained twenty-one years, but if B. shall not have then attained twenty-one years, then to B. if and when he attains that age, there would be alternative gifts to B., one being a remainder and the other an executory devise, and which ultimately took effect would depend on whether B. had or had not attained the age of twenty-one at the death of A." [13]

The doctrine that executory interests were indestructible made it necessary for the courts to provide safeguards against land being tied up indefinitely by means of remote contingent interests. The policy evolved to control such interests became embodied in what is known as the Rule against Perpetuities.[14] That Rule, as finally developed, may be stated as follows: a future interest which, by any possibility, may not vest within twenty-one years after a life or lives in being at the time of its creation is void in its inception. Although the rule may be stated thus simply, its application gives rise to so many problems that an adequate

---

[12] [1908] 2 Ch. 256.

[13] The rule of Purefoy v. Rogers was generally accepted by American courts as an integral part of the doctrine of destructibility of contingent remainders although the number of cases applying the rule was not large. The rule, as well as the destructibility doctrine itself, is of diminishing importance in modern times not only because of the prevalence of statutes making contingent remainders indestructible but also by reason of the fact that most future interests created today are interests created under a trust (equitable interests) or are interests in personal property, e. g. stocks and bonds. For an extensive treatment of the subject matter of this section, see 1 American Law of Property, §§ 4.53–4.63; Simes & Smith, Future Interests, §§ 191–209.

[14] The foundations of the Rule were laid in The Duke of Norfolk's Case, 3 Ch.Cas. 1 (1681).

treatment would be beyond the scope of this elementary treatise.[15]

SECTION 11.   EXECUTORY INTERESTS IN MODERN LAW

In the modern law of future interests, executory interests play an important role.   By employing the device of shifting and springing interests it is possible for the property owner to exercise more flexible control in the disposition of his property by will or by deed.   He may, for example, create a vested remainder in one person subject to divestment on a specified contingency in favor of another person.   Or he may give a life estate to one person and make a gift over to take effect later than the termination of the life estate.[1]

Although executory interests came into the law originally in the form of shifting and springing uses that were converted into legal interests by force of the Statute of Uses, it is no longer necessary to employ the machinery of the Statute of Uses in order to create executory interests.   The Statute of Uses, it is

---

[15] It may be some consolation to the practising lawyer (but not to the law student) to know that the Supreme Court of California has held that an attorney who drafted a will containing a limitation that violated the Rule against Perpetuities was not liable for negligence to the intended beneficiaries who sustained a loss by reason of the invalidity of the limitation.   Lucas v. Hamm, 15 Cal.Rptr. 821, 364 P.2d 685 (1961), reversing Lucas v. Hamm, 11 Cal.Rptr. 727 (1961).   After quoting Professor Leach's description of the Rule as "a technicality-ridden legal nightmare" and "a dangerous instrumentality in the hands of most members of the bar" (67 Harv.L.Rev. 1349) the court concluded that "it would not be proper to hold that defendant failed to use such skill, prudence, and diligence as lawyers of ordinary skill and capacity commonly exercise."

[1] For example, in Loats Female Orphan Asylum v. Esson, 220 Md. 11, 150 A. 2d 742 (1959) A devised property to B for life or until she marry, then to a charitable corporation to be organized within twenty years from A's death. B married and thereafter the corporation was organized.   The court held that after B's marriage the title was in A's heirs subject to an executory devise in the corporation.   When the corporation was organized the fee automatically vested in the corporation.

true, is deemed to be in force in many of the states, and, therefore, the modern deed can be given effect as a deed of bargain
and sale. Occasionally, a court will expressly label a deed as one
of bargain and sale or covenant to stand seised and discuss the
doctrine of uses.[2] But even in jurisdictions where the Statute of
Uses is not deemed to be in force the modern deed is capable of
creating any type of future interest which could be created by a
conveyance operating under the Statute of Uses.[3] And since in
every state there is a statute authorizing the transfer of property
by will, the creation of executory devises is clearly permissible.

The distinction between contingent remainders and executory
interests is one of diminishing importance.[4] In most states there
are statutes abolishing the destructibility doctrine and abrogating the Rule in Shelley's Case. In such jurisdictions (except for
an occasional problem involving the Rule against Perpetuities)
contingent remainders and executory interests are practically
indistinguishable. In the few states where contingent remainders
are still destructible by merger or by failure to vest at or prior
to the natural termination of the supporting freehold estate the
distinction between these two types of interests continues to be of
some importance.[5]

At the present time, executory interests are, in the great
majority of jurisdictions, freely transferable inter vivos, de-

[2] Ricker v. Brown, 183 Mass. 424, 67 N.E. 353 (1903) (covenant to stand
seised) ; Bass River Savings Bank v. Nickerson, 303 Mass. 332, 21 N.E.2d 717
(1939) (bargain and sale).

[3] Abbott v. Holway, 72 Me. 298 (1881).

[4] See Dukeminier, Contingent Remainders and Executory Interests: A
Requiem for the Distinction, 43 Minn.L.Rev. 13 (1958).

[5] At times, the question may arise whether a future interest is an executory interest or a vested remainder. Thus, A conveys to B to have and to hold
to B and his heirs from and after the death of A. Normally, A has a fee
simple subject to an executory interest in B in fee but it is not uncommon
for the courts to describe A's interest as a life estate with a remainder in B
in fee. Basically, the question of the nature of A's estate should depend on
his manifested intention. Usually, it will make no difference which labels
are attached to the interests created ; but if A's interest is classified as a life
estate his liability for waste could be more extensive than if he is deemed to
have a fee simple subject to an executory interest.

visable by will, and descendible on the death of the owner intestate. The power to devise, or to have the interest devolve on intestacy, may, of course, be affected by a provision in the creating instrument making the executory interest subject to the contingency of survivorship to a specified time. In most of the states transferability of executory interests is made possible by statute but even in the absence of statute some jurisdictions have reached the same result.[6]

SECTION 12. UNEXECUTED USES

To return to our discussion of the Statute of Uses, it should be observed that the Statute neither prohibited the creation of uses nor did it provide for the conversion of all uses into legal estates or interests. In most cases, it is true, existing uses and uses created in the future were converted or executed into corresponding legal interests; but in some situations the Statute was held not to be applicable and in those situations the uses created existed as purely equitable interests. All such uses as were not converted into legal estates or interests were called unexecuted uses. The principal types of unexecuted uses were the following: A. A use raised on a term of years or other chattel interest; B. A use on a use; C. An active use.[1]

A. A Use Raised on a Term of Years or other Chattel Interest

By virtue of its own terminology, the Statute of Uses operates to convert a use into a like legal interest only where one person is "seised" of land to the use of another person. The word "seised" was used in its technical meaning of possession of a freehold estate in land. If, therefore, a person was possessed of a non-freehold estate to the use of another, the Statute of Uses was inapplicable. Since a term of years was a non-freehold estate, a use

---

6 See 1 American Law of Property, §§ 4.64–4.76; Simes & Smith, Future Interests, §§ 1852–1859, 1883, 1902; 2 Powell, Real Property, §§ 283, 284.

1 There were also other situations where a use would not be executed, e. g. a use raised on a conveyance of copyhold lands and a use raised on a conveyance in fee tail.

raised thereon was unexecuted. Thus, A, having an estate for ten years in Blackacre, conveys his estate to B to the use of C. C's use is unexecuted. B holds the legal title to the term in trust for C. C's interest is purely equitable. Although a use raised on a term of years is unexecuted, it does not follow that all use estates for years are unexecuted. A use raised on a freehold estate for a term of years is clearly within the application of the Statute. Thus, A, being seised of an estate in fee simple, enfeoffs B and his heirs to the use of C for ten years, then to the use of D and his heirs. C has a legal estate for years.

A use raised on personal property in the nature of chattels or choses in action is clearly beyond the scope of the Statute and, therefore, unexecuted.

B. A Use on a Use

Prior to the Statute of Uses, the Chancellors held that a use could not be limited on a use, that is, a use could not be given to one person to be held to the use of another person. If A, for value received, bargained and sold land to B and his heirs to the use of C and his heirs, the use declared in C was held void on the ground that it was repugnant to the use raised in B by virtue of the consideration paid by him. So also, if A enfeoffed B and his heirs to the use of C and his heirs to the use of D and his heirs, the use declared in favor of D was deemed void as being repugnant to C's use.

After the Statute of Uses, the courts of law, when called upon to consider the validity of a use limited on a use, applied the Chancery doctrine and held that the second use was unexecuted. Thus, in Tyrrel's Case,[2] A, in consideration of four hundred pounds paid by B, bargained and sold land to B and his heirs to the use of A for life, and after her decease to the use of B and the heirs of his body, and in default of issue, to the use of the heirs of A. The court held that the limitation of the uses was void "because an use cannot be engendered of an use." Since the use declared in A was not executed by the Statute, and was in-

---

[2] Dyer, 155a (1557).

valid in equity as a use on a use, no interest whatsoever passed to A by virtue of the conveyance.

It may be asked why such a conveyance as that in Tyrell's Case would have been drawn in that form. The most probable answer is that it was due to a mistake on the part of the conveyancer; that he intended the uses to be executed but overlooked the point that since a bargain and sale creates an implied use the further limitation of the second use would be a use on a use. The Statute of Uses was a complex Act attended by much uncertainty and confusion. Misunderstanding of its operation was not uncommon. Yet if the Chancellor were to grant relief against such mistakes there would be the danger of reviving uses. And, as Holdsworth reminds us,[3] the Chancellor was a great officer of state as well as an equity judge; he would not risk defeating or impairing the policy behind the Statute. Nevertheless, when in 1634 another case involving the limitation of inconsistent uses arose, application was made to the Chancellor for relief against the mistake and relief was granted by ordering the holder of the legal title to convey to the second cestui que use.[4] This was not a holding that a use on a use would be enforced in Chancery in the same way that uses were protected before the Statute of Uses. It was still too early for the Chancellor to recognize the second use as an equitable interest. With the enactment of the Statute of Tenures in 1660, however, there came a change of attitude. The economic purpose of the Statute of Uses had ceased to be a relevant consideration after the abolition of feudal dues. No reason of state now stayed the Chancellor from recognizing the use on a use as an equitable interest in land. By a process not altogether clear, it became established in the late seventeenth century that although a use on a use was not executed into a legal estate it would be protected in Chancery as

---

[3] Holdsworth, Historical Introduction to the Land Law 160–161 (1927).

[4] Sambach v. Dalston, Tothill 188. For an account of this case, see Strathdene, Sambach v. Dalston; an Unnoticed Report, 74 L.Q.Rev. 550 (1958); Yale, The Revival of Equitable Estates in the Seventeenth Century: An Explanation by Lord Nottingham (1957) Camb.L.J. 72, 78.

an equitable estate.[5] By 1676 the great Chancellor, Lord Nottingham, could state: "If an use be limited upon an use, though the second use be not good in law nor executed by Statute (of Uses), it amounts to a declaration of trust and may be executed (enforced) in Chancery." [6]

With the recognition of the use on a use in Chancery, the law had come full circle. It was again possible for the landowner to split the ownership into a legal and equitable title by deliberately creating a use on a use. The unexecuted use became known as a trust. Prior to 1536 the terms "use" and "trust" were synonymous and in the Statute of Uses itself the phrase "use, confidence or trust" appears repeatedly. But with the renascence of equitable interests in the form of the use on a use, the term "use" was restricted to a use executed by the Statute and the term "trust" was applied to an unexecuted use or equitable interest. Such trusts become common in the eighteenth century. The standard form of limitation to create a trust in a conveyance by lease and release was: "to X and Y and their heirs, unto and to the use of X and Y and their heirs, in trust for C." [7] The trustees obtained the legal title by force of the common law conveyance, not by an executed use, but the declaration of a use to the trustees had the effect of making the second use in favor of C a use on a use.[8]

The recognition and protection accorded the use on a use in Chancery marks the beginning of the modern law of trusts.

---

[5] For an excellent account of the evolution of the use on a use, see Simpson, Introduction to the History of the Land Law 186–194 (1961).

[6] Grubb v. Gwillim, Selden Society, Vol. 73, p. 347. A use on a use must be distinguished from a use after a use. The former is a contradictory or conflicting use; the latter is a successive use. Thus, A enfeoffs B and his heirs to the use of C for life, then to the use of D and his heirs. D's use is a use after a use, not a use on a use, and is executed by the Statute. The state of the title is: life estate in C, vested remainder in D in fee.

[7] This was the basis of Lord Hardwicke's famous crack that the Statute of Uses "has had no other effect than to add at most three words to a conveyance." The three words, apparently, are "in trust for." Hopkins v. Hopkins, 1 Atk. 581 (1738). The statement is a witty exaggeration.

[8] Doe v. Passingham, 6 B. & C. 305 (1827).

In essence, the trust was the old use in a new form but in dealing with trusts the Chancellors were not bound by ancient doctrine and were free to fashion the trust into an effective instrument for the management and disposition of property. In course of time the trust acquired its own distinctive characteristics but the underlying concept remained the same—the holder of the legal title to property is under a duty enforcible in equity to deal with the property for the benefit of the cestui que trust, the designated beneficiary.

The statement is sometimes made that the Statute of Uses failed to accomplish its purpose of abolishing dual ownership of land since by the doctrine of unexecuted uses a separation of the legal and equitable interests was effected. Such a statement is open to the criticism that it mistakes the purpose of the Statute and ignores its subsequent history. It is true that the object of the Statute was to prevent the separation of legal and equitable interests in land but this was merely a means to the end and that end was to put a stop to the drainage of royal revenues by the evasion of feudal dues through the practice of conveying to uses. The Statute did effectually put a stop to this drainage.[9] It was not until one hundred years after the Statute that Chancery gave protection to the use on a use and by that time feudal dues were no longer an important source of revenue to the Crown. By the time the use on a use was protected in equity the Statute of Uses had already accomplished its primary purpose. Active uses and uses raised on terms for years were, indeed, held to be beyond the reach of the Statute but they were, at that time, neither numerous nor important.

[9] As noted previously (c. 1, § 7, n. 1, supra), in 1540 a special court, The Court of Wards and Liveries, was set up to supervise the collection of the feudal dues to which the King was entitled. Under the efficient operations of this court (a combination of Tax Court and Internal Revenue Service) collections rose to a new high. See Bell, The Court of Wards and Liveries 190 et seq. (1953); Hurstfield, The Profits of Fiscal Feudalism, 1541–1602, 8 Econ. Hist.Rev.2d 53 (1955).

C. *Active Uses*

An active use exists wherever duties are imposed on the grantee to uses over and above those to which the feoffee to uses was subject before the Statute of Uses. Prior to the Statute, such a feoffee had the passive duty to allow the cestui que use to take the rents and the profits, and also the affirmative duties to protect the estate against disseisors and to convey the legal title at the direction of the cestui que use. Now, if the grantee to uses was directed by the terms of the conveyance to collect the rents and profits and pay them over to the holder of the use, the imposition of such additional affirmative duties was said to make the use an active use. Within ten years after the enactment of the Statute, it was held that an active use or trust was unexecuted and this decision was steadily followed.

There is nothing in the wording of the Statute of Uses that would make it inapplicable to active uses and the doctrine that such uses are unexecuted may be a questionable piece of judicial construction. It is true that to hold an active use to be executed would defeat the intention of the grantor by preventing the grantee to uses from performing the administrative duties assigned to him but the Statute was not designed to operate only in the case where the grantor's intention would not be thwarted. The probable reason for exempting active uses from the operation of the Statute was that such uses did not involve some of the evils against which the Statute was directed inasmuch as the feoffee to uses was in possession of the land and the ostensible owner. In any event, active uses or trusts were not common until the eighteenth century.

SECTION 13.   THE STATUTE OF USES IN THE UNITED STATES

Prior to the Revolution, the Statute of Uses was deemed to be in force in the American colonies and upon the formation of the states it was incorporated into their legal systems as a part of the common law. As stated by Parsons, C. J., in Marshall v.

Fisk: [1] "The statute of uses being in force in England when our ancestors came here, they brought it with them, as an existing modification of the common law, and it has always been considered a part of our law." Some states, New York for example, later abrogated the Statute by legislation and enacted substitute statutes to deal with conveyancing and trusts. Other states substantially re-enacted the Statute of Uses. At the present time the Statute of Uses, or a statutory substitute therefor, can be said to be in force in the great majority of the states. [2]

As a result of the Statute of Uses being in force in the several states, transfers of estates in land by means of a bargain and sale or a covenant to stand seised were, and are, valid methods of conveyancing. [3] Since the Statute of Enrolments, by reason of its local nature, was never deemed to be in force in America, land could be conveyed by a simple deed of bargain and sale and there was no need to resort to the more cumbersome English device of lease and release. [4] Conveyances by way of bargain and sale were, therefore, in frequent use. In practically all states there are statutes authorizing the conveyance of land by a simple form of deed that greatly resembles the old common law "grant" but, unlike the common law grant, the modern deed of grant

---

[1] 6 Mass. 24, 31 (1809).

[2] As to the situation in the several states, see 1A Bogert, Trusts, § 208 (1951). Incidentally, the Statute of Uses was repealed in England in 1925.

[3] But not all of the complex learning on the subject of uses was mastered by American courts. In Massachusetts, for example, it has been held that a freehold estate cannot be created to commence in futuro by a deed of bargain and sale. Welsh v. Foster, 12 Mass. 93 (1815). Yet the same court has held that a covenant to stand seised can create a freehold estate to commence in futuro. Moreover, the Massachusetts court holds that a covenant to stand seised can be supported by a pecuniary consideration even though the parties are not related by blood or marriage. By treating a deed of bargain and sale as a covenant to stand seised the conveyance is held effective to create the future freehold estate. Trafton v. Hawes, 102 Mass. 533 (1869).

[4] Conveyances by lease and release were common in New York in the eighteenth century. See e. g. Van Der Volgen v. Yates, 9 N.Y. 219 (1853). This was due to the practise of lawyers following English form books on conveyancing.

can be used to transfer both present and future estates. The statutory deed is, in reality, a substitute for the common law conveyance by way of feoffment.

The doctrine of unexecuted uses is recognized in jurisdictions where the Statute of Uses is in force. In such states, a use on a use creates an equitable interest only; and an active use or trust must be distinguished from a passive use or trust. In those states where land can be conveyed either by bargain and sale or by statutory deed equivalent to a feoffment, it sometimes becomes necessary to determine the mode in which the conveyance operates. Thus, for value received, A "gives, grants, bargains and sells" land to B and his heirs "in trust for, and to the use of" C and his heirs. If the deed is considered as one of bargain and sale, the use declared in favor of C is a use on a use and, therefore, unexecuted. The legal title is in B and the equitable title in C. If the deed is held to be a statutory substitute for feoffment, B stands seised to the use of C and C's use will be executed by the Statute of Uses so as to vest in him the legal title. In passing on a question of this nature the courts seek to effectuate the intention of the parties and will treat the deed as operating under that type of conveyance which will accomplish the result intended by the parties.[5]

In the modern law of trusts, the terms "active trust" and "passive trust" are generally employed instead of "active use" and "passive use." Since an active trust is not executed by the Statute of Uses but a passive trust is executed, a determination whether in a particular case the "trust" is active or passive may become of importance. Thus, in Burnham v. Baltimore Gas &

---

[5] Carr v. Richardson, 157 Mass. 576, 32 N.E. 958 (1893); Eckman v. Eckman, 68 Pa. 460 (1871). See Burnham v. Baltimore Gas & Electric Co., 217 Md. 507, 144 A.2d 80 (1958). Occasionally, a statute clarifies the situation. Mass. Gen.Laws Ann. c. 183, § 14 provides: "When a conveyance or devise of real estate is made to a grantee or devisee to a use intended to be executed by the statute of uses, the word 'use' shall be employed in declaring the use; and provisions introduced by the words 'in trust' or other expressions that might otherwise create uses, shall be deemed to create trusts and not uses."

Electric Co.[6]   A conveyed land to B and her heirs "in trust for the use and benefit of" B's two minor daughters, C and D, during their joint lives and for the life of the survivor, then to their heirs in fee simple.   The question arose, after the death of the two daughters, as to the nature of the estates created.   Since no active duties were imposed on the trustee in respect of the remainder interest, the remainder was a legal remainder.   The central problem was whether the life estates given to the two daughters were legal or equitable.   This in turn depended on whether the trust during the life of the daughters was active or passive.   If passive, it was executed and since the life estates and the remainder would be legal interests the Rule in Shelley's Case would apply.[7]   But if the trust was active, the life estates given to the daughters were equitable and the Rule in Shelley's Case would not be applicable since the life estates and the remainder to the heirs would not be of the same quality. The court held that the trust for the daughters was passive (hence executed) and the Rule applied.[8]

---

[6] 217 Md. 507, 144 A.2d 80 (1958).

[7] The deed had been executed prior to the enactment of the Maryland statute abrogating the Rule in Shelley's Case.

[8] For an excellent summary of the law with respect to active and inactive trusts, see Restatement, Second, Trusts, § 69 (1959).

Chapter 10

CONCURRENT OWNERSHIP

From an early date the common law recognized the capacity of two or more persons to own concurrent interests in the same estate in land. In time, the various kinds of concurrent interests were classified under four headings: joint tenancy, tenancy in common, coparcenary, and tenancy by the entirety. With the exception of coparcenary, these types of concurrent interests form the basis of the modern law of co-ownership of real and personal property.[1]

SECTION 1. THE CONCEPT OF JOINT TENANCY

Joint tenancy is a form of co-ownership subsisting between two or more persons in respect of an interest in real or personal property whereby such persons own the one interest together and each person has exactly the same rights in that interest as his cotenant or cotenants. The quality that differentiates a joint tenancy from other types of co-ownership is the unity of owner-

---

[1] Two additional types of co-ownership of considerable importance in American law are community property and tenancy in partnership. Community property is a system of marital property rights derived from the Spanish law and exists in eight states: Arizona, California, Idaho, Louisiana, Nevada, New Mexico, Texas and Washington. Under this system husband and wife are co-owners of all real and personal property acquired by either or both during the marriage otherwise than by gift, bequest, devise or inheritance. For details, see 2 American Law of Property, §§ 7.1–7.36.

Tenancy in partnership is, as the name indicates, a unique form of co-ownership by which specific partnership assets, both real and personal, are held by partners. The concept of tenancy in partnership is a creation of the Uniform Partnership Act, § 25. The Act has been adopted in forty states. See 7 U.L.A. 7 (Supp.1961).

ship of the joint tenants. Blackstone,[1] in a frequently quoted passage, described this quality as a four fold unity: "the unity of interest, the unity of title, the unity of time and the unity of possession; or in other words, joint tenants have one and the same interest, accruing by one and the same conveyance, commencing at one and the same time, and held by one and the same possession."[2] This description of Blackstone is helpful in that it emphasizes the factor of identity of interest and enumerates the requisites for the creation of a joint tenancy, but it describes the attributes of joint tenancy instead of analyzing the concept itself. That concept is the rather metaphysical one of a fictitious unity of persons as co-owners.[3] Put more simply, this amounts to saying that for some purposes the joint tenants are viewed as a unity but for other purposes they are recognized as having individual rights in respect of the property. This notion was expressed in the ancient maxim that joint tenants are seised *"per my et per tout"*—of a moiety or share and of the whole.

SECTION 2. CREATION OF A JOINT TENANCY

A joint tenancy is always created by act of the parties, never by descent or operation of law. At common law a conveyance or devise to two or more persons (other than husband and wife) was held to create a joint tenancy in the absence of a clear expression of the transferor's intention to create a tenancy in common. This constructional preference in favor of joint tenancy with its quality of survivorship arose from a desire to avoid splitting the feudal services due to the lord of the fee. After the decline of feudal tenure as a significant factor in the land law, the courts showed a disposition to seize upon any words that could be construed to

---

[1] 2 Bl.Comm. 180. The requirement of unity of possession does not mean actual possession. There may be a joint tenancy in a future interest, such as a remainder. A unity of right to possession is sufficient.

[2] Courts, in discussing the creation of joint tenancies, usually refer to the four unities. See e. g. Palmer v. Flint, 156 Me. 103, 161 A.2d 837 (1960).

[3] For a discussion of the nature of joint tenancy, see 2 American Law of Property, § 6.1.

indicate an intention to create a tenancy in common rather than a joint tenancy. This hostility of the courts to joint tenancy arose from the view that in the absence of a clear intention to that effect the ultimate ownership of the property should not depend on the accident of survivorship. This view has been reflected in legislation. In a few states joint tenancies have been abolished by statute. In a minority of states there are statutes abolishing the characteristic of survivorship of joint tenancy.[1] In the majority of states joint tenancies continue to exist in real and personal property as at common law but the common law presumption favoring the creation of a joint tenancy has been abrogated by statute.[2] These latter statutes usually provide that a conveyance or devise to two or more persons (except fiduciaries such as trustees or executors) shall create a tenancy in common unless the creating instrument expressly declares that such persons shall take as joint tenants or otherwise clearly manifests an intention to create a joint tenancy. Considerable litigation has arisen under such statutes in cases where the conveyance has not followed closely the statutory language but it is claimed that the language used manifests an intention to create a joint tenancy. Thus, if A conveys to "B and C and to the survivor of them, his heirs and assigns" do B and C take as joint tenants in fee, or do B and C take a life estate as tenants in common with vested cross-remainders for life, with a contingent remainder in fee in the survivor? Or, A may convey "to B and C as joint tenants and to the survivor of them, his heirs and assigns." Do B and C take as joint tenants in fee, or as joint tenants for life with a contingent remainder in fee in the survivor? Different answers have been given by the courts to these questions.[3] The language

---

[1] See e. g. Fla.Stat.Ann. § 689.15. For a hybrid type of statute, see Conn. Gen.Stat.Ann. § 47–14a.

[2] For a collection of these statutes, see 4 Powell, Real Property, § 602, n. 12.

[3] In Michigan, for example, a conveyance to B and C or survivor has been held to create a life estate in B and C with a contingent remainder in fee in the survivor. Rowerdink v. Carothers, 334 Mich. 454, 54 N.W.2d 715 (1952). An opposite result was reached in Coffin v. Short, 82 R.I. 132, 106 A.2d 262 (1954). In Ames v. Cheyne, 290 Mich. 215, 287 N.W. 439 (1939) it was held

of the applicable statute may be controlling;[4] but in the absence of controlling statutory language the principal issue is whether the provision for survivorship in the conveyance expresses an intention to create a joint tenancy or a contingent remainder in the survivor.

Another situation which has given rise to a diversity of opinion among the courts is where the property owner attempts to convey directly to a third person and himself as joint tenants. Thus, A conveys "to A and B and their heirs as joint tenants and not as tenants in common." At common law a man could not convey to himself, hence the effect of the conveyance would be to give B an undivided half interest as tenant in common with A. Since the unities of time and of title are lacking, no joint tenancy results. In the absence of statute, some courts have held to the common law rule;[5] others have refused to be bound by the "outmoded unities rule."[6] In about half the states there are statutes permitting a direct conveyance to the grantor and other persons as joint tenants. In a jurisdiction where there is no such statute and no judicial decision clarifying the law, it is still necessary for A to convey to a straw man and then have the straw reconvey to A and B as joint tenants.[7]

that a deed to B and C "as joint tenants and not as tenants in common, and to the survivor thereof" creates a joint life estate with a contingent remainder in fee to the survivor, not a joint tenancy in fee. Contra, Palmer v. Flint, 156 Me. 103, 161 A.2d 837 (1960). For a good analysis of the problem, see Comment, Joint Tenancy, 38 Mich.L.Rev. 875 (1940).

[4] In some states (e. g. Massachusetts, New Mexico and Utah) the statutes regulating the creation of joint tenancies expressly provide that a transfer to two or more persons and "the survivor of them" is sufficient to create a joint tenancy.

[5] A leading case applying the old common law rule is Deslauriers v. Senesac, 331 Ill. 437, 163 N.E. 327 (1928). The rule in Illinois has since been changed by statute. Ill.Smith-Hurd Ann.Stat. c. 76, § 1b.

[6] Therrien v. Therrien, 94 N.H. 66, 46 A.2d 538 (1946); Matter of Horler's Estate, 180 App.Div. 608, 168 N.Y.S. 221 (1917). The cases are collected in 44 A.L.R.2d 595 (1955).

[7] An alternative device, rarely used, is to have A convey by deed of grant or feoffment (not by bargain and sale) "to X and his heirs to the use of A

SECTION 3. CHARACTERISTICS OF A JOINT TENANCY

The most important characteristic of a joint tenancy is the right of survivorship or *jus accrescendi*. On the death of one of the joint tenants his interest does not descend to his heirs or pass under his will; the entire ownership remains in the surviving joint tenants. The interest of the deceased joint tenant disappears and the whole estate continues in the surviving tenants or tenant.[1] The widow of the deceased tenant has no dower rights and his creditors have no claim against the enlarged interest of the surviving tenants.[2]

The incident of survivorship attaching to the joint tenancy explains the popularity of this form of co-ownership, particularly with respect to certain types of personal property such as bank accounts, stocks and bonds.[3] The property owner who desires to

and B and their heirs as joint tenants and not as tenants in common." Johnson v. Johnson, 7 Allen 196 (Mass.1863). A and B take the legal title as joint tenants in fee simple.

[1] The problem of the simultaneous deaths of all the joint tenants is taken care of by the Uniform Simultaneous Death Act, adopted in all states except Georgia and Louisiana. § 3 of the Act provides: "Where there is no sufficient evidence that two joint tenants or tenants by the entirety have died otherwise than simultaneously the property so held shall be distributed one-half as if one had survived and one-half as if the other had survived. If there are more than two joint tenants and all of them have so died the property thus distributed shall be in the proportion that one bears to the whole number of joint tenants." 9C U.L.A. 164 (1957). Kansas and Massachusetts in their version of the Act substitute for the second sentence in the quotation the following: "Where more than two joint tenants have died and there is no sufficient evidence that they died otherwise than simultaneously the property so held shall be divided into as many equal shares as there were joint tenants and the share allocable to each shall be distributed as if he had survived all the others."

[2] The right of a creditor having an attachment, mortgage or other lien on the interest of a joint tenant may be preserved, by statute, despite the death of the debtor tenant. See e. g. Conn.Gen.Stat.Ann. § 47–14f; West's Wis.Stat. Ann. § 230.455.

[3] A number of different theories, including that of joint tenancy, have been advanced by the courts in the so-called "joint" bank account cases. But even where a court purports to apply the concept of joint tenancy to such cases,

have the property go on his death to a particular person (usually a spouse or close relative) frequently creates a joint tenancy in the property as a substitute for a will. The reasons for so doing may be a distrust of wills, or a desire to avoid the delay and expense of probate proceedings, or an erroneous belief that the property will not be subject to estate and inheritance taxes.[4] While the joint tenancy may well serve a useful purpose, particularly in the case of small estates, it is the subject of considerable misunderstanding among lay persons and the danger of such misunderstanding has led to legislation in a few states eliminating the right of survivorship as an incident of joint tenancy.

A joint tenant may freely alienate his interest in the jointly held property and such a transfer creates a severance of the joint tenancy. If A and B are joint tenants and A conveys his interest to a third person the joint tenancy comes to an end and the transferee and B hold as tenants in common. The transfer destroys the unities of title and of time since the transferee acquires his interest by a different title and at a different time than did B. If A, B and C are joint tenants and A conveys his interest to a third person, B and C remain joint tenants with respect to an undivided two-thirds interest. So also, if A, B and C are joint tenants and A conveys his interest to B the latter becomes a tenant in common with respect to the one-third interest conveyed by A but B and C remain joint tenants of a two-thirds interest. On

not all of the normal incidents of joint tenancy are held to govern the relations of the co-tenants. See Kepner, The Joint and Survivorship Bank Account—A Concept Without a Name, 41 Calif.L.Rev. 596 (1953); Kepner, Five More Years of the Joint Bank Account Muddle, 26 Univ. of Chi.L.Rev. 376 (1959).

4 For a rare instance of special tax advantages resulting from holding property in joint tenancy, see Mass.Gen.Laws Ann. c. 65, § 1 (exemption from inheritance tax of single family residence owned by husband and wife as joint tenants or tenants by entirety and occupied by them as a domicile; partial exemption for multiple family residence). See Marshall, Joint Tenancy, Taxwise and Otherwise, 40 Calif.L.Rev. 501 (1952).

B's death a one-third interest will pass under his will but a two-thirds interest will accrue to C as surviving joint tenant.[5]

The problem frequently arises as to what acts or conduct by a joint tenant in relation to his interest in the property, other than an absolute conveyance of that interest, will create a severance of the joint tenancy.[6] A mortgage of his undivided interest by one joint tenant will create a severance in a jurisdiction adhering to the common law rule that a mortgage transfers the legal title to the mortgagee.[7] In a state following the lien theory of mortgages, the mortgage creates a partial severance: the mortgage itself is effective against the surviving tenant but the equity of redemption accrues to the survivor.[8] A contract by a joint tenant to convey his interest will effect a severance on the theory that in equity the purchaser becomes the owner of the seller's undivided interest. Whether a lease of his undivided interest by one of the tenants completely severs the joint tenancy or leaves the reversion of the lessor-tenant subject to the joint tenancy is not clear.[9] Logically, it would seem that the execution of the lease destroys the unity of interest and causes a total severance. The commencement of a suit for partition will not cause a severance but the entry of a judgment for partition will have that effect even prior to the execution of the judgment.[10] A judgment

---

[5] Jackson v. O'Connell, 23 Ill.2d 52, 177 N.E.2d 194 (1961).

[6] See Swenson and Degnan, Severance of Joint Tenancies, 38 Minn.L.Rev. 466 (1954).

[7] Van Antwerp v. Horan, 390 Ill. 449, 61 N.E.2d 358 (1945); Tracy-Collins Trust Co. v. Goeltz, 5 Utah 2d 350, 301 P.2d 1086 (1956).

[8] Wilkins v. Young, 144 Ind. 1, 41 N.E. 68 (1895). It has been held in California, contrary to Wilkins v. Young, that the lien of the mortgage expires on the death of the mortgagor-tenant and the surviving tenant takes the entire property free of the mortgage. People v. Nogarr, 164 Cal.App.2d 591, 330 P.2d 858 (1958). In Connecticut and Wisconsin the lien of the mortgage is preserved by statute when the mortgagor-tenant predeceases his co-tenant. See n. 2, supra.

[9] See 2 American Law of Property, § 6.2. Cf. Swenson and Degnan, n. 6, supra at 472–475.

[10] Minnehan v. Minnehan, 336 Mass. 668, 147 N.E.2d 533 (1958); Sheridan v. Lucey, 395 Pa. 306, 149 A.2d 444 (1959).

lien on the interest of one of the joint tenants obtained by his creditor during the existence of the joint tenancy will not, prior to sale, sever the joint tenancy.

The courts are not in agreement as to the effect on the joint tenancy of a contract by all of the cotenants to sell the jointly held property to a third person. It is difficult to see why the contract should be held to create a severance with respect to the legal title but some courts have reached that result.[11] A conflict also exists as to whether the purchase money itself is held by the cotenants as joint tenants or tenants in common.[12]

It is possible for the cotenants to terminate the joint tenancy by a contract or agreement to sever the tenancy or by an agreement to deal with the property in a way inconsistent with their interests as joint tenants.[13]

At common law neither a joint tenant nor a tenant in common could compel a partition, that is a division of the land into separate parcels and the allocation of one or more parcels to each tenant. The remedy of the writ of partition was made available to joint tenants and tenants in common by a statute in the reign of Henry VIII.[14] Later, Chancery assumed jurisdiction of suits for partition. At the present time, the availability of the remedy and the procedures governing it are universally covered by statute.[15] Voluntary partition by the cotenants was always permissible.

[11] Re Baker's Estate, 247 Iowa 1380, 78 N.W.2d 863, 64 A.L.R.2d 902 (1956); Buford v. Dahlke, 158 Neb. 39, 62 N.W.2d 252 (1954). Contra, In re Hayes' Estate, (1920) 1 Ir.R. 207 (C.A.); Simon v. Chartier, 250 Wis. 642, 27 N.W.2d 752 (1947). Cf. Watson v. Watson, 5 Ill.2d 526, 126 N.E.2d 220 (1955).

[12] Holding that the proceeds of the sale are owned in joint tenancy in the absence of an agreement to the contrary: Teutenberg v. Schiller, 138 Cal.App. 2d 18, 291 P.2d 53 (1955); Hewitt v. Beige, 183 Kan. 352, 327 P.2d 872 (1958); Lawrence v. Andrews, 84 R.I. 133, 122 A.2d 132 (1956); Contra, Illinois Public Aid Comm. v. Stille, 14 Ill.2d 344, 153 N.E.2d 59 (1958); Greenberg v. Greenberg, 141 Me. 320, 43 A.2d 841 (1945); In re Cossitt's Estate, 204 App.Div. 545, 198 N.Y.S. 560, affirmed 236 N.Y. 524, 142 N.E. 268 (1923).

[13] The cases are collected in 64 A.L.R.2d 918 at 941 (1959).

[14] 31 Hen. VIII, c. 1 (1539).

[15] For details, see 4 Powell, Real Property, §§ 609–613.

SECTION 4. TENANCY IN COMMON

Tenancy in common is a type of co-ownership of real or personal property whereby each of the cotenants has a distinct and separate interest in the property but the right to possession is common to all of the cotenants. The only unity essential to a tenancy in common is the unity of possession. As Blackstone put it: "For indeed tenancies in common differ in nothing from sole estates but merely in the blending and unity of possession." [1] By unity of possession is meant that each of the tenants is entitled to possession of the whole property and every part thereof subject to the same right in the other tenants. [2] Since the unities of time, title and interest are not required for a tenancy in common, such tenants may acquire their respective shares by different conveyances and at different times, their shares may be unequal, [3] and the quantum of estate held by each may be dissimilar. Because there is no unity of interest, there is no right of survivorship. On the death of a tenant in common in fee simple his share descends to his heirs or passes under his will subject to dower rights of his widow.

Under modern law, the common law presumption favoring the creation of a joint tenancy on a conveyance to two or more persons no longer obtains. Therefore, at the present time the normal effect of a conveyance or devise to two or more persons is the creation of a tenancy in common in the absence of a manifested

[1] 2 Bl.Comm. 180.

[2] Thus, if A and B are tenants in common of Blackacre it is not correct to say that A is entitled to possession of one half of the parcel and B is entitled to possession of the other half. A has a right to possess all of Blackacre, and so does B.

[3] A transfer of property to two or more persons presumptively creates equal undivided interests in each of the transferees. Suppose, however, that A and B acquire title to land as tenants in common, that the purchase price is $15,000, and A contributes $5000 and B $10,000. The presumption of equal interests would be rebutted; A and B would have undivided interests proportionate to their contributions—one-third in A, two-thirds in B. See 2 American Law of Property, § 6.5.

intention that the transferees should hold under a different form of concurrent ownership.

SECTION 5. RELATIONS OF COTENANTS INTER SE

Apart from matters involving the right of survivorship, the mutual rights and duties of joint tenants and tenants in common are the same. They are, therefore, treated together.

Since each of the tenants is entitled to possession of the entire property subject to a reciprocal right in his cotenants, if one of the tenants excludes the others from the possession or enjoyment of the whole or any part of the land his conduct amounts to an ouster and an action of ejectment will lie in favor of the excluded tenants. Sole possession by the occupying tenant or appropriation of all of the rents and profits, without more, is not an ouster. There must be a repudiation of the rights of the cotenants and a claim of sole ownership; otherwise, the cotenants may properly assume that the possession of the occupying tenant is not hostile to their interests. The occupying tenant may acquire sole title by continuous adverse possession for the statutory period but the courts demand clear proof of the hostile character of the possession and of notice of the adverse claim to the other cotenants. Actual knowledge by the non-occupying tenants of the repudiation of their ownership is not necessary but the conduct of the occupying tenant must be such as to give adequate notice to his cotenants of the occupant's claim of sole ownership before the occupant can acquire exclusive title by adverse possession. The courts are understandably reluctant to allow the title of the non-occupying tenants to be extinguished by the presumptively permissive possession of the occupying tenant.[1]

The question of the liability of a tenant who assumes sole possession of the whole or a portion of the premises to account to his cotenants for the economic benefits derived from such sole occupancy is somewhat complex. We must distinguish between the

---

[1] See e. g. Williams v. Fulton, 4 Ill.2d 524, 123 N.E.2d 495 (1955); McKnight v. Basilides, 19 Wash.2d 391, 143 P.2d 307 (1943).

liability of an ousting occupant and the liability of one whose possession is not in defiance of the rights of his co-tenants; between liability for use and occupancy and liability for rents collected from third persons; between use of the land that depletes its value and use that does not involve substantial exploitation of the natural resources of the land.

When the occupying tenant's possession is held under such circumstances as to amount to an ouster of his cotenants, but he has not gained title by adverse possession, he is liable to account to his cotenants for their share of the fair rental value of the property. If the sole occupancy is not accompanied by an ouster, the occupant is not accountable to his cotenants for either use and occupancy or for profits derived from his use of the land, according to the majority of courts.[2] This view would seem to be a logical consequence of the proprietary nature of the interest of the occupant. All of the cotenants are free to enjoy their ownership and the non-occupying co-owners should not, by abstaining from the exercise of their right to possession, be able to convert the status of the occupying tenant from that of co-owner to rent paying tenant.

At common law the cotenants had no remedy against a tenant who assumed sole charge of the property and collected rents from third persons for its use, in the absence of an agreement by such tenant to act as bailiff or manager of the property. A remedy was provided by the Statute of 4 and 5 Anne[3] which gave an action of account to a joint tenant or tenant in common against his cotenant "as bailiff, for receiving more than comes to his just share or proportion." In a few states this statute is deemed to be in force as a part of the received common law; in most states a similar statute has been enacted. The majority of American courts have followed the interpretation placed on

[2] Larson v. Thoresen, 36 Cal.2d 666, 219 P.2d 492 (1950); Howland v. Stowe, 290 Mass. 192, 194 N.E. 888 (1935); Bennett v. Bennett, 193 Misc. 553, 81 N.Y. S.2d 653 (1948). Contra, Cohen v. Cohen, 157 Ohio St. 503, 106 N.E.2d 77 (1952); McKnight v. Basilides, n. 1, supra.

[3] 4 & 5 Anne, c. 16, § 27 (1705).

the Statute of Anne by the English courts and have restricted the application of it and similar statutes to the situation where rents and profits have been received from third persons. They have refused to treat the statutes as imposing liability on an occupying tenant for the reasonable rental value of the land or for profits derived from the nondepleting use of the land.[4] Where the occupying tenant depletes the land by developing its natural resources, such as mineral deposits, oil and gas, he is accountable to his cotenants for their proportionate share of the net profits.[5]

Troublesome questions arise as to the respective rights and obligations of the parties where one tenant pays more than his proportionate share of the cost of improvements, repairs, taxes, and carrying charges on the property. Involved in these problems is the matter of available remedies. It is well settled that a tenant who causes improvements to be made to the property owned in joint tenancy or in common, without the express or implied agreement of his cotenants, cannot maintain an action against his cotenants to compel them to contribute to the cost of such improvements. The reason generally assigned is that a man cannot be improved out of his estate. If the cotenants cannot agree as to the necessity or desirability of making the improvements the appropriate remedy is partition. This does not mean, however, that the tenant who bore the cost of the improvements is entirely without right of reimbursement. In a partition proceeding or in an action for accounting for rents and profits an equitable adjustment will be made where possible. Thus, on partition of the land by physical division the improver may have the improved part assigned to him where this can be done without prejudice to the others. Where the property is ordered sold in the partition suit, the improver is entitled to receive that part of the proceeds attributable to the improvements, over and above the share otherwise due him.[6] And in a suit for

---

4 For a collection of cases, see 51 A.L.R.2d 388 (1957).

5 See 2 American Law of Property, §§ 6.14–6.15.

6 See e. g. Batchelder v. Monroe, 335 Mass. 216, 139 N.E.2d 385 (1957); Rainer v. Holmes, 272 Wis. 349, 75 N.W.2d 290 (1954). Cf. Cosgriff v. Foss, 152 N.Y. 104, 46 N.E. 307 (1897).

accounting of rents and profits the improver is credited with any increase realized from the improvements.

The common law denied a right of action for contribution against his cotenants to the tenant who paid the cost of necessary repairs to the common property, and this view is still followed by some courts where the cotenants had not agreed to share the costs.[7] Other courts, perhaps a majority, allow contribution where the cotenants were requested to join in the making of reasonably necessary repairs but refused.[8] It is generally agreed, however, that the tenant causing such repairs to be made will be credited with their cost in adjusting the amounts due to the co-owners in an accounting for rents or in a partition suit.

Where one of the cotenants pays more than his share of the taxes, interest on a mortgage encumbering the property, or the principal of the mortgage he is entitled to contribution from his cotenants. The usual remedy given to the tenant making such expenditures is to credit him with the overpayment in adjusting the rights of the co-owners in distributing the proceeds of a partition sale or in an accounting for rents and profits. An equitable lien on the shares of his cotenants may be given him to enforce his right of contribution. In some jurisdictions the tenant making the payment is allowed to enforce his right of contribution by a direct action at law against his cotenants.[9]

In dealing with the common property, joint tenants and tenants in common owe a duty of good faith to one another. In some respects they stand in a fiduciary relationship and are not free to act with respect to the property as though they were strangers. This fiduciary concept is usually invoked where one of the cotenants acquires for himself an outstanding encumbrance on the common property, such as a mortgage or tax lien. The

---

[7] A leading case is Calvert v. Aldrich, 99 Mass. 74 (1868).

[8] This is the view taken by the Restatement of Restitution, § 105. But compare 2 American Law of Property, § 6.18. Where the tenant making the repairs has received the benefit of them through sole possession of the property he will normally be denied the right of contribution.

[9] See e. g. Howland v. Stowe, 290 Mass. 142, 194 N.E. 888 (1935).

tenant acquiring an outstanding title or encumbrance will be compelled to hold it for the benefit of all of the cotenants if the others offer to contribute their proportionate share of the acquisition cost within a reasonable time. Most courts apply the same rule when one of the co-owners purchases the property at a mortgage foreclosure sale or at the foreclosure of a tax lien.[10]

SECTION 6.   TENANCY BY THE ENTIRETY—THE COMMON LAW CONCEPT

For many purposes the common law treated husband and wife as one legal person. This concept of the legal unity of the spouses resulted in the recognition of a peculiar kind of co-ownership between husband and wife—the tenancy by the entirety. In most respects this form of tenancy resembled the joint tenancy. It was characterized by the four unities of time, title, interest and possession. Yet the manner of holding the estate was said to be different—joint tenants were seized of a share and of the whole (*per my et per tout*), but tenants by the entirety were seised of the whole and not of a share (*per tout et non per my*).[1] As in the case of a joint tenancy, the incident of survivorship attached to a tenancy by the entirety but it was an indestructible right of

---

[10] Salter v. Quinn, 334 Mass. 220, 134 N.E.2d 749 (1956) (delay of seventeen years did not necessarily preclude cotenant from asserting claim to an interest in the property); Beers v. Pusey, 389 Pa. 117, 132 A.2d 346 (1957) (delay of twelve years not fatal to claim of cotenants where wife of one of the tenants acquired title at sale of property for unpaid taxes). Holding that any of the cotenants may purchase at a public sale for his own benefit: Starkweather v. Jenner, 216 U.S. 524, 30 S.Ct. 282, 54 L.Ed. 602 (1910); McNutt v. Nuevo Land Co., 167 Cal. 459, 140 P. 6 (1914).

[1] If you find this concept difficult to grasp, you are not alone. In his dissenting opinion in King v. Greene, 30 N.J. 395, 413, 153 A.2d 49, 60 (1959) Chief Justice Weintraub had this to say: "The estate by the entirety is a remnant of other times. It rests upon the fiction of a oneness of husband and wife. Neither owns a separate distinct interest in the fee; rather each and both as an entity own the entire interest. Neither takes anything by survivorship; there is nothing to pass because the survivor always had the entirety. To me the conception is quite incomprehensible."

survivorship. Both spouses could join in a conveyance of the property to a third person but neither alone could create a severance of the tenancy or by any act defeat the right of survivorship of the other spouse. No right of partition existed. The right of survivorship was an attribute of the ownership by each spouse of the entire estate from the time it was conveyed to them; it was not a contingent future interest in the surviving spouse, superadded to a joint life estate.

At common law a conveyance to grantees who were husband and wife created in them an estate by the entireties. It was not necessary that they be described as husband and wife or that the conveyance manifest an intention that they take as tenants by the entirety. Indeed, it would seem that under English common law the spouses were incapable of holding as joint tenants or as tenants in common.[2] Upon the creation of the tenancy the rights of the spouses were not equal during coverture. The husband alone was entitled to possession, use and enjoyment of the property. This superior right of the husband, however, would seem not to be a peculiar attribute of the tenancy by the entirety but rather a consequence of the husband's position as guardian of his wife. The analogy to the husband's estate *jure uxoris* in lands solely owned by the wife is apparent.

SECTION 7. THE TENANCY BY THE ENTIRETY IN MODERN LAW

As might be expected, the tenancy by the entirety has met with a mixed reception in the United States. Its underlying concept of an artificial unity of husband and wife is repugnant to modern views of the status of married women. It is incompatible with the basic theory of the community property system of a conjugal partnership in acquisitions and gains and, therefore, was never recognized in the eight community property states. Among

[2] Green v. King, 2 Wm. Blackstone 1211, 96 Eng.Rep. 713 (1777); Co.Litt. 291; 2 Bl.Comm. 181. But cf. Challis, Real Property 305 (1887). Tenancy by the entirety was abolished in England by the Law of Property Act, 1925.

the common law states, some have held that the Married
Women's Property Acts, by granting to wives the right to own
and control property as though sole, abolished this unique type
of co-ownership.   Others have reached the same result by construing statutes relating to conveyances to two or more persons
as eliminating the entirety estate.   The net result is that at the
present time the tenancy by the entirety exists in twenty-two
states.[1]   In those jurisdictions which recognize this tenancy as a
permissible type of concurrent ownership, it usually exists in a
modified form, shorn of some of its common law attributes.

In all of the states recognizing the tenancy by the entirety,
the spouses are also allowed to hold property as tenants in common; and except in those states where joint tenancy has been
abolished, they may hold as joint tenants.   In many of these
states a conveyance to husband and wife creates a tenancy by
the entirety in the absence of a manifested intention that the
grantees take as tenants in common or as joint tenants.[2]   In
some states the presumption of a tenancy by the entirety is so
strong that a conveyance to husband and wife "as joint tenants"
or "in joint tenancy" is held to create an estate by the entirety.[3]

[1] The following jurisdictions have retained the tenancy by the entirety in
real property: Arkansas, Delaware, District of Columbia, Florida, Hawaii,
Indiana, Kentucky, Maryland, Massachusetts, Michigan, Missouri, Montana,
New Jersey, New York, North Carolina, Oklahoma, Oregon, Pennsylvania,
Rhode Island, Tennessee, Vermont, Virginia and Wyoming. Not all of these
jurisdictions recognize a tenancy by the entirety in personal property.   The
tenancy does not exist generally in personal property in Indiana, Michigan,
New Jersey, New York, North Carolina, Oregon and Wyoming. See Anno-
tation, Estates by Entirety in Personal Property, 64 A.L.R.2d 8 (1959).

[2] See e. g. Matthews v. McCain, 125 Fla. 840, 170 So. 323 (1936); Mosser
v. Dolsay, 132 N.J.Eq. 121, 27 A.2d 155 (1942); Roberts v. Roberts, 206 Misc.
779, 134 N.Y.S.2d 877 (1954). But in some jurisdictions retaining the tenancy
by the entirety, a conveyance to husband and wife without specifying the
manner of their holding presumptively creates a tenancy in common. See
e. g. D.C.Code, § 45–816 (1961); Mass.Gen.Laws Ann. c. 184, § 7.

[3] See e. g. Franz v. Franz, 308 Mass. 262, 32 N.E.2d 205 (1941). The cases
following this view, as well as those holding that the conveyance creates a
joint tenancy, are collected in 161 A.L.R. 457 (1946). In jurisdictions, such
as Massachusetts, it is necessary expressly to recite in the deed that the grantees are not to take as tenants by the entirety in order to avoid such con-

The latter estate is viewed as essentially a joint tenancy modified by the common law doctrine of the unity of husband and wife. At common law, a conveyance to husband and wife and a third person gave to the husband and wife a one-half interest as tenants by the entirety, and to the third person the other one-half interest as a joint tenant with the spouses. This resulted from a logical application of the theory that the husband and wife were one legal person. At the present time, such a conveyance would, presumptively, create the same estate in the spouses but the third person would hold his half interest as a tenant in common.[4]

Since the tenancy by the entirety is necessarily predicated on the legal unity of husband and wife, it cannot be created in grantees who are not lawfully married at the time of the conveyance. The courts are not in agreement as to the effect of a grant to two persons, who are not husband and wife, to hold "as tenants by the entirety." Some courts, perhaps a majority, find in the declaration that the grantees are to take as tenants by the entirety an expression of an intention to create a right of survivorship and hold, therefore, that a joint tenancy, rather than a tenancy in common, results.[5] Where husband and wife hold by the entireties and the marriage is ended by divorce, the tenancy also comes to an end and is converted into a tenancy in common.

At common law a man could not convey a legal estate to himself, to himself and his wife, or to himself and another person

struction where the conveyance is intended to create a joint tenancy. Thus, A conveys "to H and W, as joint tenants and not as tenants by the entirety."

[4] Fulton v. Katsowney, 174 N.E.2d 366 (Mass.1961) (deed to "A, H and W, his wife, as joint tenants and not as tenants in common;" A takes one half interest as tenant in common and H and W take other half as tenants by entirety). But because of the Mass. statute (see n. 2, supra) creating a presumption of tenancy in common in a conveyance to two or more persons, including husband and wife, if the deed had run simply "to A, H and W, his wife" without more, it would seem that the three grantees would each take a one-third interest as tenants in common.

[5] Coleman v. Jackson, 286 F.2d 98 (D.C.C.A.1960); Bove v. Bove, 394 Pa. 627, 149 A.2d 67 (1959). Contra, Perrin v. Harrington, 146 App.Div. 292, 130 N.Y.S. 944 (1911).

jointly. A tenancy by the entirety, therefore, could not be created by a direct conveyance from a husband to himself and his wife. In most of the states permitting tenancies by the entirety this rule has been changed by statute and a direct conveyance by either spouse to both spouses as tenants by the entirety is effective to create the intended estate. In the absence of a controlling statute, the courts are divided on the question.[6] Where the spouses hold property by the entireties, either spouse can, by the majority view, release his or her interest directly to the other spouse.[7]

The characteristics of the modern tenancy by the entirety differ substantially in most jurisdictions from the common law attributes of the tenancy. While the indestructible right of survivorship is universally retained, the rights of the spouses during the marriage have been radically altered. In the great majority of jurisdictions the husband and wife have equal rights with respect to the possession, use and revenues of the property.[8] The exclusive right to possession and profits which the common law gave to the husband is usually held to have been abolished by the Married Women's Property Acts, although those statutes do not, in terms, purport to deal with tenancies by the entirety. In a few jurisdictions the rights of the spouses remain the same as at common law, with the husband having the exclusive right to possession, enjoyment and income.[9]

The courts are not in agreement as to the capacity of one of the spouses to transfer to a third person his or her interest in the property during the marriage, or as to the power of a creditor

6 For a collection of cases, see Annotation, 44 A.L.R.2d 595 (1955).

7 Hale v. Hale, 332 Mass. 329, 125 N.E.2d 142 (1955); Howell v. Davis, 196 Tenn. 334, 268 S.W.2d 85 (1954).

8 See e. g. Columbian Carbon Co. v. Kight, 207 Md. 203, 114 A.2d 28 (1955); King v. Greene, 30 N.J. 395, 153 A.2d 49, 75 A.L.R.2d 1153 (1959); Hiles v. Fisher, 144 N.Y. 306, 39 N.E. 337 (1895); Lindenfelser v. Lindenfelser, 396 Pa. 530, 153 A.2d 901 (1959).

9 Massachusetts is the leading exponent of this view. Licker v. Gluskin, 265 Mass. 403, 164 N.E. 613 (1929). Accord, Arrand v. Graham, 297 Mich. 559, 298 N.W. 281 (1941); Lewis v. Pate, 212 N.C. 253, 193 S.E. 20 (1937).

of one of the spouses to subject the debtor-spouse's interest to satisfaction of his claim. All courts agree that the right of the surviving spouse to the entire estate cannot be defeated by any transfer, voluntary or involuntary, made by the other spouse [10] but diversity of opinion exists as to the ability of one of the spouses to convey his or her right to share in the possession and income of the property together with the contingent right of survivorship. On this point the courts may be classified into three main groups. The largest group holds that neither spouse can individually transfer his or her interest during the marriage or alienate his or her contingent right of survivorship.[11] These courts adopt the view that although the rights of the spouses are equal neither has a separate interest capable of alienation. A second group of four states [12] treats the modern tenancy by the entirety as essentially a tenancy in common with an indefeasible right of survivorship and permits either spouse to transfer his or her right to possession, income and profits together with his or her contingent right of survivorship. A third group of states, three in number,[13] adheres to the common law view and allows the husband, but not the wife, to alienate his interest, including therein his contingent right of survivorship.

The question has been raised whether the tenancy by the entirety serves a justifiable social purpose in modern times. Admittedly, this tenancy is an anomaly based on an anachronism. In situations where the marriage relationship is unstable, the tenancy can operate to the disadvantage of one or both of the

[10] But by statute in Oklahoma a creditor of either spouse may force a sale of the debtor spouse's interest and thereby compel a severance of the tenancy. West's Okl.Stat.Ann. tit. 60, § 74.

[11] In this group are: Delaware, District of Columbia, Florida, Indiana, Maryland, Missouri, Pennsylvania, Rhode Island, Vermont, Virginia and Wyoming. For a summary of the law of the several states, see Phipps, Tenancy by Entireties, 25 Temp.L.Q. 24 (1951).

[12] Arkansas, New Jersey, New York and Oregon.

[13] Massachusetts, Michigan and North Carolina. As to the rights of creditors, see Huber, Creditors' Rights in Tenancies by the Entireties, 1 Bos.Coll. Ind. & Comm.L.Rev. 197 (1960).

spouses. The inability of either spouse to compel partition or to effectuate a severance, or in some states to convey a separate interest to a third person, can create a deadlock with respect to the property. The legitimate claims of creditors can be defeated in those jurisdictions which do not permit a levy of execution on the interest of the debtor spouse. Despite these objections, however, the tenancy by the entirety continues to be a popular form of co-ownership in several states [14] and it is unlikely that appeals for its abolition will be heeded.[15] In a sense, this peculiar form of marital co-ownership operates as a substitute for a community property system in the common law states which still retain it.

SECTION 8. TENANCY IN COPARCENARY

An estate in coparcenary existed at common law where lands descended from the ancestor to two or more females, in default of a male heir, or where, by special custom in certain localities, lands descended to two or more males. Coparceners, or parceners as they were frequently called, constituted together but one heir and had but one estate. The name "parcener" is derived from the fact that apart from statute such a tenant had the right to compel a partition at a time when joint tenants and tenants in common had no such right. In many respects a tenant in coparcenary occupied a position intermediate between a joint tenant and a tenant in common. Like joint tenants, coparceners had a single estate, they could sue and be sued jointly in respect of the land, and one parcener could convey her share to her co-

14 In Massachusetts, for example, the greater portion of residential property is held by husbands and wives as tenants by the entirety. The popularity of this tenancy is due to special tax advantages under the state inheritance tax, the immunity of the wife's interest to claims of creditors, and a desire to dispense with probate proceedings on the death of either spouse.

15 For criticisms of the tenancy by the entirety, see Report of Committee on Changes in Substantive Real Property Principles, in Report of Proceedings of the Section of Real Property, Probate and Trust Law Division, A. B. A. (1944); Ritter, A Criticism of the Estate by the Entirety, 5 Fla.L.Rev. 153 (1952).

tenants by a release. As in the case of tenants in common, no right of survivorship existed among coparceners, the share of a deceased parcener going to her heir who would hold in coparcenary with the surviving parceners. "And so long as the lands continue in a course of descent, and united in possession, so long are the tenants therein, whether male or female, called parceners. But if possession be once severed by partition, they are no longer parceners but tenants in severalty; or if one parcener aliens her share, though no partition be made, then are the lands no longer held in coparcenary but in common." [1]

The doctrine of estates in coparcenary was correlative to the rule of primogeniture prevailing in England whereby lands descended to the eldest male only, when there were two or more males related in equal degree to the deceased owner. This rule was never in force in this country and as a consequence estates in coparcenary were not generally recognized. In nearly all states heirs take as tenants in common. Although the term "coparceners" or "parceners" is sometimes used in statutes or decisions to describe persons taking land by descent,[2] the tenancy itself as a separate type of co-ownership is generally obsolete and only the name survives.[3] The ancient tenancy in coparcenary has been absorbed in the tenancy in common.

[1] 2 Bl.Com. 188, 189.

[2] See e. g. Fla.Stat.Ann., § 66.04 (1943); Md.Code Ann. art. 16, § 154 (1957); W.Va.Code Ann., § 3640 (1955).

[3] But cf. Gilpin v. Hollingsworth, 3 Md. 190, 56 Am.Dec. 737 (1852) (doctrine of worthier title not applicable to devise to heirs as tenants in common because their estate as tenants in common is different in quality than the estate they would take by descent as coparceners).

TABLE OF CASES

Abel **v.** Girard Trust Co.—**p.** 100.

Abbott v. Holway—p. 206.

Aetna Life Ins. Co. v. Hoppin—**p.** 147.

Ames **v.** Cheyne—**p.** 218.

Anderson v. Ries—p. 84.

Archer's Case—**pp.** 131, 145.

Armstrong dem. Neve v. Wolsey—**p.** 186.

Arrand v. Graham—**p.** 233.

Aste v. Putnam's Hotel Co.—**p.** 75.

Audley's Estate, In re—**p.** 50.

Automobile Supply Co. v. The Scene-in-Action Corp.—**p.** 72.

Bails v. Davis—**pp.** 144, 146.

Baker **v.** Forsuman—**p.** 147.

Baker's Estate, Re—**p.** 223.

Bandera v. Donahue—**p.** 79.

Barnard Realty Co. v. Bonwit—**p.** 72.

Baseball Pub. Co. v. Bruton—**p.** 68.

Bass River Sav. Bank v. Nickerson—**pp.** 201, 206.

Batchelder v. Monroe—**p.** 227.

Beeman v. Stillwell—p. 34.

Beers v. Pusey—p. 229.

Bekins v. Smith—p. 50.

Beliveau v. Beliveau—**p.** 60.

Belleville Sav. Bank v. Aneshaensel—**p.** 143.

Bennett v. Bennett—p. 226.

Bennett v. Morris—**p.** 146.

Benton v. Williams—**p.** 85.

Benz v. Fabian—**p.** 49.

Beverley's Case—**pp.** 139, 140.

Bhar Realty Corp. v. Becker—**p.** 82.

Biederman v. Seymour—**p.** 154.

Bishop v. Williams—**p.** 141.

Blackman v. Fysh—**p.** 198.

Board of Chosen Freeholders v. Buck—**p.** 37.

Bottimore v. First & Merchants Nat. Bank—**p.** 160.

Bove v. Bove—**p.** 232.

Bowman v. Brown—**p.** 51.

Braswell v. Braswell—**p.** 154.

Bridge Hardware Co. v. Disosway & Fisher, Inc.—**p.** 68.

Brown v. Independent Baptist Church of Woburn—**pp. 102, 197.**
Bruckner v. Helfaer—**p. 72.**
Buford v. Dahlke—**p. 223.**
Bullock v. Seymour—**p. 44.**
Burchell, Matter of—**pp. 158, 159.**
Burnham v. Baltimore Gas & Electric Co.—**pp. 147, 214.**

Cahill v. Cahill—**p. 146.**
Calvert v. Aldrich—**p. 228.**
Carlton Chambers Co. v. Trask—**p. 79.**
Carr v. Richardson—**p. 214.**
Carruthers v. Spaulding—**p. 99.**
Cassidy v. Welsh—**p. 79.**
Cauffiel v. Cauffiel—**p. 62.**
Charlotte Park and Recreation Commission v. Barringer—**p. 100.**
Chester A. Baker, Inc. v. Shea Dry Cleaners, Inc.—**p. 85.**
Chestnut v. Chestnut—**p. 34.**
City Bank Farmers Trust Co. v. Miller—**p. 158.**
City of. See under name of city.
Clarke v. Fay—**p. 113.**
Coe v. Clay—**p. 68.**
Coffin v. Short—**p. 218.**
Cohen v. Cohen—**p. 226.**
Cole v. Lake—**p. 33.**
Cole v. Sewell—**p. 201.**
Cole v. Steinlauf—**p. 33.**
Coleman v. Jackson—**p. 232.**
Colligan, Matter of—**p. 60.**
Columbian Carbon Co. v. Kight—**p. 233.**
Combs v. Jackson—**p. 20.**
Conger v. Lowe—**p. 60.**
Consolidated School Dist. No. 102 v. Walter—**p. 101.**
Copps Chapel Methodist Episcopal Church, In re—**p. 99.**
Cordon v. Gregg—**p. 154.**
Cosgriff v. Foss—**p. 227.**
Cossitt's Estate, In re—**p. 223.**
Cotter v. Cotter—**p. 198.**
Coudert v. Cohn—**p. 66.**
Creech v. Crockett—**p. 66.**
Crowell v. City of Riverside—**p. 75.**
Curtis v. Galvin—**p. 84.**

Dalton v. Eash—**p. 92.**
Darling Shops Delaware Corp. v. Baltimore Center Corp.—**p. 66.**
D'Arundel's Case—**p. 31.**
Davidson v. Minnesota Loan & Trust Co.—**p. 78.**
Davis v. Francis Scott Key Apartments, Inc.—**p. 69.**

Davis v. Vidal—p. 77.
Davis v. Thompson—p. 82.
Dean v. Dean—p. 203.
DeHart v. Allen—p. 79.
Dennen v. Searle—p. 33.
Deslauriers v. Senesac—p. 219.
Dial v. Dial—p. 92.
Dickson v. Alexandria Hospital, Inc.—p. 51.
Doctor v. Hughes—pp. 155–158.
Dodsworth v. Dodsworth—p. 106.
Doe v. Cole—p. 171.
Doe v. Passingham—p. 210.
Doe d. Planner v. Scudamore—p. 198.
Dormer v. Packhurst—p. 133.
Duke of Norfolk's Case, The—p. 204.
Dumpor's Case—p. 75.
Duncomb v. Duncomb—p. 133.
Dunlap v. Bullard—p. 77.
Dyer v. Siano—p. 100.

Eckman v. Eckman—p. 214.
Edgewood Park Junior College, Inc., In re—p. 73.
Edward John Noble Hospital v. Board of Foreign Missions—pp. 100, 103.
Edwards v. Hammond—p. 122.
Elliott v. Birrell—p. 81.
Ellis v. Page—pp. 150, 154.
Ellis v. Paige—p. 82.
Elm Farm Foods Co. v. Cifrino—p. 65.
Elwell v. Miner—p. 33.

Farris v. Hershfield—pp. 65, 83.
Fatheree v. Gregg—p. 32.
Ferri v. Liberatoscioli—p. 66.
Festing v. Allen—pp. 121, 201.
Fetting Mfg. Jewelry Co. v. Waltz—p. 82.
F. H. Stoltze Land Co. v. Westberg—p. 66.
Fifth Avenue Bldg. Co. v. Kernochan—p. 71.
First Universalist Society v. Boland—p. 111.
Foley v. Gamester—p. 84.
Foot v. Baumann—p. 30.
Forte v. Caruso—p. 57.
Fowler v. Bott—p. 71.
Franz v. Franz—p. 231.
Fulton v. Katsowney—p. 232.

Gaertner v. Donnelly—p. 68.
Gale v. Coburn—p. 191.
Gale v. York Center Community Cooperative, Inc.—p. 34.

Gardiner v. William S. Butler & Co.—p. 70.
Ghoti Estates, Inc. v. Freda's Capri Restaurant, Inc.—p. 65.
Gilpin v. Hollingsworth—p. 236.
Goodman v. Southern Pac. Co.—p. 106.
Grainger v. Hamilton—p. 33.
Gray v. Blanchard—p. 105.
Gray v. Kaufman Dairy & Ice Cream Co.—p. 79.
Green v. King—p. 230.
Greenberg v. Greenberg—p. 223.
Gretkowski v. Wojciechowski—p. 85.
Grubb v. Gwillim—p. 210.
Guido v. Thompson—p. 42.
Gunsenhiser v. Binder—p. 65.

Haggerty v. City of Oakland—p. 65.
Hale v. Hale—p. 233.
Harbel Oil Co. v. Steele—p. 65.
Haskins v. Kelly—p. 65.
Hayes v. Hammond—p. 46.
Hayes' Estate, In re—p. 223.
Hayward v. Spaulding—pp. 134, 202.
Hazzard v. Hazzard—p. 43.
Hermitage Co. v. Levine—p. 73.
Herrick v. Lain—p. 48.
Hewitt v. Beige—p. 223.
Hiles v. Fisher—p. 233.
Hill v. Towson Realty, Inc.—p. 100.
Hilliker v. Rueger—p. 92.
Hopkins v. Hopkins—p. 210.
Hopper v. The Corporation of Liverpool—p. 97.
Horler's Estate, Matter of—p. 219.
Hough v. Farmers Bank & Trust Co.—p. 146.
Howard v. Batchelder—p. 121.
Howell v. Davis—p. 233.
Howland v. Stowe—pp. 226, 228.
Hughes v. Westchester Development Corp.—p. 73.
Hunt v. Thompson—p. 74.
Hutchinson v. Bramhall, Deane & Co.—p. 65.

Idalia Realty & Development Co. v. Norman—p. 65.
Illinois Public Aid Commission v. Stille—p. 223.
Israel v. Beale—pp. 80, 81.
Ivey v. Peacock—p. 33.

Jaber v. Miller—p. 77.
Jackson v. O'Connell—p. 222.
Jackson ex dem. Hudson v. Alexander—pp. 180, 190.
Jackson ex dem. Wood v. Swart—p. 191.

Johnson v. Johnson—p. 220.
Johnson v. Whiton—p. 34.

Kautz v. Kautz—p. 51.
King v. Greene—pp. 229, 233.
Knowles v. South County Hospital—p. 50.
Kramer, Matter of—p. 34.
Kulawitz v. Pacific Woodenware & Paper Co.—pp. 72, 78.

Lace v. Chantler—p. 65.
Langlois v. Langlois—p. 49.
Larson v. Thoresen—p. 226.
Lawrence v. Andrews—p. 223.
Leach v. Jay—p. 92.
Lechmere & Lloyd, In re—p. 203.
Leibowitz v. 18 East 41st Corp.—p. 75.
Leonard v. Autocar Sales & Service Co.—p. 73.
Lepsch v. Lepsch—p. 83.
Lewis v. Baxter Laundries—p. 68.
Lewis v. Pate—p. 233.
Licker v. Gluskin—p. 233.
Lindenfelser v. Lindenfelser—p. 233.
Lloyd v. Murphy—p. 73.
Loats Female Orphan Asylum v. Esson—p. 205.
Loddington v. Kime—p. 125.
Loewenberg v. Wallace—p. 92.
Loring v. Eliot—p. 160.
Lucas v. Hamm—p. 205.
Lutwich v. Mitton—p. 189.
Lydick v. Tate—p. 143.

McGrath v. Shalett—p. 79.
McKenna v. Seattle-First Nat. Bank—p. 156.
McKnight v. Basilides—pp. 225, 226.
McNeilly v. Wylie—p. 154.
McNutt v. Nuevo Land Co.—p. 229.
Machell v. Weeding—p. 45.
Magness v. Kerr—p. 101.
Marcelle, Inc. v. Sol & S. Marcus Co.—p. 74.
Margosian v. Markarian—p. 85.
Markey v. Smith—pp. 37, 196.
Marshall v. Fisk—p. 213.
Masury v. Southworth—p. 74.
Matlack v. Arend—p. 57.
Matthews v. McCain—p. 231.
Mattison's Estate, Re—p. 51.
Mayor, etc., of New York v. Mabie—p. 65.
Medico-Dental Bldg. Co. v. Horton & Converse—p. 73.

Merrill v. Bullock—p. 86.
Mertenns v. Hill—p. 16.
Minnehan v. Minnehan—p. 222.
Minnig v. Batdorff—p. 119.
Mitchell v. Bagot—p. 34.
Moore v. Littel—pp. 117, 127, 128, 149.
Moore v. Stanfill—p. 34.
Morris v. Smith—p. 34.
Morse v. Goodard—p. 71.
Mosser v. Dolsay—p. 231.

Nassau Hotel Co. v. Barnett & Barse Corp.—p. 74.
National Shawmut Bank v. Joy—pp. 154, 156.
New York, City of v. Coney Island Fire Dept.—pp. 98, 106.
New York (Farragut Road), Matter of City of—p. 98.
New York Trust Co. v. Eisner—p. 1.
Nichols v. Haehn—p. 101.
Nicoll v. New York & E. R. Co.—p. 97.

Oldfield v. Stoeco Homes, Inc.—pp. 99, 100.
119 Fifth Ave., Inc. v. Taiyo Trading Co.—p. 73.

Paeff v. Hawkins-Washington Realty Co.—p. 106.
Palmer v. Flint—pp. 217, 219.
Parsons v. Winslow—p. 153.
PCK Properties, Inc. v. City of Cuyahoga Falls—pp. 99, 108.
Pells v. Brown—pp. 45, 199, 200.
People v. Emery—p. 146.
People v. Klopstock—p. 75.
People v. Nogarr—p. 222.
Perrin v. Blake—p. 141.
Perrin v. Harrington—p. 232.
Peters v. East Penn Township School Dist.—p. 99.
Petta v. Host—p. 57.
Phoenix State Bank & Trust Co. v. Buckalew—p. 154.
Pierce v. Pierce—p. 65.
Post v. Weil—p. 105.
President and Fellows of Middlebury College v. Central Power Corp.—p. 105.
Proprietors of Church in Brattle Square v. Grant—pp. 37, 97, 103, 196.
Proprietors of Locks and Canals v. Commonwealth—p. 98.
Public Service Co. v. Voudoumas—p. 84.
Purefoy v. Rogers—pp. 133, 201–204.
Pure Oil Co. v. Miller-McFarland Drilling Co.—p. 102.
Putnam v. Davis—p. 84.

Rainer v. Holmes—p. 227.
Ramsey v. Holder—p. 51.
Raymond v. Raymond—p. 92.

Reeve v. Long—p. 130.
Reid v. Wiessner Brewing Co.—pp. 75, 76.
Rice v. Boston & Worcester Railroad Corp.—p. 108.
Richardson v. Richardson—pp. 158, 160.
Ricker v. Brown—p. 206.
Roberts v. Casey—p. 69.
Roberts v. Roberts—p. 231.
Rogers v. Atlantic, Gulf & Pacific Co.—p. 58.
Rothrock v. Sanborn—p. 75.
Rouse v. Paidrick—p. 134.
Rowerdink v. Carothers—p. 218.
Rupp Hotel Operating Co. v. Donn—p. 65.

St. John v. Dann—p. 42.
Salter v. Quinn—p. 229.
Sambach v. Dalston—p. 209.
Samuels v. Ottinger—p. 76.
Sands v. Old Colony Trust Co.—p. 156.
Santa Monica, City of v. Jones—p. 98.
Say v. Stoddard—p. 83.
Scattergood v. Edge—p. 200.
Seaver v. Coburn—p. 75.
Seavey v. Cloudman—p. 85.
Sewell v. Thrailkill—p. 48.
Sexton v. Chicago Storage Co.—p. 77.
Sharrington v. Strotton—p. 191.
Shelley's Case—pp. 27, 127, 138, 139, 142, 148, 149, 151, 155, 160, 161, 206.
Sheridan v. Lucey—p. 222.
Shindler v. Milden—p. 72.
Shoolman v. Wales Mfg. Co.—p. 76.
Shorter v. Shelton—p. 84.
Simon v. Chartier—p. 223.
Simon v. Kirkpatrick—p. 67.
Simonds v. Simonds—pp. 201, 202.
Smith v. Groton—p. 32.
Smith v. McEnany—p. 72.
Smith v. Town of Groton—p. 136.
Spiritwood Grain Co. v. Northern Pac. Ry. Co.—p. 80.
Stagecrafters' Club, Inc. v. District of Columbia Div. of American Legion—
    p. 64.
Stanmeyer v. Davis—p. 65.
Starkweather v. Jenner—p. 229.
Stockbridge Iron Co. v. Cone Iron Works—p. 108.
Storke v. Penn. Mut. Life Ins. Co.—pp. 36, 37, 100.
Sutliff v. Aydelott—p. 160.
Suydam v. Jackson—p. 71.
Sybert v. Sybert—pp. 141, 146.

Taltarum's Case—p. 39.
Taylor v. Cleary—p. 145.
Taylor v. Continental Southern Corp.—pp. 97, 105.
Taylor v. Farrow—p. 51.
Teutenberg v. Schiller—p. 223.
Therrien v. Therrien—p. 219.
Thompson v. Baxter—p. 84.
Tinkham v. Wind—p. 58.
Tips v. United States—p. 69.
Tolley v. Wilson—p. 44.
Tracy-Collins Trust Co. v. Goeltz—p. 222.
Trafton v. Hawes—p. 213.
Trustees of Union College v. City of New York—p. 100.
Tyrrel's Case—p. 208.

United States v. Shafto—p. 74.
University Club v. Deakin—p. 73.
Upington v. Corrigan—p. 109.

Van Antwerp v. Horan—p. 222.
Van Der Volgen v. Yates—p. 213.
Van Gruten v. Foxwell—p. 141.

Wadsworth's Estate, In re—p. 34.
Wagner v. Kepler—p. 80.
Walker v. Rednalloh Co.—p. 76.
Warren's Estate, In re—p. 153.
Watkins v. Cohen—p. 65.
Watson v. Watson—p. 223.
Welsh v. Foster—p. 213.
Westland Housing Corp. v. Scott—p. 72.
Wheeler v. Boston Housing Authority—p. 81.
White v. Summers—pp. 202, 204.
Whitehouse Restaurant, Inc. v. Hoffman—p. 106.
Whittemore v. Equitable Trust Co.—p. 158.
Wichelman v. Messner—p. 102.
Wilkins v. Young—p. 222.
Wilkinson, Roe ex dem. v. Tranmer—pp. 128, 185, 191, 194.
Willett v. Pilotte—p. 69.
Williams v. Fulton—p. 225.
Wilson v. Harrold—p. 141.
Wunsch v. Donnelly—p. 65.

Zimmerman v. Shreeve—pp. 58, 59.

INDEX

References are to pages

ACTIVE USE, 212, 214

AIDS, 20, 24

ALIENABILITY
Contingent remainder, 135–137.
Entirety, tenancy by, 233–234.
Estate for years, 74–77.
Executory interests, 206–207.
Fee simple, 30–31.
Fee simple conditional, 37–38.
Fee tail, 39, 43.
Life estate, 59.
Possibility of reverter, 101–102.
Quia emptores, effect of, 21, 30.
Right of disseisee, 90–92.
Right of entry for condition broken, 107–109.

ALIENATION
See also Conveyancing, Methods of.
By subinfeudation, 22–23.
By substitution, 22–23.
Fines for, 21.
Quia emptores, effect of, 22–23.

ALLODIAL OWNERSHIP, 26

ASSIGNMENT
Estate for years, 74–77.

ATTORNMENT, 74

BARGAIN AND SALE
After Statute of Uses, 188–190.
As a method of conveyancing, 213–214.
Nature of, 179–180.
Prior to Statute of Uses, 179–180.

BASE FEE, 95 *(＋ Burgage)*

Barring the Entail p. 39

BOROUGH ENGLISH, 15, 25

CESTUI QUE USE
Effect of Statute of Uses, 182–184.
Nature of interest of, 173–176.

CHATTEL REAL, 64

COMMENDATION P. 7

COMMON OCCUPANT, 50

COMMON, TENANCY IN
Characteristics, 224.
Creation, 221, 224–225.
Relations of cotenants, 225–229.

COMMUNITY PROPERTY, 216

CONCURRENT ESTATES
See Common, Tenancy in; Community Property; Coparcenary; Entirety, Tenancy by; Joint Tenancy.

CONDITIONAL LIMITATION, 37, 196

CONTINGENT REMAINDERS
After term of years, 169, 177.
Alienability, 135–137.
Construction problems, 121–123.
Defined, 123.
Destructibility of, 128–135.
Distinguished from executory interest, 197–205.
Distinguished from vested remainder, 112–114.
Doctrine of Worthier Title, 149–162.
Remainders subject to a condition precedent, 124–125
Remainders to unascertained persons, 125–128.
Rule in Shelley's Case, 138–149.
Rule of Purefoy v. Rogers, 200–202.
Trustees to preserve, 133, 202.
Vesting of, 123.

CONVEYANCING, METHODS OF
Assignment, 73–77.
Bargain and sale, 179–180, 183, 188–190.
Common recovery, 39, 135, 165–166.
Covenant to stand seised, 190–191.
Deed, 164, 170–172.
Effect of Statute of Uses, 185–191.
Feoffment, 163–165.
Fine, 35, 135, 165–166.
Frauds, Statute of, 66, 78, 164.
Grant, 164, 170–172.
Lease and release, 188–190.
Release, 172.
Surrender, 78–79, 171–172.

COPARCENARY, 235–236

COPYHOLD, 15–17

COVENANT DISTINGUISHED FROM CONDITION, 104–105

COVENANT TO STAND SEISED, 190–191

COVENANTS IN LEASES, 69–73

CURTESY, TENANCY BY, 54–55

CUSTOMARY TENURE, 15–17

DE DONIS, STATUTE OF, 38–39   *Demesne lands p. 15*
DEMESNE ct. Tenure
DETERMINABLE FEE SIMPLE, 35, 95–100
See Reverter, Possibility of.

DISSEISIN
Powers of disseisor, 90.
Remedies of disseisee, 88–89.
Distress p. 9   *Docketing p. 39*
DOMESDAY SURVEY, 7–8

DOWER
Equitable estates, 56.
Fee tail, 58.
Nature of, 55.
Statutory modification of, 56–57.

EJECTMENT, 90–91

ENROLMENTS, STATUTE OF, 188–189

ENTIRETY, TENANCY BY, 216, 229–235
Alienability of spouse's interest, 233–234.
Common law concept, 229.
Creditors, rights of, 233–234.
Modern law, 230–231.
Simultaneous death of tenants, 220.

ENTRY, RIGHT OF
Alienability, 107–109.
Creation, 104–105.
Defined, 103–104.
Incident to reversion, 108.
Statutory modification, 109.
Waiver, 106.

EQUITABLE ESTATES AND INTERESTS
See Uses.

ESCHEAT, 21, 27

ESTATES
At sufferance, 85–86.
At will, 83–85.
Concept, 28–29.
Concurrent estates, see that title.
Fee simple, 29–37.
Fee tail, 37–48.
For years, 65–79.
Freehold, 28–29.
Future estates, 93–137, 192–207.
Non-freehold, 63–64.
Periodic, 79–83.

ESTOPPEL BY DEED, 101–102, 136

EVICTION
See Years, Estate for.

EXECUTORY DEVISE, 195–196

EXECUTORY INTERESTS
Alienability, 206–207.
Characteristics, 196–199.
Distinguished from contingent remainders, 199–205.
Indestructibility, 199–200.
Origin and nature, 192–194.

FEALTY, 18

FEE SIMPLE
Alienability, 30–31, 34.
Characteristics, 29–30, 34–35.
Creation, 32–34.
Defined, 29–30.
Determinable, 35–36, 95–100.
Development of, 29–31.
Qualified or defeasible, 35–37.
Subject to condition subsequent, 36–37, 103–106.
Subject to executory interest, 37, 192–193, 205–206.

FEE SIMPLE CONDITIONAL, 37–38, 43.

FEE TAIL
Alienability, 39, 43.
Creation, 40, 44–48.
De donis, 38–39.
Dower, 58.
In United States, 41–43.
Origin, 37–38.
Varieties of, 39.
Wild's Case, rule in, 46–48.

FEOFFEE TO USES, 173–176

FEOFFMENT, 163–165, 214

FEUDALISM, 4–21

FINE
Conveyance by, 39, 165.
For alienation, 21–24.

FORFEITURE, 21, 23

FRANKALMOIN TENURE, 14, 24–25

FRAUDS, STATUTE OF, 66–67, 78, 164, 166

FREEHOLD ESTATES, 28–29, 63–64

FREE TENURE, 10–11

FUTURE INTERESTS
See also Entry, Right of; Executory Interests; Remainders; Reversions;
Reverter, Possibility of; Uses.
Alienability, 101–102, 107–108, 135–137, 207.
Common law types, 93–137.
Concept, 93.
Effect of Statute of Uses, 191–207.
Restrictive common law rules, 169–170.

GAVELKIND, 15, 25

GRAND SERJEANTY, 6, 12–14, 24

GRANT
Conveyance by, 170–171.
Feudal grants, 2–7.

HOMAGE, 4, 9, 18, 24

INCIDENTS OF TENURE, 18–22, 24–25

INHERITABILITY
Burgage tenure, 15, 43.
Canons of Descent, 43.
Estate for years, 64.
Estate pur autre vie, 50.
Evolution of, 30–31.
Fee Simple, 29–32.
Fee Tail, 39–40.
Gavelkind, 15, 43.

INHERITANCE, ESTATES OF, 32, 34, 39–40

INHERITANCE, WORDS OF, 31–32, 40

INTERESSE TERMINI, 67, 166–167

ISSUE
Definite failure of, 43–45.
Indefinite failure of, 43–45.
Meaning of, 39.
Rule in Wild's Case, 46–47.

JOINT TENANCY
Characteristics, 220–223.
Concept, 216–217.
Creation, 217–219.
Partition, 222–223.
Relations of tenants inter se, 225–229.
Severance, 221–223.
Simultaneous death of tenants, 220.
Statutory modification, 218.
Survivorship, 220–221.

JURE UXORIS, 52–53

KNIGHT SERVICE, TENURE BY, 4–5, 11–12, 24

LEASE
See also Years, Estates For.
Assignment, 73–77.
Covenants in, 69–73.
Recording requirement, 67.
Statute of Frauds, 66.

LEASE AND RELEASE, 172, 188–190

LICENSE, 68–69

LIFE ESTATES
Characteristics, 58–61.
Conventional life estates, 48, 51.
Creation, 48–49.
Curtesy, 54–55.
Defined, 48.
Dower, 55–58.
Duties of life tenant, 60–61.
Estate by the marital right, 52–53.
Fee tail after possibility of issue extinct, 51.
Forfeiture of, 59, 130–131.
Legal life estates, 48, 51–58.
Pur autre vie, 50.
Wild's Case, Rule in, 47.

LIMITATION, WORDS OF, 31–32, 46, 138

LIVERY OF SEISIN, 90, 163–172

MANORS, 15–17, 26

MARRIAGE, INCIDENT OF, 19–20, 22, 24

MARRIED WOMEN'S PROPERTY ACTS, 53–54, 233

MERGER
Defined, 131.
Destruction of contingent remainder by, 131–135.
Relation to Rule in Shelley's Case, 139, 142–143.

MILITARY TENURE, 4–6, 11–12, 24–25

NON–FREEHOLD ESTATES
    See also Periodic Tenancy; Sufferance, Tenancy At; Tenancy at Will;
        Years, Estates For.
Creation, 166–167.
Defined, 28, 63–64.
Use raised on, 207–208.

NORMAN SETTLEMENT, 2–8

PERIODIC TENANCIES, 79–83

PERPETUITIES, RULE AGAINST, 200, 204–205

PETTY SERJEANTY, 13

POSSESSION
Distinguished from seisin, 63, 87–88.
Duty of lessor to deliver possession, 67–68.
Right of cotenants, 217, 224–226.

POWER OF TERMINATION
See Entry, Right of.

POWERS OF APPOINTMENT, 120

PRIMER SEISIN, 17–18, 24

PRIMOGENITURE, 15, 43, 195

PURCHASE, WORDS OF, 31–32, 46, 138

QUIA EMPTORES, STATUTE OF
Background, 22.
Effect on possibility of reverter, 96–97.
Effect on tenure, 23.
In United States, 25–27.

REAL ACTIONS, 88–89

RECOVERY, COMMON, 39, 135, 165–166

RELIEF, 18–19, 24, 25, 139–140

REMAINDERS
See also Contingent Remainders; Vested Remainders.
Characteristics, 111.
Classification of, 114–115.
Defined, 110.
Distinguished from executory interests, 197–199.
Distinguished from reversion, 111.
Historical development, 112–114.

RENT
Assignee, liability for, 76–77.
Commercial frustration, 73.
Defenses, 71–73.
Destruction of premises, effect of, 71.
Remedies of lessor, 70, 78–79.
Sub-lessee, liability for, 76–77.
Tenant at sufferance, liability for, 85–86.

RESULTING USES
After Statute of Uses, 186–187.
Defined, 180.
Prior to Statute of Uses, 180.

REVERSIONS
After term of years, 94.
Defined, 94.
Resulting from sub-lease, 77.
Worthier Title, Doctrine of, 149–162.

REVERTER, POSSIBILITY OF
Alienability, 101–102.
Creation of, 99–100.
Defined, 95–96.
Distinguished from right of entry, 97–98.
Quia emptores, effect of, 96–97.
Statutory regulation, 102–103.

SEISIN
Actions for recovery of, 88–89.
Concept, 87–88.
Livery of, 163–164.
Operation of Statute of Uses, 182–184.
Rule against abeyance of, 90, 113.

SERJEANTY TENURE, 12–13.

SHELLEY'S CASE, RULE IN
Operation of, 141–147.
Origin, 139–140.
Stated, 138.
Statutory abolition of, 148–149.

SHIFTING AND SPRINGING USES
See Uses.

SOCAGE TENURE, 11, 15, 24–25

STATUTE OF TENURES, 24

STATUTE OF USES
Attainment of objective, 211.
Background, 181–182.
Effect on conveyancing, 185–191.
Effect on future interests, 192–207.
In United States, 212–215.
Operation, 182–184.

STATUTE OF WILLS, 195–196

SUBINFEUDATION, 22–23

SUBSTITUTION, ALIENATION BY, 22–23

SUFFERANCE, TENANCY AT, 85–86

SURRENDER, 78–79

TENANCY AT WILL, 83–85

TENURE
Ancient demesne, 16.
Burgage, 15, 43.
Classification of, 10–11.
Consequences of, 27.
Copyhold, 15–17.
Customary, 15–16.
Frankalmoin, 14, 24–25.
Gavelkind, 15, 43.
Incidents of, 18–22.
In United States, 25–27.
Military, 4–6, 11–12, 24–25.
Serjeanty, 12, 13.
Services, 6–7, 10–11, 22–24.
Socage, 11, 15, 24–25.
Statutes affecting, 22–25.
Sub-tenure, 5–7.
Unfree, 15–16.

TORTIOUS FEOFFMENT, 130–131

TRUST
Active trust, 212, 214–215.
Passive trust, 214–215.
Revocation of, 157–159.
Trust to preserve contingent remainders, 133–134.
Use on a use, 208–211.

USES
Alienability, 175.
Characteristics, 175–179.
Creation of, 179–180, 190–191.
Execution of, 182–184.
Nature of, 173–175.
Origin, 173–174.
Resulting, 180–181, 186–187.
Shifting and springing, 178–179.
Statute of Uses, 181–207.
Unexecuted, 207–215.

VESTED INTEREST, 113–114

VESTED REMAINDERS
Absolutely vested, 118–119.
After contingent remainder in fee, 125.
Classification of, 117–118.
Defined, 116.
Vested subject to complete divestment, 120–123.
Vested subject to partial divestment, 119–120.

VILLENAGE, TENURE IN, 15–17

WARDSHIP, 19, 22, 24

WARRANTY, 9, 31, 101–102

WILD'S CASE, RULE IN, 46–47

WILLS, STATUTE OF, 195–196

WORTHIER TITLE, DOCTRINE OF, 149–162

YEARS, ESTATES FOR
Assignment, 73–77.
Covenants, 69–71.
Creation, 65–67.
Defined, 63.
Destruction of premises, 71.
Eviction, 71–73.
Historical background, 63–64.
Holdover tenant, 82.
Sub-lease, 76–77.
Surrender, 78–79.
Termination, 78.